"DEAR WORLD,

you don't know how happy I am that Ritchie's book is finally coming out.

Read it and you won't regret it.

You will be getting more information on us, the peaceniks of the 60's

having worked on Giving Peace a Chance.

Yes, it still good to keep repeating it until we get World Peace.

GIVE PEACE A CHANCE,

GIVE PEACE A CHANCE,

GIVE PEACE A CHANCE.

Thank you, Ritchie, for reminding people how important this is."

YOKO

Contents

ACKNOWLEDGMENTS		3
1.	ECHOES OF TOKYO ROSE	4
2.	WAR ON THE HOME FRONT	9
3.	WHERE THE PEACE GREASE INTERACTED WITH THE LENNON'S CONCERN FOR HUMANITY	18
4.	THE AMERICAN ATTACKS FROM MONTREAL AND THE BED-IN	28
5.	I AM THE WALRUS	47
7.	THE LENNONS ENCAMP TO CANADA FOR CHRISTMAS	68
8.	MARSHALL MCLUHAN MEETS A WORD MAGICIAN	84
9.	THE TRUDEAU-LENNON GATHERING AND THE BEGINNING OF POLITICAL POP	92
10.	DUELLING WITH THE DEVIL IN DENMARK	106
11.	THE WORLD PEACE TOUR BEGINS	122
12.	TOKYO PIRATE RADIO INVADES AMERICA'S VIETNAM	131
13.	A GONG IN HONG KONG	137
14.	PEACE HITS THE HEADLINES IN HONG KONG	150
15.	BANGING THE PEACE DRUM IN BANGKOK	157
16.	MEETING IN THE LION'S DEN	162
17.	HEADING BACK HOME TO FROZEN LAKES	170
18.	MEANWHILE SOMEWHERE BACK IN ENGLAND	181
19.	THE NEW YORK YEARS	190
20.	THE INSPIRATIONAL WORLD OF YOKO	203
21.	MEANWHILE BACK AT THE VATICAN	219
22.	IS IT THE END OR IS IT THE BEGINNING?	221
i		229
ii		230

ACKNOWLEDGMENTS

The author would like to extend his sincere gratitude and LOVE to a number of special souls including his partner and Muse, Minnie Cherry.

He wishes to thank his children (in order of appearance) Samantha, Chris, Ian and Emily, and grand children Lachlan, Zoe, Hamish, Milo and Matilde. Not forgetting newer family members in the form of Judd, Lilly, John and Anastacia.

Many good folk have contributed to the research aspects of this book. In particular Minnie, Chris von Sanden and Hamish Hill. And Darryl Bailey.

Members of Yoko's staff at Studio One in New York have been particularly helpful.

Yoko herself has been extraordinarily generous with her time, caring and understanding.

From an editing standpoint, my thanks to Chris von Sanden, Theo Wisdom, Tyrone Noonan and M. B.

Of particular note is the contribution of the noted Australian artist Starr who provide the striking artwork for the cover of this book.

I naturally acknowledge the enormous depth and breadth of John Lennon's regard and respect around the planet.

                    LOVE IS ALL YOU NEED.

1. ECHOES OF TOKYO ROSE

Lawd almighty, it was like a scene out of a James Bond movie. Weapons of war and violence were stacked everywhere - handguns, rifles, hand grenades, riot shields, sharpened metal poles, automatic weapons, tear gas canisters, shells, ammunition. This was an arsenal bristling with the hardware of military madness - more than enough to supply a huge uprising or demonstration.

Here we were in the Japanese headquarters of Japan's anti-war movement in the early days of the 1970s. From the outside, it was a harmless-looking suburban warehouse in a side alley of suburban Tokyo. But inside - after the back wall did its little reverse swing thing - we were confronted by this menacing armory.

As a representative of John Lennon and Yoko Ono's *War Is Over If You Want It* peace campaign, I was appalled by what I saw. But somehow - on a lighter note - it was hard not to conjure up visions of Sean Connery and Roger Moore.

My travelling partner, Ronnie Hawkins (aka the Hawk)* had served in the US Army and was more familiar with the scene in front of us. He looked around and shrugged. ``Pretty wild stuff, but what the fuck?'' he muttered.

I was horrified and confused. This place represented the opposite of my own ethos of non-violence. It was a lesson in the idiosyncrasies of the peace campaign in 1969/70. That's how events often unfolded - innocently and totally out of the blue - back in the (golden waning) days of the '60s!

But fate had brought us here, and we were, in truth, messengers of peace. We had been led to this nondescript warehouse by a Japanese friend and media contemporary of Yoko Ono Lennon. Perhaps it's best not to mention his name. After our arrival in Tokyo, I had made contact with this gentleman, who suggested we meet for a traditional tea ceremony.

During our conversation, he produced two stark black and white photographs, which left me speechless. I could hardly believe what I saw. This was direct, dramatic, deadly serious imagery. Remnants of bodies being held aloft by grinning Marines. No picture could come close to capturing the abject misery and pathos that was the Vietnamese war. A place where hope and peace and human love had died in the boiling napalm oil-stained mud.

An evocative line of John's comes to me as I write this. The occasion was the busting of his Bag One lithographs at the London Arts Gallery in January of that same year, 1970. Police seized eight of the 13 prints on grounds of obscenity. John's public response was simple and true: ``I can't call any person's drawings of a lover obscene - actually I call dropping boiling oil on the peasants of Vietnam obscene!''

These were and will remain religious words for me, testaments to my faith, and a hearty endorsement of what I believe - and what I believe to be false and ignorant. You might pause to consider them yourself. This book, a long overdue account of my involvement in John and Yoko's peace campaign, bares what I believe to my soul.

So it was that during this strangely symbolic Japanese tea ceremony with Mr X, Yoko's student radical friend ever-so-politely asked me to pass these shocking photos along to her and John. He didn't doubt their support for the peace cause at large but wasn't convinced that they had a truly realistic indication of what was going on as part of the ugly US invasion of Vietnam.

As life unfolded, I never did show Yoko or John those pictures. But Yoko will undoubtedly see them shortly, through the publication of this book. I hope she will not be offended, for they are as offensive as any news picture could be. In their graphic impact, ancient racial resentment and hatred reaching new lows.

Aware of my peace agenda, Yoko's friend then gave me the chance to become instantly actively involved in the anti-war media campaign beaming out of Japan. I didn't know it then - and how could I, as a callow 26-year-old? - but this urbane, articulate Japanese man was about to play a major role in my life. What would soon unfold would change the course of my life's journey.

After Mr X observed my wildly emotional reaction to the battlefield scenes from Vietnam, he quietly asked if I would be interested in spreading the message. Specifically, taking John and Yoko's anti-war message to the airwaves and speaking directly to the troops.

``You can actually talk and present your case,'' he enthused across the pristine white tablecloth, ``to the soldiers and marines over the airwaves. They're out there listening to all you say. And you can play them music that you personally request … you can just get on there and tell them what Yoko and John really think about what they're doing … what the Lennons think about this horrible, horrible war,' he said with a knowing smile, in impeccable English.

I was sold. What a fabulous opportunity, proof that what we were aspiring towards was precisely what the universe had chosen for us. Profound endorsement from the higher realm helps any cause! I was deeply and almost desperately thrilled at the prospect.

Mr X ordered a taxi to whisk the Hawk and me out to the pirate radio station. As we drove through suburban Tokyo, past endless rows of double storey warehouses, I noticed they were all fairly new constructions, built of mass-produced post-war materials. Older buildings were notably absent, even in 1970. In a stilted attempt at communication, I asked the taxi driver what had happened to older forms of Tokyo suburban architecture. ``Fire bombing - World War II,' he said, gesticulating towards the sky.

On the nights of February 24/25, 1945, 279 B-29 bombers dropped thousands of tonnes of bombs and incendiaries on Tokyo, razing half the city. Officially the death count was 83,000 but many other sources suggest a figure of more than 100,000. The Tokyo Fire Department estimated a toll of 97,000 killed and 125,000 wounded. The statistics themselves are bad enough, but the chilling fact is that most of the victims were women, children, babies and the elderly, because able-bodied men were away fighting the war elsewhere.

You have to wonder about the morality of warmongers at that time. Tokyo's suburbs were not a military target. The victims and enemy were not soldiers fighting against the US and its Allies. When we're thinking about ``good'' and ``bad'' sides in wars, we should consider this: THERE IS NO GOOD SIDE IN THIS SCENARIO!

As a passionate believer in the peace cause, I was itching to run our message up the flag pole. Darn it, I thought, I'm in the deep end here. And I'm too far gone to turn around.

My rap to the massed armed forces tuned in to the pirate radio station signal was pretty straightforward. Straight from the heart. As I sat down in front of the microphone, I simply let fly the whole crescendo of my feelings about war and violence, ignorance and aggression.

1. ECHOES OF TOKYO ROSE

The station's operations operator handed me a procedural sheet. ``This is radio station Camp mustgo,' it read. ``Our radio program includes news, anti-war messages, forums, music and even weather forecasts and commercial messages, all of which are dedicated to the protest against the American aggression over Vietnam." They gave me a shout-out sheet outlining their ``Appeal to Soldiers."

I offer it to you now as it came to me.

1. We've got to be friends for peace and liberation.
2. End the war now.
3. Army go home.
4. GIs join us.
5. Soldiers! You'd better go home where you belong.
6. Don't get lost in the Army.
7. Leave the camp of war (silence or hate) and join the camp of peace (free speech).
8. You can easily find friends. We are your friends.
9. Before returning to your homes, rise and unite against the war and oppression.
10. Rise and unite against the world and oppression.
11. Smash Japan-US Security Treaty.
12. Okinawa to the people.
13. The camp must go.
14. All power to the people!

Broadcasting a message of peace from an arsenal packed to the roof with weapons of war was not the only irony that struck me that day. As the Hawk and I were driven back to our hotel, I remembered the infamous Tokyo Rose**. Like the despised Lord Haw Haw in Europe, she polluted the airwaves with war-mongering messages intended to spread fear and undermine the morale of Allied troops in the Pacific. But my conscience was clear, for I had been promoting the moral imperative of human kindness. A feeling of deep satisfaction settled in at the end of that memorable day.

*Rompin' Ronnie Hawkins had produced a string of distinctive rockabilly hits such as Mary Lou, Bo Diddley and Forty Days in the late '50s. He'd moved to Canada in 1958 on the advice of another Southern white singer named Conway Twitty and put together a backing group called The Hawks. Later, creatively frustrated, they left the Hawk (as he'd become known) and renamed themselves The Band. A subsequent link with Bob Dylan led The Band to the top of the critics' elite favourites list.

Somewhere in the upsurge of The Band's musical velocity, Ronnie was unintentionally left behind. But after I'd written a ``tits-and-all''expose of his speckled history for Rolling Stone magazine in the fall of 1969, the Hawk had been besieged with recording deals.

On my advice he signed with my long-time mentor and mate Jerry Wexler, executive vice-president of Atlantic Records, often described as the 'godfather of rock'n'roll'. That deal took Ronnie and his protege, Richard Newell, aka the King Biscuit Boy, to Muscle Shoals to work with the famed local rhythm section and the budding guitar genius Duane ``Skydog'' Allman imported from Macon, Georgia.

After all this, Ronnie owed me at least a few brownie points, so when I suddenly needed to come up with a place to stay for the Lennon party when they travelled to Toronto, Canada, for the launching of their *War Is Over* peace initiative, I was able to call in a favour. So the Lennons went to stay at the Hawkins' spread (... more on that within).

Ronnie Hawkins was a natural and hopefully calming tour companion. That was the initial aim, but it didn't quite work out that way, as will soon be revealed.

**Tokyo Rose was not a single broadcaster but a collective nickname given to several English-speaking women, some of whom were believed to be American citizens living in Japan. As such they were despised as traitors. Rather than sapping Allied morale, their broadcasts were mocked and scorned. Such was the notoriety of the so-called Tokyo Rose, she even rated a mention in the song *There is Nothing like a Dame*, from the Rodgers and Hammerstein musical South Pacific, and was featured in several post-war films.

2. WAR ON THE HOME FRONT

Father came home from World War II in 1943 a deeply troubled man, with a kitbag of traumas that would ultimately impact on all around him.

When he'd left Australia swaddled in dreams of glory and as part of a chosen mission, he and his comrades had mistakenly believed they were on some sort of God-given task to save humanity. The reality was about as far away from this as a soldier could get. It wasn't so much about glory as about gore and horror at the senseless, indiscriminate violence of modern warfare. Not for the faint of heart. Not for those who allow compassion in. It was a case of kill or be killed. Maim or be maimed. Hurt and be hurt.

Alfred George Annable, always Father to me but "Snow" to his mates, served with the Australian anti-tank battalion in the deserts of North Africa and witnessed some very nasty episodes. As an infant, I would soon discover that the war zone was not confined to overseas soil. It could be transferred back to the home front and continue to cause pain and suffering to all those involved. It would impact on the rest of my life. As the great American anti-war novelist Kurt Vonnegut (1922-2007) wrote in 2005: "... Anzacs were pretty good soldiers. But in the North African desert you were just cannon fodder."

That's the sort of revelation dear old Dad would occasionally dig up from his kitbag of WWII reflections - caustic memories of watching a close mate having his head blown off in the trenches by random tank fire. Vonnegut gave the North African scenario perspective; the sort of overview that a participant could never allow himself.

War extended into the lives of everybody connected with the participants on the battlefield. I would soon figure out that my father's frustrations at trying to stuff hand grenades into the wheel tracks of military tanks rolling over his trench had a great deal to do with my turbulent upbringing.

I'll always remember returning to Australia in 1972 on holidays from Canada and visiting my home town of Brisbane. My father, to whom I hadn't spoken in 12 years since our disengagement, was keen to receive me at his home. I arrived there one evening, full of platitudes about peace and the futility of war, and he was flabbergasted. Not that he disagreed with anything I was saying. Just that it was a radical departure from any conversation I had undertaken with him in our painful past of beratings and bashings.

War, I strongly declared, was wrong on any level. People killing other people was just not acceptable, for any reason. There can be no justification for violence. My father looked at me and nodded. Looking back over his life, he could see that violent behavior had been instigated by his own dismal experiences.

John Lennon - who grew up across the world from me in Liverpool, England - also suffered from a lack of paternal love, and a father named Alfred. We were both children of war. Kindred spirits. German bombs were raining down on Liverpool as John Winston Lennon took his first breath on October 9, 1940. Within a couple of years, his ship steward father had sailed away, and his parents would be legally separated by the time John started formal education.

John went to live with his Aunty Mimi, while his mother Julia took up with a new partner. It was a tough journey for a young bloke trying to find his way, made even more complicated by the death of his mother Julia, run down by an off-duty policeman.

``She was killed after visiting my aunty's house by an off-duty cop who was drunk,' John later reflected. ``I wasn't there at the time. She was just at a bus stop. (Later) a copper came to the door to tell us about the accident. It was just like it was supposed to be, the way it is in the films.

Asking if I was her son and all that. Then he told us, and we both went white. It was the worst thing that ever happened to me.

``I thought, 'I've no responsibilities to anyone now'. That was another big trauma for me. I lost her twice. When I was five and I moved in with my aunty, and then when she physically died. That made me more bitter; the chip on my shoulders, a youth, got really big then. I was just re-establishing the relationship with her and she was killed.'' Traumatic stuff, brilliantly well documented in the 2009 film, *Nowhere Boy*.

``I was torn between being (*The Wild Ones* actor) Marlon Brando and the sensitive poet - the (writer) Oscar Wilde part of me with the velvet, feminine side,' Lennon said. But he felt he had the world figured out from an early age, as much as it may have pained him. He told actor Victor Spinetti (who had roles in The Beatles' films *A Hard Day's Night* and *Help*) for BBC2 radio's art program release in June, 1968: ``I think our society is run by insane people for insane objectives and I sussed that when I was 16 and 12, way down the line. But I expressed it differently all through my life. But now, I can put it into that sentence that I think we're being run by maniacs for maniacal ends! If anybody can put on paper what our government ... what they are actually trying to do, and what they think they're doing ... I'd be very pleased to know. I think they're all insane. But I'm liable to be put away for being insane for expressing that. That's what's insane about it. It's insane, it's not just a bit strange, it's insane!".

Later Lennon had declared: "It (peace) was just a gradual development over the years. Last year was *All You Need is Love*. This year it's *Give Peace a Chance. Remember Love*. The only hope for any of us is peace. Violence begets violence. If you want to get peace, you can get it as soon as you like if we all pull together. You're all geniuses and you're all beautiful. You don't need anybody to tell you who you are or what you are. You are what you are. Get out there and get peace. Think peace, live peace and breathe peace and you'll get it as soon as you like. OK?"

Some might affirm that John found a substitute father figure in manager Brian Epstein, whom he met in 1961 at barely the age of 21. He lost him in August, 1967, when Epstein committed suicide. Things were never quite the same in The Beatles' camp again. In the April before Epstein's death, when he was ill in hospital, John sent him an enormous bouquet of flowers with a note saying, "I hope you get well soon, because I love you, and you know I mean it. John".

It was that sort of connection, but I vigorously refute the suggestions of homosexuality that have been laid in their direction. They, too, were kindred spirits, just as John and Yoko Ono's anti-war message resonated around the world and found millions of kindred spirits and sympathisers.

My involvement with John Lennon's peace movement began in 1968 when, as Toronto newspaper The Globe and Mail's inaugural full-time columnist covering the rock music culture, I established contact with individual Beatles. During my regular jaunts to London documenting the astonishing evolution of the British music scene, I had crossed paths with John on several occasions. The Beatles' Apple Corps PR offices sought me out to provide coverage of Apple activities in Canada's national daily (and assorted freelance outlets throughout the world), and I was not reluctant to supply plenty of copy to delighted editors.

At first I found John's global stature foreboding, his intellect and wit a tad intimidating. But I soon clambered over those self-imposed barriers and began to know a beautiful, noble and hugely talented human being. Finally, this rock'n'roll music of ours had spawned a person who truly appreciated the finer notions of our moral responsibility to give something back. Lennon was a compassionate man who believed it was equally satisfying to give as to receive.

As the final years of the '60s zoomed past, John and his second wife, Yoko, became increasingly motivated by the politics of planetary injustice and warfare. I was passionately caught up in the groundswell. It was all so obvious. Deeply despairing of the planetary predicament and the ugly excesses of the machine-driven madness of the Vietnam War, I found the Lennon conduit to a new and better world absolutely irresistible. Rock'n'roll music, founded on adolescent angst and rebellion under the shadow of the nuclear age, takes an inherently anti-establishment stance. John steered these characteristics to a logical conclusion: a united reaction against the corrupt but convenient status quo. He went about doing something positive to change the way it was, instead of merely moaning and whingeing about society's ills. Through John and Yoko's undoubted clout with the mass media, we could present the facts of the world political situation to the populace at large.

Or so we hoped, perhaps naively. When in December, 1969, a few days before Christmas, the opportunity arose for me to join the Lennons' *War Is Over If You Want It* peace campaign as their peace envoy, I did not need a lot of arm-twisting. And when the Toronto Globe and Mail editors confronted me with an ultimatum that I could no longer work for both Lennon and the newspaper, it wasn't a difficult choice. I recall thinking it over for about two seconds, before bidding farewell to the Globe. So began one of the most astounding and enlightening eras any person could dream of being involved in.

I would be privy to some of the most basic - and most profound - human utterances on the violence-splattered 20th century. Here are some samples, expressed by John Lennon off the cuff and out of the blue.

(On hope): ``The Beatles had nothing to do with the hope. The Beatles made it four years ago and they had all the money they wanted and all the fame they wanted, and then they found out they had nothing. And then we started on our various trips of LSD and the Maharishi and all the rest. And the old gag about money and power and fame is not the answer. We didn't have any hope just because we were famous. You see, (ill-fated actress) Marilyn Monroe and all the other people had everything The Beatles had, but it's no answer. So John and Yoko had the same problems and fears and hopes and aspirations that any other couple on earth does, regardless of the position we were in. We had exactly the same paranoia as everybody, the same petty thoughts, the same everything … we had no super answer that came through Beatles or power.''

(On God) : ``I believe that God is like a powerhouse where you keep electricity, like a power station. And that he's a supreme power, and that he's neither good nor bad, nor left, right, black or white. He just is. And we tap that source of power and make of it what we will. Just as electricity can kill people strapped to a chair, or you can light a room with it. I think God is."

(On illegal drugs): ``The liquor problem is even worse. I think the drug problem is a hang-up and a drag, but if we hadn't had methedrine and all the rest of it, they would have been alcoholics ... the ones that are going through that trip. Everybody seems to need something in the way society is because of the pressure. So it would have been alcohol or something. The problem is not what they're on; it's what made them go on whatever they're on."

(On the peace movement): ``We think that the '60s was the beginning of the end and that it was a positive decade, not a depressing one which people have tried to put around. It's been the decade of all the music, the generation and the freedom and sort of awareness and the moratoriums and the (music festivals) Woodstocks and the Isle of Wights and everything. This is just the beginning: what we've got to do is keep hope alive. It's all about keeping hope alive. Because without it we'll sink!"

As writer Stephen Holden noted in his contribution to the excellent anthology *The Ballad of John & Yoko* (Doubleday/Dolphin, 1982): ``John Lennon believed passionately that popular music could and should do more than merely entertain, and, by acting out this conviction, he changed the face of rock'n'roll forever. By taking such huge risks he sometimes failed or seemed silly. Yet, in retrospect, even his failures take on the glow of nobility: the fact that he cared so much shines through his occasional shortcomings."

Holden continued: ``For Lennon rock music was an intellectual and moral platform for discussing the large questions that troubled his generation - the Vietnam War and the capitalist system, personal freedom and sexual equality and, ultimately, the future of humanity. He accepted the responsibilities the counterculture handed him and set about making the world a gentler, more peaceable place. Even though his commitment to radical causes had all but evaporated by the end of the'70s, what Lennon stood for, both as a Beatle and an ex-Beatle, ultimately transcended issues. Inspired and encouraged by his wife, Yoko Ono, he was rock music's supreme solipsist - someone whose art and life were so inextricably bound that they were practically indistinguishable. The public response to his assassination in December, 1980, was overwhelming testimony to the fact that Lennon still had the power to influence masses of people by simply being who he was - a utopian dreamer with extraordinary artistic gifts who believed in giving power to the people, in giving peace a chance."

The message lingers on. Interestingly enough, the last surviving British soldier to have fought in the sodden trenches of World War I (1914-1918), Harry Patch, who died in July 2009 at the age of 111, inspired contemporary British rock supergroup Radiohead to compose an ode to the horrors of war.

The song *Harry Patch (In Memory Of)* was reportedly inspired by a radio interview with the soldier who had been involved in the notorious Battle of Passchendaele in 1917, in which more than 70,000 British soldiers were killed. A horrific bloody encounter, by any definition.

It was a song John Lennon might well have written. And surely would endorse. Its composer, Thom Yorke, has noted: "I had heard a very emotional interview with Harry Patch a few years ago... the way he talked about war had a profound effect on me. It became the inspiration for a song we happened to record a few weeks before his death."

The singer added: "It would be very easy for our generation to forget the true horror of war, without the likes of Harry to remind us. I hope we do not forget. As Harry himself said, 'Irrespective of the uniforms we wore, we were all victims'."

The moving song features such lyrics as, "I am the only one that got through, the others died wherever they fell" and finishes with the line "I've seen hell upon this earth, the next will be chemical but they will never learn".

And of course John's actions would inspire others who turned up down the track on the evolutionary trail of rock history. People such as Live Aid organiser Bob Geldof, singer with the Boomtown Rats: "The Beatles overwhelmed me musically with their sense of optimism. The way John spoke was the way I felt,' Geldof said. "But John was much more of an idealist than me. I'm a pragmatist. John didn't think there was anything wrong with pursuing an object which didn't have a logical end. Peace is something worth striving for, but probably not possible to attain. But that certainly doesn't mean you should stop aspiring towards it."

U2's Bono is another who pursued a pacifist agenda, at a time when spin was everything. Politicians and corporate leaders seized the notion of connecting with Bono because of the message that it sent of their supposed concern.

Even an early-21st-century luminary such as the Black Eyed Peas' Will. I. Am allowed: "I love John Lennon! He was such an incredible campaigner for peace. Songs like *Give Peace a Chance* were definitely inspiring for us when we were writing *Where Is the Love?* And I think that, with things in the world being the way they are, his message is more relevant than ever."

2. WAR ON THE HOME FRONT

Tom Morello, Audioslave's politically charged artisan, gave three distinct reasons for admiring John Lennon: ``*Imagine, Working Class Hero*, and the way he fearlessly attempted to use his life and his art to make the world a better place. John Lennon was a great spirit.''

Chris Martin, the affable frontman for mega group Coldplay, said simply: ``I love him. I really do. How much? Well, you know Leningrad in Russia? I think they should rename it Lennongrad in honour of him.''

And finally the redoubtable Ozzy Osbourne: ``John Lennon, in my opinion, is the greatest music legend to ever walk this earth. My biggest regret in life is that I never got to meet him.'' I suspect John would have been less than impressed by Ozzy's rampant opportunism!

The meeting of John Lennon and Yoko Ono's creative minds brought about profound changes in attitudes - theirs and ours. ``That's why we ended up doing things like Bed-Ins, and Yoko ended up doing things like pop music,' John said in his last interview. ``With our first attempts at being together and producing things together, whether they were Bed-Ins or posters or films, we crossed over into each other's fields, like people do from country music to pop. We did it from avant-garde left field to rock'n'roll left field.

We tried to find a ground that was interesting to both of us. And we both got excited and stimulated by each other's experiences. The things we did together were all variations on a theme really. We wanted to know what we could do together, because we wanted to be together. We want to work together. We don't just want to be together on weekends. We want to be together and live together and work together. So the first attempts were the Bed-Ins.

``The media all came charging through the door (at the Amsterdam Hilton Bed-In) thinking we were going to be screwing in bed. And of course we were just sitting there with peace signs.''

After John's death, Yoko committed to keeping the peace message which she had initiated through her concept of performance art, alive. She worked tirelessly and unselfishly for peace. While she could have lazed on a country estate like so many other wealthy widows, she pursued the peace platform at no little cost to herself.

And at the age of 82, she was keeping the peace message alive through a succession of widely acclaimed anti-war exhibitions and statements. Of great contemporary interest was her *Imagine: The Peace Ballad of John and Yoko* exhibition which drew tens of thousands of people to the Museum of Fine Arts in Montreal, Canada in 2009. She was accorded a Lifetime Achievement award at the Venice Biennale. Yoko deservedly has been recognized for the wonderful job she has done in keeping the Lennon legacy in tune with contemporary times.

It's particularly apt to reflect on John's comments in his last major interview before his death, with Playboy magazine's David Sheff in September, 1980, about the profound impact of Yoko's arrival in his life: ``The old gang of mine was over the moment I met her (Yoko). I didn't consciously know it at the time but that was what was going on. As soon as I met her, that was the end of the boys, but it so happened that the boys were well known and weren't just the local guys at the bar. These were guys everybody else knew. But it was the same thing - but everybody got so upset about it and angry! Only, Yoko and I were so involved with each other we just went and made the records and did the Bed-Ins and somehow blasted our way through it. But there was a lot of shit thrown at us, a lot of painful stuff.

``I didn't mind being the brunt of all that nastiness and ignorance, but it wasn't fair to Yoko. And that really bothered me. It bothered me and at times angered me deeply, but I couldn't let it get me down,' John told me during a private moment. ``All the knockers and the critics, many of them hacks in bloody London newspapers, were dying for us to give up the peace grease and get back to being rock'n' rollers. But we weren't giving up that easily.

``Yoko and I are quite willing to be the world's clowns if by so doing it will do some good. I know I'm one of those 'famous personalities'. For reasons known only to themselves, people do print what I say. And I'm saying 'peace'. We're not pointing a finger at anybody. There are no good guys and bad guys. The struggle is in the mind. We must bury our own monsters and stop condemning people. We are all Christ and we are all Hitler. We want Christ to win. We're trying to make Christ's message contemporary. What would he have done if he had advertisements, records, films, TV and newspapers? Christ made miracles to sell his message. Well the miracle today is communications, so let's use it.''

But John was no sentimentalist, ripe for a cheap romance novel. ``My thing is out of sight, out of mind,' he declared in his final interview. ``That's my attitude to life. So I don't have any of the romanticism about any part of my past. I think of it only in as much as it gave me the pleasure of helping me grow psychologically. That is the only thing that interests me about yesterday. I don't believe in yesterday by the way. You know I don't believe in yesterday - I am only interested in what I am doing now.''

Right to the end John was questioning himself. ``I always was a rebel because of whatever sociological thing gave me a chip on the shoulder. But on the other hand, I want to be loved and accepted. That's why I'm on stage, like a performing flea. It's because I would like to belong. A part of me would like to be accepted by all facets of society and not be this loudmouth lunatic, poet/musician. But I cannot be what I am not. What the hell do you do? You want to belong but you don't want to belong because you cannot belong." What a graphic description of the life energies which divided John Lennon!

But still war and suffering drag on. In the past year, 24 million people were displaced by various ill-fated wars, bringing the total of the world's refugees to 42 million. It is a sobering thought to realise that 44 per cent of all refugees are children. Another damning statistic. During World War I (1914-1918), 95 per cent of war casualties were armed participants and 5 per cent were civilian casualties. Almost a century later, 97 per cent of war casualties are civilians. What the hell are we doing allowing this absurd behaviour on this planet? Where is love and compassion when you need it?

3. WHERE THE PEACE GREASE INTERACTED WITH THE LENNON'S CONCERN FOR HUMANITY

"Our interest in peace built up over a period of years, but the thing that struck it off was a letter we got from a guy called Peter Watkins, who made a film (documentary-style, for the BBC) called *The War Game*. It was a long and detailed letter stating what's happening - how the media is controlled, how it's all run, and it ended with: 'What are you going to do about it?,' John explained in 1969.

"He said people in our position and his position have a responsibility to use the media for world peace. And we sat on the letter for three weeks and thought it over and figured, at first, that we were doing our best with songs like *All You Need is Love*.

"Finally we came up with the Bed-In event and that was what sparked it off. It was like getting your call-up papers for peace. Then we did the Bed-In event. The idea came directly from Yoko. She had decided that whatever action she took, it was for a specific reason. Her reason, of course, was peace.

"I'd been singing about love, which is another word for peace. So our actual peace demonstrations were Yoko-style events. They were also pure theatre, which was her wont. The Montreal Bed-In was one of the nicest ones and I participated almost like a spectator, because really it was Yoko's way of demonstrating and making the point."

``I was very thankful that John was so open to using his media influence, and functioning as the head of my `marketing department',' Yoko commented in 2010. ``John was so open to that. I don't think anybody else could have been so open to it. He understood immediately the significance of it. He was a very, very intelligent guy in the first place, and also not just intelligent, but the fact that he would listen to a woman (spoke for itself).''

I mention that John had demonstrated that outlook in his great song, *Woman is the Nigger of the World*, and Yoko laughs. He had discovered the phrase in a magazine interview Yoko did in 1969.

The War Game, an Oscar-winning film which was banned for two de-

3. WHERE THE PEACE GREASE INTERACTED WITH THE LENNON'S CONCERN FOR HUMANITY

cades apart from a limited theatrical release in 1966, is a powerful work focusing on the aftermath of a nuclear attack by the Soviet Union on Britain. It is only 47 minutes long and is filmed in dramatic black and white. It is presented in the style of a news magazine show with several different threads which resonate throughout, including news footage of the nuclear strikes and their horrific impact on civilians, along side brief vox-pop interviews with passers-by are queried about their awareness of nuclear war issues.

In the film, China's invasion of South Vietnam ignites the confrontation; tensions escalate when the US decides on tactical nuclear warfare against the Chinese, although the Soviet and East German forces threaten to invade West Berlin if the US does not rescind that decision. The US does not bow to communist demands and the communists occupy West Berlin; two US Army divisions attempt to take back Berlin, but the Russian and East German forces defeat them in battle. The US President launches a nuclear attack and during the war that erupts between the East and West, nuclear missiles rain on Britain.

The chaos of the prelude to the attack, when city residents are forcibly evacuated to the country, leads to the story's centre in Rochester, Kent, which is struck by an errant missile aimed at Heathrow Airport. Key targets in Kent are RAF Manston and the Maidstone barracks. The results of that missile's explosion are the instant blinding of those who see it and a firestorm caused by the heat blast. Scenes of the subsequent collapse of society caused by radiation sickness, psychological damage and failed infrastructure are horrific.

In support of Watkins's efforts to have his film aired, controversial and outspoken British critic Kenneth Tynan later claimed *The War Game* might be "the most important film ever made". It quickly became a focus for the Campaign for Nuclear Disarmament (CND). Watkins fronted a write-in campaign demanding the BBC to permit a limited theatrical release, a compromise approved in March 1966. But since the BBC retained all rights, Watkins never received any income from theatrical or video releases of *The War Game*.

This was the man who sent John and Yoko's consciences into high gear and set the stage for their *War Is Over If You Want It* peace campaign. Armed with a lot of thought about their upcoming peaceful protest, John and Yoko approached their looming wedding on March 20, 1969, with a measure of special resolve.

Originally they thought of Paris as an ideal location but red tape officialdom would have meant delays, a no-no in John's *Instant Karma* attitude.

He wanted the event to take place right away, not later.

John said the day after his marriage: "Our wedding in Gibraltar yesterday was the most fantastic happening. We are both tremendous romantics. We would like to have been married in a church by the Archbishop of Canterbury, but it was impossible because of the press and because they do not marry divorced people. Intellectually, of course, we don't believe in getting married. But one does not love someone just intellectually."

"We worked for three months thinking out the most functional approach to boosting peace before we got married,' Yoko has revealed. "And we spent our honeymoon talking to the press in bed in Amsterdam. For us, it was the only way. We couldn't go out in Trafalgar Square because it would have created a riot. We can't lead a parade or a march because of all the autograph hunters. We had to find our own way of doing it. And for then, Bed-Ins seemed to be the most logical way. We think that Bed-Ins can be effective."

After their wedding in Gibraltar (chosen, said John, because it was "quiet, friendly and British"), the Lennons booked into the presidential suite, Room 920, of the Amsterdam Hilton and invited the world's media to join them in a protest against all forms of violence. Because of the notoriety of other recent Lennon media events, such as the nude cover of their *Two Virgins* album, there was a big turnout of media reps.

Asked why they'd chosen Amsterdam, John said: "Well, if we did it in Paris, all they would talk about was things like Monsieur Humeur or whatever who had a happening there in 1930, you know, and they would have only seen it in that light. If we did it in London, the press would say, 'Oh it's those freaks again'. So we knew we'd make more effect on Britain if we were abroad. We're not doing a (US presidents) Johnson or Nixon-cum-Queen of England shake-your-hands PR tour, you know, we're here to meet the press and TV, because they are the modern-day communicators."

On the first day, March 25, an abundantly curious contingent of more than 50 journalists, photographers, radio DJs and camera crews turned up to find the Lennons dressed in identical white robes, reclining in an enormous king-size bed. Around them was a montage of hand-drawn slogans and peace messages - *"Bed Peace"*, *"Hair Peace"*, *"I love John"* and *"I Love Yoko"*.

John was comfortable and compassionate in how he approached the subject matter and answered questions flowing from the minds of professional skeptics. "We are both artists! Peace is our art. We believe that because of everything I was as a Beatle and everything that we are now, we stand a chance of influencing other young people. And it is they who will rule the world tomorrow."

John also addressed the issue of sexual presumption at the Bed-In. "These press guys were sweating to get in first because they thought we were going to be making love in bed. That's where their minds were at. I hope we weren't a letdown for them. We wouldn't make love in public - that's an emotionally personal thing."

Later in an interview entitled *Lennon Remembers* with Rolling Stone co-founder Jann Wenner, Lennon would observe: "Our first peace event was the Amsterdam Bed-In. It was a nice high. We were in the Hilton - overlooking Amsterdam - it was very crazy; the press came, expecting us to be fucking in bed. They'd all heard John and Yoko were going to fuck in front of the press for peace. So when they all walked in - about 50 or 60 reporters flew over from London, all sort of very edgy, and we were just sitting in pyjamas saying 'Peace, brother'."

Privately, John explained to me in Toronto, Canada, on a lazy snowy December 1969 afternoon at Ronnie Hawkins' Mississauga farmhouse, ``It was really quite scary at the time. These Fleet Street bloodsuckers were looking for anything controversial or sex-related that they could cotton onto and nail down Yoko and I. They came to our room in Amsterdam expecting all manner of things. They thought they'd make some headlines with Yoko and I taking our clothes off. Of course that didn't happen which left them pretty disappointed and depressed."

For the next seven days, John and Yoko talked relentlessly from 10am until 10pm about the prospects of peace in a war-torn world. The Lennons never faltered in their enthusiasm for the cause and their belief in the righteousness of any peace endeavor. It was a tale written straight out of the history book accomplishments of the likes of Mahatma Gandhi, Desmond Tutu and Martin Luther King, other prominent peaceniks of the 20th century.

The biased attitudes of the British press were particularly galling to Bed-In observers and staff. "They were harsh and critical, and the way in which they hurled abuse, mercilessly lampooning John and Yoko, was unnecessary and deliberately hurtful,' observed Anthony Fawcett, personal assistant to the Lennons, who'd helped to organise the Bed-In event. One London columnist suggested "this must rank as the most self-indulgent demonstration of all time". Yet another British journo suggested, "John seems to have come perilously near to having gone off his rocker".

"It was very hard for John and Yoko,' recalled Peter Brown, who had been executive assistant to Brian Epstein and had co-ordinated the Gibraltar wedding. He was one of the Lennons' closest confidantes at that time. "A lot of it was because they took such controversial positions, as in the Bed-In. They were setting themselves up, to a certain extent. The English press is really awful. They loathe success. So they went after John and Yoko and it was terrible!"

Despite the low-rent attitudes of some members of the gutter-leaning UK media, the Bed-In did gain valuable coverage and was the start of a long and continuing campaign by the Lennons (later by Yoko as a widow), to draw people's attention to their passive war against violence and injustice.

"We're very shy and straight and ordinary. We're just trying to do the best we can. But we're in an abnormal situation," John explained. "The blue meanies (John's all-encompassing name for members of the Establishment and other conservative forces), or whoever they are, are promoting violence all the time in every newspaper, every TV show and every magazine. The least Yoko and I can do is to hog the headlines and make people laugh. I'd sooner see our faces in a bed in the paper than yet another politician smiling at the people and shaking hands."

And so they kept on talking about peace and non-violence in a media dominated by more distressing developments in Vietnam. "The Bed-Ins were the best idea we'd had yet,' John commented. "Better than wriggling about in a black bag or stripping naked for people who don't appreciate what we're trying to do or why. Just suppose we had wanted to go to the Isle of Capri in Italy for a secret honeymoon like (former US first lady) Jackie Kennedy had, the press would have been bound to find out. So we thought we might as well do something constructive about the publicity."

The Lennons, of course, were familiar with negative publicity. "People criticised us for spending all that money protesting about Biafra and such like, when the money would have been more useful had I sent it directly there,' John said. "But I'd already done that. I've always respected the sentiments behind that kind of charity and I always will do. But it doesn't solve the problem ... in a capitalist society like ours, people are much more effective if they have money. And we have. Our name is known and so we're using our fame and our money to advertise for peace. Some people say this is a pretentious ambition but we feel that the big problems are where you have to start."

This was headline-making stuff after years of self-enforced Beatles' silence on the subject of violence. In the early days in America, Brian Epstein had beseeched the band members not to comment publicly on the touchy topic of the Vietnam War*. After several tours when The Beatles had studiously avoided the topic, Lennon could contain himself no longer. "Listen, when they ask next time, we're going to say we don't like that war and we think we (the West) should get right out! The continual awareness of what was going on made me feel ashamed I wasn't saying anything. I burst out because I could no longer play that silent game anymore - it was just too much for me. So I had to say something!"

Later John noted: "We're all responsible for war. We all must do something, no matter what - by growing our hair long, standing on one leg, talking to the press, having Bed-Ins to change the attitudes. The people must be made aware that it's up to them. Bed-ins are something everybody can do and they're so simple. We're willing to be the world's clowns to make people realise it."

After seven days in Amsterdam, and as the lyric in their song *The Ballad of John and Yoko* explains ("made a lightning trip to Vienna, the newspapers said ..."), the Lennons headed for Vienna where they undertook a Bagism press conference. Bag Productions was set up during the summer of 1969 to administer and take care of John and Yoko's film catalogue and other projects or merchandising ideas. He didn't want to share the proceeds of his non-Beatles-related creative efforts with the other members of the band. "I always knew at the back of my mind that I'd finish up well off,' John said. "I think I always wanted to be an eccentric millionaire - and I am. My only regret is that we originally set up Apple in an attempt to get away from all the big-business men giving us orders. Now we've finished up worse than we were before, and poorer. I've even had to set up my own company with Yoko - Bag Productions - to keep some of the pennies from going down the Apple drain."

Personal assistant Anthony Fawcett noted that the Lennons had made an attempt to lure New York accountant Allen Klein into investing in Bag Productions, but he waffled out of it. Functioning out of the front office in the Apple building in Savile Row as Bag Productions, Bagism became an all-encompassing generic term for all the Lennons' creative activities. Similarly, a set of lithographs John had been working on was dubbed the Bag One lithographs.

Two days after leaving Amsterdam, back in the more secure territory of London, they began to wonder what it was all about. Later Yoko explained: "Because people kept saying we were crazy, we went into a very, very deep depression. We thought, `Oh well, they were right'. We didn't do very much. And it didn't help the world. We were very sad, because there was no response. But then we started to get a tremendous, beautiful response around the end of the year. And that gave us hope."

That measure of hope would come through a meeting with Canada's Prime Minister, Pierre Trudeau. As it turned out, Trudeau was one of only a handful of world leaders who bothered to respond to the Lennon's mail out of acorns for peace. After returning to England, they arranged to send out acorns ("from tiny acorns, mighty oak trees can grow") to an array of world leaders as a symbol of peace. Pierre Trudeau, Israel's Prime Minister Golda Meir and King Hussein of Jordan planted theirs.

In April, John also wrote a new autobiographical song, *The Ballad of John and Yoko*, a literal account of the recent weeks in the Lennon lives. It talked of their marriage, the Amsterdam BedIn, the side trip to Vienna and the battles for peace. It reflected a new sense of immediacy in his connection with all media. And it contained an epic chorus line which would resonate down through the ages: ``Christ you know it ain't easy, you know how hard it can be, the way things are going, they're going to crucify me ...'' Truer words were seldom presented on the pop charts.

John was so headstrong in his desire to record the new song that he couldn't wait for George or Ringo to return from holiday and a film shoot, so he and Paul McCartney - tunefully toiling amicably together, which surprised some close observers given the state of the principal's relationship - went into the studio on April 14. Paul contributed bass, drums, piano, maraccas and background vocals to what would be the last Beatles' song specifically recorded as a single. John provided the lead vocal plus lead guitars, acoustic guitar and miscellaneous percussion.

John admitted that the closing guitar riff was inspired by the Dorsey and Johnny Burnette song, Lonesome Tears in My Eyes, which The Beatles had covered earlier in their career. It was released on May 30 during the second Bed-In for Peace in Montreal and would be the 17th and final UK No. 1 single for The Beatles. It also rocketed to the top of the charts in Germany, Australia, Holland, Norway, Spain, Belgium, Denmark and Malaysia. Unfortunately it peaked at only No. 8 in the US for a very simple reason. More than half of America's Top 40 rock radio stations refused to play a song that mentioned Christ, no matter what the context. Many other stations beeped the allegedly offensive use of the word. Some US radio program directors described the chorus reference to the religious deity as profane, sacrilegious, offensive and generally objectionable.

In a Rolling Stone story headed "Christ they know it ain't easy", my colleague Ben Fong-Torres wrote: ``In San Francisco, Bill Gavin, influential record programmer (at that time in 1969), turned thumbs down on the Beatles record - 'I personally found it offensive' he explained - while admitting, in his newsletter, that 'the instrumental track is great and Lennon sings with conviction'. He is keeping the record off his Recommended Playlist."

Among stations banning the record, Gavin said, were WMCA in New York, WLS in Chicago, and almost all of the (key Top 40) stations around the country. In an informal poll of his 112 correspondents, Gavin found only 21 stations playing the single. This rose to about 50 percent "but some of them are playing edited versions - they've beeped out the objectionable parts or cut out the lines about 'peace in bed'." (The line, sung in answer to reporters' questions at John and Yoko's Amsterdam Bed-in, goes, "We're only trying to get us some peace". For some listeners, it's just a little too close to "trying to get us a piece".) These are the inanities the Lennons were faced with in their quest to enlighten the world on the devastation of war.

I listened in Montreal as Lennon explained the meaning of the "Christ" line while calling US radio stations from his Queen Elizabeth Hotel Bed-in site with Yoko. "It has two meanings,' he told Bob Lewis of WABC-FM in New York. "It's like a prayer. You know, 'Jesus, you alone should know it ain't easy'. And it has that street language connotation, too. But even when it's used irreverently, it's in effect a prayer, too. It's a gospel song. I'm a big fan of Christ -the song is a prayer."

"Why is it being banned?" Lewis asked. "Man, you know why,' Lennon replied.

The especially spiritual Lennon was never sacriligious or irreverent in my presence but I know he had serious reservations – as did we all – about the relative intelligence of some of the followers of the faith. John found this to be incredibly frustrating and at times, downright depressing. Far too many souls just didn't get it.

"Sometimes I just can't wait to get something (musically) new out,' John told me in December, 1969. "They (the record company Apple and The Beatles) let me put *The Ballad of John and Yoko* out but I wanted it out as news, not as something like the film of the event. I wanted the video of the event happening then, and that's it, really. I offered *Cold Turkey* to The Beatles but they weren't ready to record a single, so I did it as the Plastic Ono Band. I don't care what it goes out as... as long as it goes out."

I asked John what he really thought of radio stations freaking out and censoring ``Christ'' out of his Ballad of John and Yoko - a not-for-publication reaction - and he didn't beat around the bush. ``I was really dumbfounded about it. I really couldn't believe it myself. Although I suppose I should have expected it. There are a lot of hypocrites in America wanting to ban things and stop messages getting through. There's no point in getting upset about ignorant people. I just try to ignore it if I can. It's a pity the song didn't reach more people in America.

``How out of touch can these programming people be? I had begun to realise just how deeply this paranoia was set in. They would do anything to prevent their Lord's name being taken in any context. Now I knew for sure that I couldn't talk about religious people in any way without offending these people. Even when I was being complimentary.''

In his last interview with David Sheff of Playboy magazine, Lennon observed: "With Yoko and my first attempts at being together and producing things together, we crossed over into each other's fields, like people do from country music to pop. We did it from avant-garde left field to rock'n'roll left field. We tried to find a ground that was interesting to both of us. And we both got excited and stimulated by each other's experiences.

"So the first attempts were the Bed-Ins. We attempted to make music together, but that was a long time ago. People still had this idea that The Beatles were some kind of thing that shouldn't step outside of its circle, and it was hard for us to work together then. We think either people have forgotten or they've grown up. Now we'll make the foray into the place where she and I are together and it's not 'some wondrous prince from the rock world dabbling with this strange Oriental woman', which is the picture projected by the press."

``That's why we ended up doing things like Bed-Ins, and Yoko ended up doing things like pop music,' John said in his last interview. ``With our first attempts at being together and producing things together, whether they were Bed-Ins or posters or films, we crossed over into each other's fields, like people do from country music to pop. We did it from avant-garde left field to rock'n'roll left field.

``We tried to find a ground that was interesting to both of us. And we both got excited and stimulated by each other's experiences. The things we did together were all variations on a theme really. We wanted to know what we could do together, because we wanted to be together. We want to work together. We don't just want to be together on weekends. We want to be together and live together and work together. So the first attempts were the Bed-Ins.

Asked in Amsterdam if the whole Bed-In thing was "just one big put on", John responded: "We are not laughing at you any more than you're laughing at us. It was just our protest against violence. Everybody has their own bag and this is ours. The way we look at it is this: in Paris, the

Vietnam peace talks have got about as far as sorting out the shape of the table they are going to sit around. These talks have been going on for months. In one week in bed, we achieved a lot more."

But the cynical censorship in the US of *The Ballad of John and Yoko*, which is the story of the wedding and the Amsterdam Bed-In, was the type of media response that John Lennon had to face in the aftermath of his misinterpreted comment about how The Beatles were more popular than Jesus Christ, which caused an international scandal. He was quickly learning that in the good old Godly USA there was no such thing as freedom of expression. As always, Gods and guns ruled!

*FOOTNOTE

The Vietnam War was a conflict between the north and south of that country which became an international engagement of the Cold War, with the US and its allies backing the south while the communist countries supported the north. It ran from 1955 to 1975 with the north prevailing.

4. THE AMERICAN ATTACKS FROM MONTREAL AND THE BED-IN

By the time late April, 1969, had rolled around, the Lennons realised it was imperative to take their *War Is Over* peace campaign to North America. To the United States, the centre of militarism - and the principal perpetrators of a war against the internal affairs of another country, Vietnam.

But there was a major hurdle - John was barred from entry into the US because of a minor marihuana bust in 1968, when he and Yoko were staying in Ringo Starr's inner-London flat. They were charged with possession of a small amount of hash and, hoping to simplify the legal minefield, John pleaded guilty and the charges against Yoko were dropped. The blot on his record would be used as a reason to deny John immigration status in the US for several years. We draw your attention to the fact that these charges were drummed up by a crooked cop, as shall be revealed herein.

Initially John and Yoko flew to the Bahamas and spent a night at the Sheraton Oceanus Hotel, where they were charged $(US)130 for a room service orange juice and pushy hotel staff demanded tips for services rendered - before they were rendered. Beatles' confidante and publicist Derek Taylor was not impressed by this rip-off. ``It was too hot down there, too far from the US and the hotels were terrible,' he declared.

So the party flew on to Toronto. I was sitting at my desk in the Toronto Globe and Mail on a day full of the promise of spring when a call came through from the King Edward Sheraton Hotel, one of Toronto's pre-eminent hostelries. It was Derek Taylor, my esteemed colleague from Apple Corps.

``Ritchie, hi there, it's Derek. Look mate, we're in Toronto and wondered if you could come over for a bit of a chat? We've got a bit of a problem you may be able to help us with, Ritchie.''

"Well, of course I can,' I replied and was soon heading along King Street to the King Eddie. I found John and Yoko, along with Derek, in very convivial spirits, but looking for a bit of guidance. Here they were in Canada, and after undergoing a gruelling immigration interview, they had been granted temporary visitor status for a period of 10 days. They'd found the Bahamas prohibitive in several ways, and were looking for a new location for their second Bed-In for Peace, this time an event organised to reach the heartland of US media.

But where would they do it? Toronto the Good, heart of Canadian Waspville and old school straightness and conservatism? Doubtful. After some intense discussion, we (John, Yoko, Derek and myself) arrived at the conclusion that Montreal, in the French-speaking region of Quebec, nicknamed La Belle Province, would be the ideal location for the second Bed-In. It was cosmopolitan, edgy, not traditional English and most importantly, an hour distant from the US media power centre of New York City.

The ever-efficient Taylor made some calls and Montreal was settled on as the central scenario for the second Bed-In. On the afternoon of May 26, they invited me to join them on their departure for the airport and for the chance of an exclusive behind-the-scenes interview. But what an escape it would be! I had never seen Beatlemania in its full roar, but I was to be exposed to an alarming taste of it in the corridors of the King Eddie and in the limo tooling out to the airport...

It was meant to be a top-secret exit from the hotel, before flying to Montreal. We'd left several phone lines angrily buzzing, carnations littered over beds and rugs, unopened letters and telegrams, even an advance signed copy of novelist (and fellow guest at the King Eddie Hotel) Jacqueline Susann's latest semi-pornographic epic - dumped in the trash can covered with John Lennon's fingerprints. Wish I'd stopped to gather it up, on reflection, during our escape from John and Yoko's room..

A porter had gathered up the Lennons' bags and a limousine was waiting in the hotel basement. But after slipping out of the room we were assailed by a pack of fans gathering up steam down the corridor. There were several score of them, passionate and poised to pounce. Under the direction of past fan-mania master and never-panicked Derek Taylor, we blazed down the corridor towards the hordes. Along the way, the universe descended and granted us safe passage. A nearby service elevator bobbed up at our urgent button-pushing. We dived inside, just as the hordes reached us. The door closed on the jostling, shouting mob. It was a nightmare of epic proportions! In the basement, we hurried towards the limo but suddenly the fans were on us. All over us. The car was covered in a crush of slithering bodies - fervent fans desperate to find some physical connection with John Lennon of The Beatles. Just to touch him, reach him, grab him and capture him!

But the car offered protection and as it eased forward the frenzied fans slipped, jumped or fell off. Holy fucking hell! These were mere skirmishes in the everyday life of John Lennon and any of The Beatles. As the limo scooted away, John sat back and heaved a sigh of relief. He looked tired. Yoko was nonchalant. Lennon, all in white, sighed again and observed to nobody in particular: ``I think Ringo was right about us not touring.'' And later: ``The Beatles are just a democratic group of middle-aged teenagers. We just don't happen to agree on doing concert tours. I've wanted to do some for a while, but I'm not sure any more.''

It was an uneventful ride to the Toronto Airport, a welcome respite from the madding crowds. Pleasant conversation and gentle reflections pervaded the Caddie. But the punters and fans were never far from sight. We arrived unannounced at the airport but in no more than a minute a crowd had gathered and we were ushered into a small, vacant room. We sat there for over an hour while the Lennons awaited their flight to Montreal and the launch of the second Bed-In - there was John, Yoko, daughter Kyoko, who was five, a Beatles cameraman and myself.

It was a chance to catch up on a number of matters and I didn't hold back. There were a few lurking topics I was keen to raise, such as the storm of controversy that had accompanied the November, 1968, release of the *Two Virgins* album, which pictured John and Yoko naked on its jacket.

I fondly recall a *Two Virgins* cover story told me by a gentleman who worked at London Life magazine and had done some art direction and general photography work for the Lennons. Apparently he'd been handed an undeveloped roll of film by John and was asked to have it processed. He dropped the film at a London lab but when he went to collect the negs and proof sheet, he was asked if he knew what was on the film. The lab staff were more than normally curious about this particular contacts sheet. Turned out that it was a series of candid shots of the world's most famous couple in the buff, the Lennons in the nude. There was much pseudoshock all around.

``I expected some noise about the cover shot but not as much as we got,'' John sheepishly admitted. "I'd planned to produce an album with Yoko before we became lovers. Paul had (as a protege) Mary Hopkin while George had Jackie Lomax, but I wanted to do something with Yoko. I was in India meditating about the album, when it suddenly hit me. I wrote Yoko telling her that I planned to have her in the nude on the cover. She was quite surprised, but nowhere near as much as George or Paul (were surprised).. Paul gave me long lectures about it, and said, `Is there really any need for this?'. It took me five months to persuade them (to *Let It Be*).

``It was a natural turn of events that I got into the picture too. When we got the pictures back, I admit I was a bit shocked. I thought, 'Hello, we're on'. I figure that if I was mildly shocked, what would others think? But it was worth it for the howl that went up. It really blew their minds. It cleared the air a bit. People always try to kill anything that's honest. The album wasn't ugly - it was just a point of view."

Despite police confiscations and other outrages, the *Two Virgins* cover did not create as big a stir as the alleged masturbation incident involving The Doors' lead singer Jim Morrison during a Florida concert (for which he was recently granted a posthumous pardon in late 2010). ``I wasn't particularly impressed by all that,' Lennon commented. ``I suppose the show wasn't going too well so Jim decided to liven things up a bit. If he likes masturbating, that's OK. If he did do it, I would have liked to see him do it properly and actually have intercourse on stage. Actually we now have a play on Broadway called *Oh! Calcutta* which has a piece written by us (a clutch of other artists also contributed sketches) in which four guys are masturbating.''

Lennon insisted he still believed The Beatles had more influence over young people than Jesus Christ, an outlook which brought a heavy load of wrath upon him when first mentioned two years previously. ``Some ministers even stood up in their churches and agreed with it then,' John said.

``Kids are still more influenced by us than by Jesus Christ, and make of that what you will. It says a lot. As it happens, I'm very big on Jesus Christ personally. I've always fancied him because he was honest. He said in his book that anyone who followed his ways would be knocked. He was so right about that! I'm always saying his name and talking about him.'' (The word Christ is featured several times in the chorus of The Beatles' single *The Ballad of John and Yoko*, which was banned by hundreds of American radio stations. Lennon's reaction to that censorial attitude: ``It's pure hypocrisy.'') John's supposed denigration of Jesus Christ has been vastly misunderstood, especially in the bible belt regions of rural America. John certainly was not boasting about the Beatles being more popular than Jesus Christ on some philosophical Top 40 preference chart. He thought it a defining factor in contemporary life that any pop group or musical act could be more keenly followed than a spiritual pundit. This said much about the society in which we exist.

A couple of days after the Lennons had descended on Toronto en route to Montreal, I convinced my editors at The Globe and Mail that I should be present bedside at the Queen Elizabeth Hotel where the Lennons were bedded in. It was an extremely colorful scene - a potted purple gloxinia plant, signs, placards and proclamations covering the walls, John's Gibson guitar, candles, other burning objects and an expanding set of lyrics to a new and emerging Lennon song temptingly entitled *Give Peace a Chance.*

John's assorted doodlings were everywhere. Yoko's daughter Kyoko (from her marriage to US filmmaker Tony Cox) offered an alternative to all the talk of non-violent anarchy and changing the world. On first inspection, the trappings of peace were everywhere. John and Yoko were perched on the bed in white pyjamas and there were vases of pale pastel-coloured flowers, while a bunch of scribblings and sketches adorned the walls of the suite.

Just before settling on Montreal as the location for the second Bed-In there had been significant anti-war protests on US campuses. Harvard students had gone on strike, while in Berkeley, San Francisco, students had objected to private property rights and occupied a communal space called People's Park on a vacant lot owned by the University of California. As the Montreal Bed-In unfolded, university officials had asked police to clear out and destroy the park. A contingent of about 800 police officers hammered into 6000 demonstrators killing one, blinding another and injuring more than 100 others. This led to a further demonstration of 20,000 students marching in protest against police brutality and the closure of the park.

John was horrified up by these developments and was keen to play a role in a peaceful resolution of the problems. He made himself available to radio station KPFA on a regular basis to discuss the confrontation and pour some oil on very troubled waters. He was totally opposed to confrontational tactics, which inevitably lead to more violence.

``I don't believe there's any park worth getting shot for. You can do better by moving on to another city or going to Canada. Then they've got nothing to attack and nobody to point the finger at,' John declared from his bed in La Belle Province. The KPFA announcer was desperately anxious to know how John would handle the situation if he was on deck in Berkeley. ``I'd be urging a music festival to take place. Sing Hare Krishna or something. But don't move about if it aggravates the pigs, don't get hassled by the cops, don't play their games. I know it's hard. Christ, you know it ain't easy, you know how hard it can be. But everything's hard - it's better to have it hard than not have it at all.''

I sat on the floor in John and Yoko's room and listened to him expound on his principles of peace.

``You've got to entice the police! Calm them! You can make it, man! We can make it - together! Just don't fall into those same old traps.'' He continued to explain the scenario as he saw it from 2500 miles away in Montreal. ``The students are being conned. It's just like the typical school bully - he aggravates you and aggravates you until you try to hit him. And then they kill you, like has happened in Berkeley. The Establishment - it's just a name for evil. The monster doesn't care - the blue meanie is insane. We really care about life. Destruction is good enough for the Establishment. The only thing they can't control is the mind. And we have to fight for sanity and peace on that level. But the students have gotten conned into thinking they can change it with violence and they can't, you know, they can only make it uglier and worse.''

For several long days, John kept arguing against a violent response to any provocation. He conducted more than 50 radio interviews extolling the virtues of peace and it was a convincing message ... especially to a generation of peaceniks. A succession of clear-thinking left-of-centre celebrities was invited to join the Lennons at the Bed-In in Montreal, among them human rights campaigner Dick Gregory, social commentator Timothy Leary and his wife Rosemary, comedian and TV show host Tommy Smothers, British/French singer Petula Clark, Rabbi Abraham Feinberg* and music critic, Village Voice contributor and civil rights campaigner Nat Hentoff. Unfortunately Hentoff - an early supporter of the Lennon anti-war outlook - would ultimately blot his copybook by coming out in favour of the disgusting invasion of Iraq by the USA. But back in 1969, all the above were enthusiastic supporters of a peace-at-almost-any-cost philosophy. And they were joined by the Canadian chapter of the Hare Krishnas.

It wasn't always a waltz in peace-time, and eventually the enemy made an appearance. Not everybody invited to the Montreal Bed-In was a believer in peace. Cartoonist Al Capp, creator of the acclaimed L'il Abner comic strip, was a right-wing extremist and agitator, as he proved soon after entering the Lennons' boudoir. Capp had been in a trolley car accident when he was nine years old, resulting in the amputation of a leg. He maintained an ugly and bitter outlook for the rest of his rather sinister life (he died in 1979), which ultimately saw him trying to take advantage of gullible young women on the college lecture trail. This was not a splendid specimen of the human race, in my opinion, and he could act like a real scumbag, as I was about to witness.

Capp was the son of Russian immigrants who'd arrived in the US in the late 19th century. Apparently they were so poor his mother used to venture out at night to sift through other people's rubbish to find reusable pieces of coal, according to later researchers. Surviving this undistinguished scenario, Capp based his cast of characters on genuine hillbillies he met while hitchhiking through rural West Virginia as a teenager, years before the Tennessee Valley Authority Act brought basic utilities like electricity to the region. Alfred G. Caplin eventually became "Al Capp" because the syndicate which contracted for the L'il Abner strip felt his original name would not fit in a cartoon frame. Capp changed his name legally in 1949. In May 1969 he'd been invited bedside by the Canadian Broadcasting Corporation in an attempt to provide balance in their coverage of the peace protest.

I believe this scammer had been paid to come to Montreal and sabotage the John Lennon peace movement. At any rate, he tried his darndest to arouse the enmity of Lennon. It certainly worked on the rest of those present. Following his taunting of the Lennons, others in the bedroom were more than ready, this writer included, to throttle him into silence. But John remained impervious to insult. He was not about to be brought down by this degenerate.

Capp: suspiciously shuffled into the Bed-In suite and immediately sought support for his physical disability.

John: Would you like to sit at the edge of the bed, here?

Capp: I'd like something hard, for instance. There's a chair.

John: We're those famous freaks.

Capp: So far, you've been confronted mainly with admirers and I may wind up to be one, you never can tell.

John: We've had all sorts in here, believe me.

Capp: I'm sure you have. One of the things that interested me was the method you've chosen to inspire peace.

4. THE AMERICAN ATTACKS FROM MONTREAL AND THE BED-IN

John: We're trying to sell it like soap, you know, and the only way to sell it is to focus attention and sell every day.

Capp: Well, you feel that being in bed compels more attention than if you were sitting in chairs?

John: Yes, and it makes it easier for us because we talk 10 hours a day and it's functional for us to be lying down, you know.

Capp: Now, don't you think that being in bed is one thing, but you could go further. You could shower together.

John: We just did it. But I did it alone.

Capp: What about during World War II? If Hitler and Churchill had gotten into bed, which Hitler would have clearly enjoyed, do you ..

John (interrupting): I think that if Churchill and Hitler had got into bed, a lot of people would have been alive today!

Capp: I see. It's a way of doing it. Now, suppose Montgomery had gone to bed with Rommel .... John (interrupting): Beautiful!

Capp: Do you like that, John? Do you feel that this continent is one place to preach peace or will you preach equally in Peking (now Beijing)?

John: Sure. We're going to find out. I believe it's easier to get into Moscow than it is to get into the States, for a kick-off.

Capp: But don't you feel that they need you now in Peking and Hanoi (Vietnam)?

John: If we're needed at all, we're needed everywhere, but you can't be everywhere at once.

Capp: But I do hope that you plan to make them as peaceful as you've made these blood-crazed Canadians.

John: The best thing we've done so far is talk to the people at Berkeley and we think we had some influence in holding back the violence that was going to come out of that. And we believe that, and we talk to them solid every hour.

Capp: You haven't talked to them during this last week!

John: Ah, we talk to them every day. We talk on the phone, on the radio station live ...

Capp (interrupting): I saw them throwing rocks at cops just a couple of days ago. You'd better talk to them just a little more.

John: Well, no one got shot this time, did they?

Capp: No, nobody got shot.

John (interrupting furiously): And what are you doing about it?

Capp: What am I doing about it? I'm cheering the police. That's precisely what I'm doing about it.

Yoko: Why? Why?

Capp (getting agitated): Now, now, you people have a home in London. Are you permitting people to come in and defecate on the rugs, smash the furniture? No. Then why do you want them to do it in Berkeley?

John: We don't want them to do it at Berkeley. We tell them to protest in some other way. If they had stayed in bed at Berkeley, they wouldn't have got killed.

Capp: Now simmer down, simmer down, just rest.

Yoko: Can we have a conversation instead of, you know…

Capp (interrupting): I'll be delighted with any conversation.

Yoko: OK.

Capp: Good God, you're an unbelievable couple.
(Laughter fills the suite.)

John: Nice try.

Capp: I can see why you want peace. God knows you can't have much from my own observations. But anyway … from my point of view, I am sorry for you. Now, I read something that said you were very shy people.

Yoko: Yes we are.

Capp: And yet … (he brandishes the *Two Virgins* album cover).

John (interrupting): Does that prove that you're not shy?

Capp: Certainly not. Only the shyest people in the world would take pictures like that.

John: Do shy people ever become naked or not?

Capp: If that is a picture of two shy people, I'd like to know what shyness is.

Yoko: May I ask you: Would you consider yourself shy?

Capp: Oh I'm just normal. I think that everybody owes it to the world to prove they've got pubic hair. And you've got it, and I applaud you for it. (Laughter again rings around the suite.)

Yoko: If you want to prove it, you can prove it.

Capp: I don't think there's any great interest in it. Clearly, you must have felt that the world wanted to know what your private parts looked like and now the world knows. Now, you wrote a song, and one of the lines, and correct me if I'm wrong, 'Christ, it ain't easy' …

John (interrupting): Rubbish! I didn't say that. The lyrics go, 'Christ, you know it ain't easy, you know how hard it can be, the way things are going, they're going to crucify me', and you, baby.

Capp: But, in the lyric, you said they're going to crucify you.

John: Yeah, you can take it literally.

Capp: So, how did you mean it?

John: It means everything you want it to mean.

Capp: What did you want it to mean?

John: They're going to crucify me and you and everyone else.

Capp: I'm upset that they're going to crucify me. Who's going to make the time to crucify you?

John: Oh, if you're going to take everything literally.

Yoko: Me is you.

Capp: I don't permit you to speak for me. Who are you speaking for?

John: I took that liberty, Mr Capp.

Capp: That's too much of a liberty.

John: I'm speaking on behalf of people in general, you know.

Capp: You're speaking for yourselves.

John: I'm sorry that it upsets you.

Capp: It doesn't upset me.

John: I can choose to sing about whatever I want in whatever fashion I wish.

Capp: Yes, but you mustn't include me. Now, you're not my spokesman, are we agreed?

John: I'm everyone's spokesman.

Capp: You're not mine.

John: You're mine and I'm yours.

Capp: I don't say, 'I'm speaking for John Lennon.'

John: As a representative of the human race, I'm speaking for us all, whether you like it or not.

Capp: Whatever race you're representative of, I ain't a part of it.

John: What do you write your cartoons for?

Capp: I write my cartoons for money, just as you sing your songs. Exactly the same reason, and exactly the same reason much of this is happening too, if the truth be told.

John: Do you think I couldn't earn money by some other way than sitting in bed for seven days, taking shit from people like you. I could write a song in an hour …

Capp (interrupting and annoyed): Now, now, look here. You got into bed so people like me can come and see you.

John: Right, but not for money, like you're saying.

Capp: Er … it won't do you any real harm, except it might give you bedsores. I'll tell you what'll do you harm …

John (interrupting): I can earn money by easier ways than doing this.

Capp: So can I. I make a lot more drawing people like you than confronting you, and I must say it's more appetizing drawing them,' cos I can leave. What you've just done now is, when you said, 'Taking shit from people like you', now, I was invited here. You knew I was coming …

John (interrupting): So, we're not doing it for money. You indicated I was doing it for money. Do you have manners?

Capp: I'm your guest. John: And I'm yours.

Capp: No, you're not. This is your bedroom.

Capp (to Yoko): I'm delighted to have met you, Madame Nhu (a widely detested former first lady of Vietnam). You are our answer to Madame Nhu. But, I'm sure that the other three guys, the other three, are gentlemen.

John: What does that mean?

Capp: Think about it.

Derek Taylor (who had been listening to the conversation from the side of the bed): Get out!

John: I'll try and work it out now, Derek.

Capp: Oh really, come on.

Derek Taylor: I'm not having these people spoken to like that. John: We asked him here.

Derek Taylor: Forgive me.

Capp: Derek, it's not for me to forgive you. It's for your psychiatrist.

John: And yours, baby. You've just done a great deal for peace, Mr Capp. With that, this physical and mental cripple scampered out of the room.

On reflection, I see him as a master manipulator, driven by profit at any cost (imagine how much he would have been able to pocket if he had provoked John Lennon, peacenik, into physical violence). Al Capp was from the bottom of the barrel, as his subsequent history would demonstrate.

The main character of his comic strip L'il Abner was a rural hick named Yokum. Apparently the name was a combination of yokel and hokum, which Capp later explained thus: "It's phonetic Hebrew - that's what it is, all right - and that's what I was getting at with the name Yokum, more so than any attempt to sound hickish. That was a fortunate coincidence, of course, that the name should pack a backwoods connotation. But it's a Godly conceit, really, playing off a Godly name - Joachim means 'God's determination', something like that - that also happens to have a rustic ring to it."

Capp just didn't get the '60s protest movement. In a televised appearance on The Dick Cavett Show with other guests including eccentric musician Frank Zappa, Capp apparently sarcastically questioned the outspoken performer on whether he thought he was a girl because of his long hair. Whereupon Zappa, a bit of a smooth wordsmith himself, responded with the cutting question:

``You have a wooden leg: does that make you a table?'' Touché!

Two years after the Montreal Bed-In, syndicated columnists Jack Anderson and Brit Hume alleged instances of sexual harassment by Al Capp of students on a lecture tour. Capp allegedly propositioned a married student from the University of Wisconsin-Madison in his hotel room. After being charged over the incident, Capp pleaded no contest to "attempted adultery" (at the time of writing, adultery remains a crime in Wisconsin, attracting a penalty of $10,000 and/or up to 3.5 years in prison) and was fined $500. The resulting publicity led to hundreds of papers dropping his comic strip and Capp, already in failing health from a lifetime of tobacco addiction, withdrew from public speaking.

Years later, on Inside the Actor's Studio, Goldie Hawn claimed Capp had sexually propositioned her during her auditions for the 1964 New York World's Fair. There were other reports of sexual propositioning by actresses such as Grace Kelly and Edie Adams.

In 1977, he finally retired his comic strip, which had long since been compiled by an assortment of associates. He even apologized for its latter-day lack of quality. "If you have any sense of humour about your strip - and I had a sense of humour about mine - you knew that for three or four years Abner was wrong. Oh hell, it's like a fighter retiring. I stayed on longer than I should have,' Capp admitted, adding "I can't breathe any more."

He died a victim of the tobacco industry, which had fought long and hard to prevent regulation of the poisons it was pushing on health grounds so that it could continue making profits at its customers' expense. This ugly face of capitalism was a system he embraced, and so for those who believe in karma, his slow death was apt. After a life of chain-smoking, Capp died from emphysema at his home in South Hampton, New Hampshire. Comic-strip fans may have been possibly distressed but among peace supporters, Capp would not be mourned.

What had been particularly galling about Capp's attack on the Lennons was his sneering, leering attitude to Yoko, whom he dismissed as some sort of Oriental freak with a mistaken agenda. He tried to insult the woman in order to infuriate the man. Human rights campaigner and black activist Dick Gregory, a friend of the Lennons who knew them well, later noted about Yoko's presence:

"We're not used to seeing an Asian that ain't bent over, smiling, apologetic. She never was that. When was the last time people in the press interviewed any Asian, much less an Asian woman, who looked you right in the eye, and answered your question, and could be as belligerent with her answer as you are with your question?

"I've never seen a relationship that was as equal. They came together, they moved together. It would have been very easy for him to be just John Lennon - the press didn't want this Asian to be any part of it. But he said, 'It's me and her. We are one.' He demanded that you not overlook her - that takes a very special animal."

Such ups and downs notwithstanding, all through the unfolding of the Montreal Bed-In John had been scribbling away on a new set of lyrics for a song he wanted to call *Give Peace a Chance*. Hour by hour, day by day, the words came together and as they did, John wrote them out on a large piece of white board and affixed them to the hotel suite wall. It was almost a detailing of creative progress. By the end of the Bed-In, it had fixated in his mind and he was ready to call in the roving recorder. He asked his record label EMI/Capitol to provide somebody with the expertise and equipment to record an on-location, in-the-bedroom rendition of his new song.

Later John would explain: ``I'm an artist and I'm both shy and aggressive. So I always have great hopes for what I'm doing with my work and I also harbour great despair that it's all shit. I go through all of that but in my secret heart, I really wanted to create something that would take over from *We Shall Overcome*, which is great in its own right but is hardly contemporary. I used to think, 'Why doesn't somebody write something that works for people right now?' And I suppose that in the end, that's what our job is, both me and Yoko.''

Folk singer Pete Seeger remarked about the song: ``Undoubtedly some people wanted to say a lot more than '*Give Peace a Chance*'. On the other hand, history gets made when people come to the same conclusion from many different directions. And this song did hit a common denominator. There's no doubt about it.''

In response to John's request, Derek Taylor approached EMI/Capitol's Montreal-based manager Pierre Dubord, who contacted a prominent Quebec producer/engineer/musician, Andre Perry. At 32, Perry was the most influential record maker in French Canada. Versions of his story of the making of *Give Peace a Chance* have been told many times over, but never with total accuracy. We are indeed fortunate that Andre - at the ripe old age of 72 - was both happy and able to provide us with the true account of what happened in the making of the anthem for peace.

``After I got the call from Pierre Dubord, I had to track down four-track mobile recording equipment. My own set-up was in Ottawa at the Arts Centre, where I was doing a quadraphonic playback of Tommy, the rock opera. In those days, four-track recorders were not common. They were very bulky and difficult to move around. So not having mine readily available, I arranged to rent one from RCA Victor,' Andre explained.

"When I arrived at the hotel early on the Saturday evening, there were about 40 or 50 people in the suite for the recording. But if you believed all the people who have claimed to have been there, it would have been about 3000! Let me say at the outset that there are a few things to be added to what I've been saying about *Give Peace a Chance* over all these years. The thing that is hardest to understand is how disorganised the whole proceedings were. How unrehearsed everything was! It was fully improvised. If there were 40 people in there contributing to the recording, there might have been 15 or 20 people singing in tune or banging in time. The rest was just noise which kind of spoilt it for everyone else. The end result was chaos!

"I knew when I first walked in that it was going to be a difficult situation. Firstly from an acoustic standpoint, because of the audio conditions in the room. The two parallel walls would create a standing wave, which is akin to having a big speaker in a small enclosure. The enclosure cannot contain the sound without creating a wave effect. So what I did was put John's voice and guitar on one track and Tommy Smothers' guitar on another track, leaving two tracks for the background vocals and effects.

"Nothing was changed or adulterated. That energy, that spirit, that feel, everything is all natural and real. So the essence of the song was captured there. After we captured what was felt to be a satisfactory take, I played it back to John through the headphones because we didn't have speakers. He listened to it and glanced at me with a funny look. 'Yeah,' I mumbled, 'I don't think it's usable. But I'll be back in the morning and I'll go into the studio and see what it's all about'." John said that would be fine.

"You know, I never expected to have a situation where the artist I was contracted to record would not have detailed what he wanted. He didn't - he had absolute faith in me to record it for him. He had full confidence. That outlook stayed with me. I wasn't a young kid then, I was 32. The fact that he, John Lennon, had so much faith believing in me - and not guiding me along the way or nothing - was quite incredible. Actually he spent most of the pre-recording time discussing the guitar styles and parts with Tommy Smothers and working on the words of the song. And trying to give some guidance to the people gathered in the hall, preparing to join in the singalong. But they were just hanging out at a party and weren't really taking notice. That was a pity.

"John didn't even want a run-through before recording. But I did - just to check the sounds and the levels. What John wanted with that song was for it to be spontaneous, not produced and not overly weird. He wanted it au naturale. But the other part of the equation, unfortunately, was that it was unmusical. And that was a problem. So I had two choices - fix it up somehow, or bring back the tapes and admit that it wasn't really usable. It was quite a dilemma for me.

``Before I went back to the studio to try to deal with this situation, I spent a wonderfully memorable time with Yoko and John recording the B side of the single, which was *Remember Love*. It was particularly memorable because I got to know them better through the intimacy. Secondly, they had just gotten married so there was a lot of love in the room. I could feel the presence of the real guy in John - he wasn't just the guy who was trying to drive the recording of the song. He was a very humble guy. The way he actually behaved with her - and the song was very hard to sing, no doubt about it.

``There were no `punching-in' possibilities (as is prevalent today with Pro Tools and other recording software). I was rolling the tape from top to bottom. I didn't have studio facilities so we had to run the tape of the song from beginning to end every time. You couldn't just drop something in. Yoko had to endure a lot of takes: she was not known to be a great singer and this was a very difficult song to sing. I thought to myself that she'd never get through it. It was a case of take after take and I wondered if her voice was going to give out. They'd do two or three takes and then they'd get on the bed and tickle themselves and have fun and I'd get up to excuse myself and they'd say `No no!'.

``It was quite something to be there. I wouldn't say I felt embarrassed but it was kind of awkward for me in a way. They were lying in front of the bed, on the floor. And I was in front of that with the two microphones. There were many, many takes. Maybe 20. But with patience and with love, he managed to capture her great performance. This was the B side of *Give Peace a Chance* but it was very much an audiophile recording. It's very pure with no EQ (for equalization), just straight to tape, not even through a mixing board. Even today when you listen to it, it should be in mono or very close stereo because they were that close together.

``Unfortunately unbeknownst to me, somebody in England at Apple Records later decided to put the voice on the left and the guitar on the right channel. That was stupid.

``So I did the four hours on *Remember Love* at the Queen Elizabeth Hotel and then I went to the studio for a listening session. I quickly realised there was no way the original version of *Give Peace a Chance* could be saved. The voice was good and the guitar parts were good. But the rest of it was not. It was out of tune and out of time in many parts. It would not work. I realised we needed an option. Primarily I was a musician and then a sound engineer and then a producer. I had recorded well-received albums by French Canadian stars such as Jean-Pierre Ferland and Robert Charlebois. So I had enough confidence to think I might be able to come back with an option version of the song for John to evaluate. I didn't want to produce it - merely re-create it.

``To make it work, I gathered together overnight a group of professional musicians (but not necessarily singers) and some friends and we went back into the studio and cut the song again. I made sure it didn't sound slick - it really sounded natural. I placed the mics in the studio so that people would get the 3D effect. I didn't create that atmosphere synthetically. We proceeded to create the rhythm using a telephone directory book - and we kind of built that up as the song unfolded and proceeded.

``We worked all night and I went back to see John and Yoko with no sleep in the late morning. Now, I said, you have a choice. John listened to both versions and was knocked out with what we'd done to save the song. He was extremely grateful and gave me a signed Hair Peace poster with some artwork drawn on it. I was very honoured.

``A few weeks later, I received a call from EMI Capitol head office in Toronto with the news that the single was being released the next week. Official Apple credits on the record would feature my name, plus the name of my studio and even its address. It was just like a business card but printed on a John Lennon Plastic Ono Band record. Imagine.

``That's when I got John's message. It was his way of thanking me really when you think about it. I had just done what needed to be done, had to be done. It's like when you see a big movie and it has special effects but you can't detect the special effects. They're the greatest special effects much greater than the in-your-face kind of stuff. And that's what I tried to do. I tried to take the feeling that unfolded when I was there at the hotel and I tried to reproduce that in the studio without the studio production stuff. It was about an audio documentary, not a slick recording ... it stands up today, to my ears.''

Andre's pride in his re-creation of *Give Peace a Chance* is not surprising. He was delighted when I finally let him know that John many years earlier had confided to me that Andre had actually saved the recording and that it would never have been released without his intervention. He was touched to hear that. And he would go on to other great accomplishments, including the creation of one of the world's first environmental recording studios at Morin Heights in the Laurentian Mountains, 40 miles from Montreal. It was a state-of-the art facility which hosted a flock of music superstars including, just for the record, Rush, Bryan Adams, the Bee Gees, Chicago, The Police, Wilson Pickett, Keith Richards, David Bowie, Roberta Flack, Nazareth and Sting. ``I always looked on a recording studio as more of an instrument than just a facility,' Andre observed.

But there was no doubting that *Give Peace a Chance* was a particularly special John Lennon effort, created in the vortex of the second Bed-In for peace in a country notorious for its anti-war agenda. The song was meant to emerge from John Lennon's magical connection with the open-mindedness of Canada. There was much, much less concern north of the 49th Parallel with the primeval passions of America, namely gods and guns! You can hear it in this song. It would go on to instant fame as the first non-Beatles single from John Lennon (it went out under the name of the Plastic Ono Band).

Forty years and five months after the Montreal Bed-In took place, the disgraced but not dispirited former US President George W. Bush set out on his post-presidential profiteering talkfest trail. Crossing Canada, he eventually arrived in Montreal at the end of October, checking in to the Queen Elizabeth Hotel. About 1000 local businessmen paid $400 to hear Bush's justification of his controversial warlike policies and invasions of other countries for a box office gross of $400,000, not chump change.

Not surprisingly in a neutral country, there was considerable protest against Bush's blatant profiteering from what many would consider to be his own historic violence-based mistakes.

There was considerable irony in the fact that Bush delivered his invasion justification in the same hotel where *Give Peace a Chance* had been recorded 40 years earlier. I sent off the press coverage to Yoko, who replied: "Thank you for sending me the information. I've read it very carefully, and in the end, I started crying. I don't know why. That was such a long time ago, it shouldn't matter." (It was October 2009, just a few days after what would have been John's 69th birthday.)

As John had said to me at Toronto International Airport en route to Montreal: ``Really, there's no difference between what we're doing now and what we've always done. The idea of peace has always been with us. You could smell it in the early Beatles songs.''

And what did John regard as the most satisfying event for him since The Beatles were formed? He didn't pause for a second. ``Meeting Yoko,' he grinned, putting his arm around her diminutive shoulders in the back of the limousine. Yoko simply smiled sweetly.

* Rabbi Feinberg - who had gained a reputation for being quite unorthodox after making a trip in 1967 to North Vietnam with three other well-known clergymen - was a keen supporter of the Lennons' peace cause. He had written a controversial book, *Rabbi Feinberg's Hanoi Diary*, and he undertook an extensive tour of the US and Canada speaking out against the Vietnam War. He encouraged John and Yoko in a number of significant ways. He had attended the Montreal Bed In and had suggested a slight change in John's lyrics for *Give Peace a Chance*. Whereupon John had urged the rabbi to make his own album, *I Was So Much Older Then*, which was released in 1969. John and Yoko didn't have a lot of genuine friends within the ranks of the Establishment, and even though the rabbi was regarded as a radical in some circles, he reached across a significant divide to the Lennons. After his wife Ruth passed away in 1971, Rabbi Feinberg relocated to California for a new start. He died of cancer in Reno, Nevada in October 1986.

5. I AM THE WALRUS

For nigh on 40 years, the world at large has blamed Yoko Ono for the break-up of The Beatles. They are wrong. It was me. I was the walrus*.

The inevitable dissolution began to unfold before the Japanese avant-garde artist appeared on John Lennon's radar. Certainly Yoko had constantly encouraged John to believe in himself and in his individual talents, but I provided the key which opened the prison door enabling John to be free of the dependence on his old mates and the only band he had ever played with. Subconsciously, I sensed John's unease over the future of The Beatles - and that he was looking for an escape route - as I worked closely with him and Yoko on the Montreal Bed-In for peace. When opportunity knocked in the most extraordinary way, I seized it.

In his own mind, Lennon had already shut the door on The Beatles. He wanted a fresh challenge and a chance to perform in a band that enhanced his songs, rather than being forced to embellish the songs of the other Beatles, as had essentially been the case for the past couple of years. This was demonstrated most particularly true in one of the Beatles' least praiseworthy songs, *Maxwell's Silver Hammer*. Lennon despised this song - and the massive and even obsessive attention given to it in the studio - more than to almost any other Beatles' song creation. George Harrison shared his outlook.

It wasn't so much that John was aiming to leave The Beatles - he was merely aspiring to become one with himself. To burst forth from the jail the band had built around itself, in order to ensure its survival. As the ancient sages have long chronicled, the castle inevitably falls from within.

Here's how this castle fell.

It had been a pleasantly warm September afternoon in London in 1969 when I dropped into the Apple Corps offices on Savile Row. I was in England, holidaying from Canada with my wife and mixing the odd rock interview with sightseeing and museum visits. I had absolutely no idea that I was about to play a monumental role in music history. Or be part of an event that Rolling Stone magazine is reported to have described as the second-most-important in rock history.

Recently asked what was THE most important event, Rolling Stone founder and celebrated bon vivant, Jann Wenner, wasn't quite sure.

"When John met Paul; when Bob Dylan arrived in New York City; the birth of Elvis ... you've got me," Wenner wrote in response to my query. He couldn't recall the original context.

I'd dropped into The Beatles' office to confirm with publicist and comrade Derek Taylor an exclusive interview with George Harrison that Derek had managed to pull together for me as a trusted confidante of The Beatles.

Derek was a special friend - as he was to a coterie of critics and commentators - and I counted myself fortunate to have a positive connection with him. I admired his deft handling of The Beatles' media relations, which were often prickly because of the appalling attitudes of some of Fleet Street's tabloid editors. The latter-day Beatles' refusal to bend over to hypocrisy - as demonstrated by the release of John and Yoko's *Two Virgins* nude album jacket the year before only crystallized the media battlefield. Derek, an affable ex-columnist for The Daily Post and Echo in Liverpool, presented as the spokesperson for The Beatles and carried the challenge with style and grace.

The exclusive interview with George Harrison had been scheduled for the following Monday to discuss the forthcoming *Abbey Road* album. But on hearing my voice in in the corridor outside his ground-floor Bag One offices, John Lennon called me in for "some advice". (In an audiotape of the conversation in the office prior to my being summonsed, Lennon's aide, Anthony Fawcett, can be heard informing John and Yoko that "the Rolling Stone reporter with the ginger walrus moustache" was outside. Apart from my mainstream newspaper gig I was also Canadian editor of the emerging underground culture and specialist music publication.) I was one of the Lennon's links to the editorial coverage of their activities in the energetic young rock publication.

As I entered the office, I saw across the black leather desk that Lennon was speaking quizzically into the phone and Yoko was perched in a large chair next to him. Fawcett hovered nearby awaiting instructions and directions. He was slick, one had to admit, as he fielded a variety of questions and suggestions from John and/or Yoko. Fawcett would later observe in his memoir, *One Day at a Time*: "John had a special sort of power. He didn't have to exert himself to use it; it just seemed to flow from him. His personality was electric, his wit razor sharp, and his whole being radiated an alertness I had never seen before."

As I waited for John to finish his phone call, I looked around the spacious white room which was covered with wall decorations – newspaper front pages, latest-edition teaser sheets, memorable feature stories and the odd offbeat drawing. There were no framed accolades or gold albums from The Beatles. This, after all, was the headquarters of Bag Productions, John and Yoko's personal creative services company. Ultimately it had nothing to do with the rest of the band, apart from being housed in the same upmarket inner-city terrace mansion, which Apple had bought in for a reported half a million pounds in early 1969. The Lennons' mutual desk was littered with papers, file folders, black and white photo-prints, Apple teacups and takeaway hot beverage containers.

"Hi, how are you Ritchie?" John said as he slapped down the phone. "Maybe you could help us here. We just seem to be getting a bunch of lies from Canadian Immigration saying they'll give us a chartered plane to go play a rock concert this weekend. And put us up in a castle or something. What is this all about?"

John was plainly talking about the Toronto Rock'n'roll Revival, a huge event that was to feature a host of legendary '50s acts the next weekend. The show had been talked up for weeks back in Toronto and there was considerable media interest in the diverse and broad talent line-up. It promised a summertime return to the glories of the early days of rock'n' roll. Ticket sales had not been particularly strong, however, and a lot of hope had been invested in late-walk-up ticket sales. Those would surely come once the extraordinary story unfolding here in Lennon's office gained oxygen.

I told John that I certainly knew John Brower and Ken Walker (he died in early 2011), the show's promoters. "Well, we seem to be getting invites from the Immigration Department, but I'm not sure about it," added John. Yoko, clearly intrigued by the concert's prospects, asked if I could find out who and what was behind the invitation, adding, "It would be very nice of you". And, while also urging me to call Brower, John suggested that I "find out how much" they were paying, too!

He paused while Fawcett organised the connection at the secretary's desk on the other side of the room. Looking straight through me, John asked: "It won't turn into a rockers' (obviously implying motor bikers) festival, will it?" "Oh no," I replied, "It's not that sort of festival." There would be no shades of Altamont in this scenario.

"It would be nice if we could get some sort of a group together to take over there," John said, rubbing the stubble on his chin. "I wonder if George would do it?" He paused for several contemplative seconds. ``No, I doubt he'd come all the way to Canada. I don't really need Ringo, I need a group, you know. A new group of sorts."

"Would Paul go?" speculated Fawcett, knowing full well that pigs were more likely to fly over the Empire State Building than the bass player performing or doing anything, anywhere, for any reason with his song-writing partner.

"No, no. George is the only hope," Lennon insisted. "He was going to do the Hyde Park show with me." (A free concert in Hyde Park had been mooted by John and Yoko, to follow similar events at that venue by the Rolling Stones and Blind Faith, which never eventuated).

Yoko suggested that Eric Clapton might be up for the gig and Lennon asked his personal assistant to track him down. Lowering his voice as though his office might be bugged, John then confided to me that he had a secret agenda in all of this – he was very keen to see how he could cope on the performance stage without his usual comrades. "I think I can do it but I want to be absolutely sure. So I need to play a show to find out how it will work out. That's why I'm really keen to get this happening," he revealed. "I want to take the chance of finding out if I can do this in a different way. Something new without the old hassles. I'm just a wee bit tired of the old set-up. It's just not working any more. It doesn't feel right. That old magic isn't there any more." Yoko held John's hand and nodded sympathetically. She was plainly familiar with his building frustration.

John certainly didn't need to explain to me in any clearer terms that he was looking for a chance to play WITHOUT Paul, George and Ringo. I quickly got the drift. I knew John Brower from when he had promoted (with his business partner Ken Walker) the Toronto Pop Festival the previous year. I had functioned as a freelance writer/consultant for that event.

Brower had initially cold-called John and Yoko at the Apple office at the shrewd suggestion of Kim Fowley, an unusual music biz character from Hollywood who'd been hired to emcee the Revival show (Fowley passed away in 2015). A good purveyor of an intriguing pitch, Brower had been trying to convince the Lennons that they should attend the planned historic musical event. Maybe, suggested the ever-eager Brower, they would consider a performance piece at the show? Perhaps sing a couple of numbers? Maybe toss up some rock'n'roll oldies to fit with the mood of the show? The smooth-talking promoter had managed to stir a spark in John, a curiosity about what would ensue if he did in fact do this. What would they, his long-term bandmates, think of something like that? How would that upset the finely-balanced apple cart at 3 Savile Row?

It was a threatening scenario but I knew Brower and Ken Walker well enough to believe they would aim to do the right thing by an inquisitive and frustrated John. I pushed the "Yes" button:

"I'd have no hesitation in saying to you 'do it', John! And I say that as a dear friend who feels the frustrations of your current predicament, I declared." Privately, I considered that even though he hadn't played a public performance in more than three years, this could be the perfect re-entry point, the chance to get back on the live flight deck, even one step beyond The Beatles. Find out what life was like without the other three from the band. "Move forward brother!"

The timing could not have been better for John, who had recently realised that in order to produce songs like Cold Turkey (itself inspired by the pressures of the band's 1968 decay and his withdrawal from a modest heroin-smoking habit, which was rejected by The Beatles as a song the band should record), he had to recruit outside musicians who were totally in tune with his trip. But Brower initially encountered a wall of reluctance. To the possibility of attending the Revival as spectators, John said: "We can't do that. Yoko and I sitting in the audience would be like a King and Queen number."

Several calls and a couple of hours later, John was prepared to commit to the possibility of performing at the Toronto Rock'n'roll Revival. There was some light-hearted banter but every now and then a flash of bitterness would appear and John would comment, sarcastically, on some aspect of The Beatles' life. He had a biting wit and a keen sense of how to present his case. By the end of the day, the trip was on.

Two days later, the Lennons gathered at Heathrow Airport with guitarist Eric Clapton, Klaus Voormann (bass player with Manfred Mann and an old friend from The Beatles' early days in Hamburg), Alan White (drummer with Alan Price and later with Yes), Beatles' manager Allen Klein and roadie Mal Evans for the flight to Toronto and a show later that evening. But not before quite a bit of subterfuge had gone down. Voormann and White were easy to track down and eager to join the planned Plastic Ono Band. It was a new band name John had concocted for his first 45rpm single release outside of The Beatles, *Give Peace a Chance*, which had been released on American Independence Day, July 4.

Press officer Derek Taylor had explained the change of moniker for the media: "They said, 'You are The Plastic Ono Band' and that is the truth. You are and I am, and The Beatles are, any of them, or none at all. Anyone. The band may be the property of Apple, but it also belongs to everyone, because what it represents is freedom, freedom for performers to be themselves, taking no heed of who they are or what they may look like or where they have been or what their music is supposed to be. I phoned

John to ask what he would say The Plastic Ono Band was. He said he wouldn't know what to say ... except ... 'You are The Plastic Ono Band', and because you are you, you understand, don't you?"

Thus John would appear with his Plastic Ono Band at the Toronto Rock'n'roll Revival and at a Peace for Christmas show in aid of UNICEF at the Lyceum Ballroom in London in mid-December. Later, he explained: "I'm trying to get it across that The Plastic Ono Band (always) plays the unexpected. It could be anything. It could be *Blue Suede Shoes*, or it could be Beethoven's *Ninth*. People should expect something (in advance) from The Beatles or The Stones, but with The Plastic Ono Band, anything goes. I can't do variety any more."

But on the morning of the planned departure for the Toronto gig, Eric Clapton and the Lennons were not so accessible. An hour before the booked departure flight the party minus these key players had dutifully made their way to Heathrow. Anthony Fawcett, who was also passionately in favour of John stepping out of his Beatles cage, hastily put through a call to John and Yoko's Tittenhurst Park home to see if they were ready. He was told by Val, the cook, that the couple were still asleep and did not wish to be disturbed. Undaunted, Fawcett asked Val to knock on their bedroom door. "I've just got to speak to them," he begged. He later wrote in his memoir: "I realised that despite all the arrangements, our chances of seeing John Lennon on stage again were pretty remote." That view was reinforced when Val finally succeeded in getting Fawcett on the line with his boss. Cancelling the appearance, John explained to his PA: "We couldn't wake up in time, and anyway, Yoko doesn't feel well. Send them a telegram to cancel it - and send them a big bunch of white flowers saying 'Love and peace, John and Yoko'."

The irrepressible Fawcett wasn't giving up that easily. And not with me breathing down his scrawny neck. He temporarily forgot about sending the telegram and the flowers and rushed from Heathrow to nearby Tittenhurst Park in Ascot, hoping in person to encourage the couple to reconsider. He found them in better spirits after breakfast.

John was by then a tad more comfortable with both the prospect of an historic live performance and the opportunity of catching a later flight. And then the universe stepped in. Eric Clapton suddenly called, affirming his availability and keenness to take part in this bound-to-be-legendary gig, which would also involve talent of the calibre of Bo Diddley, Jerry Lee Lewis, Chuck Berry, Gene Vincent, Little Richard, Chicago Transit Authority, Tony Joe White, Alice Cooper, Cat Mother & the All Night Newsboys, Junior Walker & The All Stars, Doug Kershaw, Screaming Lord Sutch, Nucleus, Milkwood and Whiskey Howl. Tickets to the show were all of $6 and there was a budget of $100,000 to pay the artists.

Three hours later, the Lennon party had boarded Air Canada Flight 24 bound for Toronto to play the show that would end The Beatles. Clapton's agent had insisted that the guitarist was relaxing at his country cottage in the Berkshire Downs. But the guitar god had continually failed to answer his home telephone and it wasn't until a telegram (remember them!) was received by the estate gardener that Clapton was alerted to the looming Canadian gig. He quickly packed and rushed out to the airport.

Only three first-class tickets were available, so the newly formed second version of the Plastic Ono Band (Klaus Voormann, Alan White, Eric Clapton and the Lennons) gathered in the rear of the 707 jet, vamping their acoustic way through a cluster of classic rock'n' roll favourites that the principal players worshipped. It was a half-hearted effort, however. Anthony Fawcett observed: "John's mind was on heavier things, particularly his decision to leave The Beatles."

Perhaps this inspired the intense bout of honesty that unfolded on the flight, during which John informed both Eric Clapton and Klaus Voormann that he was fed up with being in The Beatles and was thinking about starting a new group. He went as far as to enquire about their interest in joining him in this new enterprise - a proposal he subsequently scuttled. He also told Allen Klein of his plans but the ever-cunning manager - trying to renegotiate existing Beatles' contracts and to stoke up a huge offer to get the band touring again - persuaded him against going public with these thoughts right away. It would have gotten in the way of vital Beatles business, Klein insisted. Klein was fiercely adamant that John must keep his feelings about leaping forth afresh to himself. There was too much business at stake!

"I had made up my mind about leaving The Beatles on the flight over to Toronto," John later revealed. "I told Allen (Klein) I was leaving. I told Eric and Klaus that I was leaving ...but that I would probably like to use them as a group. Then, later on, I thought, 'Fuck! I'm not going to get stuck with another set of people, whoever they are'. I announced it to myself and the people around me on the way to Toronto on the plane. Klein came with me and I told him, 'It's all over'. When I got back, there were a few meetings, and Allen said, 'Well, cool it', there was a lot to do, business-wise, you know, and it would not have been suitable at the time."

Considering the enormous cultural implications of the gig and John's stepping away from The Beatles, the payment John and Yoko received boggles the mind. According to John Brower, the Lennons were paid union scale. There are documents in the files of the AFM Toronto (American Federation of Musicians Toronto chapter) office stating that they received a total of $265. But as pointed out by Brower, an ever-youthful 63-year old (at the time of writing) based in Venice, California, who continues to pluck out entrepreneurial possibilities, this didn't include "the cost of airline tickets for the party, which ended up being around ten thousand bucks!" Film rights were a different story. Still, it was a bargain.

A highly enthusiastic John Brower was at Toronto Airport to meet the flight and escort the Lennon party to the venue. Rumors about Lennon's announcement of a live performance had spread like wildfire on the airwaves overnight. Fans were pouring across the US border and the Detroit/Windsor road tunnel was jammed to capacity, as emcee Kim Fowley had predicted. At the Varsity Stadium venue, John was extremely nervous. Stage fright coupled with the lines of cocaine he had snorted, resulted in him throwing up before the show. Brower had hurriedly obtained a gram from a coke dealer he knew in response to an urgent request from John upon arrival at the venue. "Imagine if you were in The Beatles from the beginning and you were never in any other band," John explained. "Then all of a sudden you're going on stage with this group who've never played live together, anywhere. We formed on the plane coming over here and now we're gonna play in front of 20,000 people."

Beatles' roadie the late Mal Evans later wrote: "The show was taking place in the Varsity Stadium and the stage was a 12-foot dais in the middle of the football pitch, facing half of the arena where the audience sat. When the crowd sensed that John was there, there was such an incredible feeling of excitement. But he and the rest of the band had other problems to worry about, and they gathered together backstage, plugged all their guitars into one small amp and started running through the numbers they were going to perform. Just imagine - John Lennon, Eric Clapton and Klaus Voormann all plugged into one small amp. Actually John wasn't feeling very well during these rehearsals, but he was determined to put on a good show."

Eric Clapton recalled that "John stood in the dressing room, which was admittedly rather tatty, beforehand, saying: 'What am I doing here? I could have gone to Brighton!' After all, it was a long way to go for just one concert."

Yoko wasn't impressed with the backstage facilities either. "I came from the avant-garde art world, which is kind of like the classical world,' Yoko would note. "They have lovely reception rooms, they treat you really well. We arrived in this dressing room, and it is a concrete locker room, it's dirty, it's ugly. I looked at John and he laughed and said, 'Welcome to rock'n'roll'." (It's worth noting that the room was a space for inter-college hockey players to dress and undress).

After the perfunctory backstage rehearsal, guest emcee Kim Fowley urged the audience to fire up their lighters and matches - and in the process light their communal fire, the early uprising of a collective consciousness - to welcome on stage the Plastic Ono Band in their debut performance. Kim, the step-grandson of Rudolf Friml, who composed the operetta Rose Marie which included the evocative hit song Indian Love Call, had no trouble recognizing history as it was unfolding. He was a songwriter and multi-level greaser of legendary proportions, and well worthy of your google attention.

"It was fantastic," Lennon would tell me back in London afterwards. "It was just getting dark and the lights were just going down. This was the first time I'd ever seen an audience light candles or lights all together ... it was incredible! I think it was the first time it happened." The night was faithfully and creatively recorded on camera by award-winning filmmaker Donn Alan "D.A." Pennebaker, to follow his *Monterey Pop* and *Don't Look Back* triumphs.

"John, Eric, Klaus and Alan went on stage and lined up just like the old Beatles set-up. Bass (Voormann) on the left, lead guitar (Clapton) next, then John on the right with the drummer (White) right behind," Mal Evans glowed. He, like other members of the Beatles' road troupe who had patiently waited four years for the Fab Four to hit the performing track again, was thrilled to watch what was unfolding in Toronto. Was it the first step towards The Beatles playing live again? Or was it what many considered to be its most insightful member breaking loose from the band's shackles? Only time would tell, but that moment was rapidly advancing. Mal Evans was sweating on the results.

An eager John bounced out on stage, bedecked in a black shirt underneath a white tropical suit, and was spellbinding with his new band. The cocaine he'd snorted before the show - and his subsequent nervous vomiting - probably had something to do with it. "We're just going to do numbers we know, as we've never played together before," he declared modestly. Later he would relate: "We started off doing things like *Blue Suede Shoes*; things that we'd rehearsed on the plane. It was a madhouse. Everybody was really together. It was really sound so we did all the *Money* and *Dizzy Miss Lizzy* bits and it was fantastic. Everybody in the audience was with us and they were leaping up and down and doing the peace sign, because they knew most of the numbers anyway."

Eric Clapton concurred: "When we walked out on stage, it was a glorified jam session. It was really refreshing to do these songs because they are very simple and uncomplicated. John and I really love that music. That's the kind of music that turned John on initially, and it's the same for me. In fact, I could go on playing *Money* and *Dizzy Miss Lizzy* for the rest of my life." Adds Mal Evans: "I'll always remember turning around during their performance and finding Gene Vincent (the originator of *Be Bop a Lula*), who was standing next to me, with tears rolling down his cheeks. He was saying, 'It's marvellous! It's fantastic, man!'."

The Toronto audience was equally uplifted. After whipping through three these rock'n'roll chestnuts - the Plastic Ono Band dug into their originals bag. A re-energised John plunged into *Yer Blues* from the White album. And then, to take proceedings to another level, the debut of a new single which would be within released five weeks and become a hard-edged classic, *Cold Turkey*. "We'd never done this before, and the audience dug it like mad," John confided. "It was the first performance.

The way that we got it together was like we'd all been playing together for years." This was followed by a centrepiece selection which John graphically set up as, "This is what we really came here for" and into the strains of his new peace anthem, *Give Peace a Chance*: "Ev'rybody's talkin"bout Bagism…" which he, Yoko and assorted luminaries had recorded in a Montreal hotel room some four months earlier.

Rolling Stone's magazine reviewer Stephen Holden would later write: "Lennon delivered blistering versions of *Blue Suede Shoes*, Money and *Dizzy Miss Lizzy* as well as powerful versions of two singles - *Cold Turkey*, a bleak, scary evocation of heroin addiction, and *Give Peace a Chance*, his first and most stirring piece of street music." Yoko added to the street-theatre vibe by performing two tunes in a bag, which turned out to be quite controversial. " Yoko did a number, which was half rock and half madness," said John, "and it really freaked them out. We finished with Yoko's number, because you can't go anywhere after you've reached that sort of pitch. You can't very well go 'Ji-jing' like The Beatles and bow out at the end of screaming and 50 watts of feedback. So, after Yoko had been on for about a quarter of an hour, we all left our amps going like the clappers and had a smoke on the stage. Then, when they stopped, the whole crowd was chanting *'Give Peace a Chance'*.

"The ridiculous thing was that I didn't know any of the lyrics. When we did *Money* and *Dizzy*, I just made up the words as we went along. The band was bashing it out like hell behind me. Yoko came up on stage with us, but she wasn't going to do her bit until we'd done our set of five songs.

Then after *Money* there was a stop, and I turned to Eric and said, 'What's next?' He just shrugged, so I screamed out 'C'mon' and started into something else. "We did *Yer Blues* because I'd done that before with Eric. It blew our minds. Meanwhile Yoko had whipped off stage to get some lyrics out of her white bag. Then we went into *Give Peace a Chance* which was just unbelievable. (He'd never played the peace anthem with a band before.) I was making up the words as we went along. I didn't have a clue. After that, we just wandered off to the back of the stage, and we lit up (cigarettes) and let go."

Back in London after a momentous and a career-changing 36 hours on Canadian soil, John was extraordinarily grateful to me for the role I personally played in getting him off his backside, across the Atlantic and, as time would prove, out of The Beatles.

Arriving at the Apple offices at noon Tuesday after a day of rest at Tittenhurst Park, the world's most famous couple were beaming as I met them at the door. "That was so great man; the Rock'n'roll Revival gave me a great feeling; a feeling I haven't had for a long time. Thank you so much Ritchie for getting me into this. That show convinced me to do more appearances, either with or without the rest of The Beatles. Everything went down so well," John enthused. "I can't remember when I had such a good time ... Gene Vincent was standing on the stage crying when we did our number. Backstage he came up to me and whispered, 'John, remember Hamburg (The Beatles honed their act on a residency in the seedier clubs of that portside German city)? Remember all that scene?'."

The after effects of John's emergence show at the Toronto Rock'n' roll Revival finally settled in John's consciousness. Just a week after the performance, a crucial and life-altering Apple board meeting was held in London with John, Paul and Ringo in attendance, along with business manager Allen Klein. (George Harrison was unable to attend as he was visiting his ailing mother in Cheshire.) It provided a platform for recently installed manager Allen Klein to reveal that he had renegotiated a royalty increase of 69c per album on all LPs sold by Capitol Records in North America. That was the positive aspect of the meeting.

The vibes were out there. Knowing that John had just played his first gig without the rest of The Beatles, Paul McCartney arrived at the Apple meeting full of bonhomie. "We had a meeting and it was getting very serious," Paul would later recall. "It was all Apple and Allen Klein, and no one was enjoying themselves. We had forgotten the music, it was just business." He told the company the band needed to re-establish its musical identity and find out who they were again, and go back to little gigs ... go back to square one and remember what it was all about.

Neither Klein nor Lennon wanted to hear this. Klein didn't like the inherent profit-lowering potential of "little gigs". He was into making monster money from mega concerts. And John just wasn't interested in going back to any performances with his old associates . Not after being what he relegated to being considered one of Paul's sidemen for many recent months - both John and George Harrison had increasingly felt like they'd become extras to Paul's musical vision in the post-Sgt Pepper period, which also followed the death of manager Brian Epstein. After that tragedy the band's members had stumbled around in a form of shocked grief, with McCartney ultimately taking control and calling the creative shots. For John and George, it was a dead period.

"Paul said something about The Beatles doing something and I kept saying, 'No, no, no' to everything he said," was Lennon's memory of the Apple meeting. Recalled McCartney: "John looked at me and his actual words were, 'Well, I think you're daft' which was a little bit of a showstopper. He said, 'Well I wasn't going to tell you until after we signed the Capitol contract, but we're breaking the group up. Klein asked me not to tell you, but seeing as you asked me, I'm leaving the group'."

Lennon: "So it came to a point where I had to say something, and Paul said 'What do you mean?' I said, 'I mean the group is over. I'm leaving!' Allen was saying, 'Don't tell'. He didn't want me to tell Paul even. So, I said, 'I'm out'. I couldn't stop it. It came out."

McCartney was mortified by Lennon's decision. "Everyone went 'Gulp!" he recalled. "The weight was dropped, our jaws dropped along with it. Everyone blanched except John, who said, 'It's rather exciting. It's like I remember telling Cynthia (his first wife) I wanted a divorce'. I think, from what he was saying, that there was an adrenalin rush that came with the telling. We signed the new Capitol deal in a bit of a daze, not quite knowing why we'd done it."

Klein kept pushing for a postponement of the breakup announcement. "A lot of business deals are based on you guys being around, and we can't have anyone thinking that you're breaking up. Jesus Christ, it would ruin everything we're getting going here." Noted John: "Paul and Allen both said they were glad I wasn't going to announce it, and that I wasn't going to make an event out of it. I don't know whether Paul said don't tell anybody, but he was darn pleased that I wasn't going to. He said, 'Oh that means that nothing's really happened if you're not going to say anything'. 'But it had been a mortal blow. Later comments by roadie Mal Evans, fresh in from the Toronto concert of anticipation, provided an insight into the devastation resulting from that crucial meeting: "All of them had left the group at one time or another, starting with Ringo, but the real ending was when John came into Apple and said, 'The marriage is over! I want a divorce', and that was the final thing. That's what really got to Paul, you know, because I drove him home and I ended up in the garden crying my eyes out."

A great fog of disillusionment had settled on Apple Corps. Down, down, down the mood sank as days drifted by until it reached rock bottom and physical violence among Beatles' members raised its ugly and very unrighteous head. The bonds had been broken. All of this would be revealed in the not very distant future.

*FOOTNOTE

I Am the Walrus occupies a particularly special place in the canon of John Lennon. It was the first studio recording made by The Beatles since the sudden death of their manager and sometime mentor, Brian Epstein, in August, 1967. It was assigned the B side of the *Hello Goodbye* single, which seems ludicrous in 2010 in regard to the durability of the respective songs. It was the follow-up to one of the band's most poignant pop moments, *All You Need is Love*, and arguably presents the Liverpool lads at the pinnacle of their creative power. The song consisted of three ideas on which John had been working, but ultimately he decided to combine them into one. The first was inspired by a police siren John heard at his Weybridge home in suburban Liverpool. The second was a short rhyme about John sitting in his garden. The third part was a nonsense lyric about sitting on a cornflake. John admitted that the first two sections arose from the starburst of two acid trips on consecutive weekends during the so-called *Summer of Love*.

There is no doubt that Lennon was vigorously working the nonsense muse in writing *I Am the Walrus*. He'd received a surprise letter from his alma mater, Quarry Bank Grammar School, informing him that the English master had instructed the class to analyse The Beatles' lyrics. In response to this, and to soothe his revolutionary spirit, Lennon wrote the most confusing lyrics he could. He gave free rein to a word-filled anarchy. "Let the fuckers work that one out," John said to a close friend as he finished the word maze that constitutes the closing half of the track. The song also - and perhaps not coincidentally - contains all musical letters of the alphabet.

The original concept of the walrus was inspired by the walrus in the Lewis Carroll poem *The Walrus and the Carpenter*. Much water flowed under The Beatles' bridge before John discovered that not only was the walrus the villain in the piece, but that the author had more menacing motives between his lines. "It never dawned on me that Lewis Carroll was commenting on the capitalist system. I never went into that bit about what he really meant. Later, I went back and looked at it and realised that the walrus was the bad guy in the story and the carpenter was the good guy. I thought, 'Oh, shit, I picked the wrong guy. I should have said, 'I am the carpenter'. But that wouldn't have been the same, would it? 'I am the carpenter...'.," John gaily sang.

6. THE LAUNCHING OF THE War Is Over PEACE CAMPAIGN

``It is the people themselves who must take the initiative, and especially if the government does not. And the way to mobilize this power is not through the use of violence. I'm often asked what I would replace all the mess we have now with. My answer to that is people. Just the idea that the individual is capable of looking after himself, that we don't need centralized government, that we don't need father-figures and leaders, that every child is an artist until he's told he's not an artist, that every person is great until some demagogue makes him less great. Government was an invention that I think didn't work.''

JOHN LENNON, 1969

After returning to London on a liberated high from the R'n'R Revival, there was a feeling of anticlimax in London's autumnal air and at Apple headquarters. At first, John and Yoko plunged whole-heartedly into their peace campaign, meeting and greeting every journalist and radio interview from their Savile Row offices to kingdom come. It was a non-stop, never-ending merry-go-round ride. According to Anthony Fawcett, John was desperate to ``produce peace''. A lot of his desire could be attributed to the ongoing decay of The Beatles - and John's need to find new meaning in life without actually cutting off his previous partners. Meanwhile Yoko was pregnant again and her doctors urged her to spend some time in the security of a hospital room.

John Kosh was a young Cockney creative type whose life was immeasurably altered in 1963 by the change of government which followed revelations of British Secretary of State for War John Profumo's sexual escapades with Christine Keeler, who was also sleeping with a Russian embassy attache. (This was during the Cold War, when such behaviour was seen as a breach of security because of Keeler's potential ability to leak information she gained during "pillow talk".) The subsequent downfall of Harold Macmillan's conservative government brought British Labour into power. Overnight, it seemed, everything about Britain changed as the new order moved into power and threw out the old guard. Doors opened to a new awareness under the Labour Party. This would lead to the emergence of a youth-driven Swinging London in the mid to late '60s. And change the unfolding modern history of the United Kingdom.

``I'd been working as a designer for the Royal Ballet and the Royal Opera House and it was all about the avant garde. (Rudolf) Nureyev was dancing with Dame Margot Fonteyn and there was a lot of experimental stuff going on in that period. Rock'n' roll stars would be in the audience - (Rolling Stones singer) Mick Jagger would be in the gallery, John Lennon would be in the stalls. It was that kind of thing,' Kosh recently recalled from the his Ten Worlds Productions offices, located in film director Alfred Hitchcock's old base at Crossroads of the World in Hollywood.

``We were all caught up in that working man's revolution which unfolded in the late '60s after the conservatives had been disgraced by the Profumo Affair. Without Christine Keeler … there wouldn't have been a Labour government. That's why you'll see a few of her pictures around my office walls. She changed my life, and for the better, as a creative person. I'd love to have had the chance to meet her and thank her personally for that. Without the election of the Labour government, there wouldn't have been that resurgence of the arts, especially among Cockney-speaking people. Frankly I had the wrong accent to be working in the arts area, especially at the Opera House. It was all `lardy-dardy' stuff around there. But the arts were indeed flourishing and it was our job to knock the Establishment, which was on its knees anyway at that point, what with the revelations in Private Eye magazine and whatever else. London was really swinging at that time, at least until big business took over.''

It was an ideal time for an aspiring creative designer to arrive in The Beatles' camp. Asked to recall how he came to design John and Yoko's *War Is Over If You Want It* slogan/handbill/advertising billboard, Kosh is understandably a tad vague. ``It was 40 years ago so the brain cells are having trouble coalescing the facts. The memories are a bit blurred because certain `substances' were involved and that was the norm.

``I met John Lennon after getting a phone call while I was working with Art & Artists magazine where I was the art designer. The Venice Biennale was on and we were putting together a box of tricks to go in the magazine. One night at home the phone rang and a voice said `This is Mr Lennon'. At first I thought that it was somebody having me on. ` We're at Hammersmith Hospital, please come and see us,' said the voice. I thought it was a bit of a con and I figured I'd end up meeting some mate in a bar somewhere. But I drove out to the Hammersmith Hospital from central London and I went to reception and asked for Mr Winston as the voice had instructed me. I was ushered to a private elevator and given a room number. I knocked on the door and lo and behold, it was John Lennon inviting me in for a cup of tea.

``The Lennons were living there in hospital while Yoko was expecting and ultimately losing a baby. I ended up visiting them there regularly for a lot for consultations and to smuggle in those chocolate cookies which John's macrobiotic diet did not allow. I called those biscuits a Vitamin B supplement but that's not what Yoko called them. John had a whole range of projects - art, music, books - that he wanted me to work on. He wanted to do a book on donation boxes, which was an idea that Robert Fraser, the art gallery owner, had come up with. Those boxes that you see on shop counters and so on soliciting donations. There was another book concept called You Are Here for which I had traced around John's hand as a cover idea. And there was another idea for a book about all the hate letters pouring in from all over the world because John was now 'living with a Japanese tart', and that was one of the milder descriptions.

``The acorn thing was just hitting its stride and then one day it just happened, John and Yoko wanted a design for this new slogan they'd come up with ... The project really appealed to me - very much so because it would represent me in my 'stark mode' - black and white and very minimal.

``I could readily imagine those block letters - Bang! Bang! Bang! - on a plain white background. Then in smaller type underneath *War Is Over* there was IF YOU WANT IT, the presentation concept of which was my idea. John originally had the whole thing in big, bold letters, and then underneath the message - in smaller letters - 'Happy Christmas from John and Yoko'. At this point, it was still designed to be a Christmas card. The thought of Times Square billboards in New York, the biggest roadside signs yet seen in that iconic location, had yet to unfold.''

Surely, I suggested to Kosh, it must have been a thrilling time to work for The Beatles with their acutely formed sense of the irreverent, their avant garde nature, the ability to express themselves in a different way. By the autumn of 1969, Kosh had become creative director for Apple Records and had been a central figure in the design of the jackets for *Abbey Road* and *Let It Be*.

``Paul always was the least radical of the band. John was the total revolutionary, George was the peacenik and Ringo was going to have fun no matter what happened. I liked all of them and I liked John a lot. He never suffered fools gladly. But he was a very, very kind man. He could sometimes be unkind but it was usually because he'd become exasperated. I do remember something that happened that was really sweet and indicative of John's state of mind and outlook.

``I'd gone along to the *Abbey Road* studios where John and Paul were recording the song *The Ballad of John and Yoko*. George and Ringo were not at the session. I can't remember why not but they were not part of the making of this track. It was right in the middle of the period where John and Paul were supposedly heaping shit on one another. But they seemed to be getting along fine in the studio. John was playing rhythm guitar and Paul was playing the drums, and it sounded good to me. Yoko was sitting under the piano. (Paul's partner) Linda Eastman went into the control room and my late wife Marjorie was there in the control room with the engineer Geoff Emerick. And Linda was incredibly rude - and I mean in-cred-ib-ly rude - to my wife. We could hear the exchange through the mikes in the studio and I thought 'that was a bit odd'. To make a very long story short, I got a phone call later that night and it was John Lennon asking to speak to my wife. Whereupon he proceeded to apologize to Marjorie for Linda's behaviour. That was one of the sweetest things I ever saw around The Beatles - a little vignette for you."

Kosh moved to Los Angeles in 1973 and proceeded to design a flock of outstanding album jackets, including such artists as the Rolling Stones (*Get Yer YaYa's Out* and *Through the Past, Darkly*), The Eagles (*Hotel California* and *The Long Run*), The Who (*Who's Next*), Jimmy Buffett (*Son of a Son of a Sailor*), E.L.O. (*A New World Record*), Humble Pie (*Smokin'* and *Eat It*), the Pointer Sisters (*Black and White*), Rod Stewart (*Atlantic Crossing* and *A Night on the Town*), James Taylor (*JT*), Ringo Starr (*Ringo's Rotogravure*), Randy Newman (*Faust*), Dan Fogelberg (*The Wild Places*) and Linda Ronstadt (three of Ronstadt's titles won Kosh Grammy Awards - *Get Closer, Lush Life* and *Simple Dreams*). A man of impeccable artistic taste, Kosh later became involved in the film documentary production world with more astounding results.

Back in the Bag One offices at Apple, life had become a bit of a struggle according to the Lennons' personal assistant, art student and devotee Anthony Fawcett. The pressures of trying to access the US kept building and began to affect John and Yoko's personal relationship. According to Fawcett, John was pleased to see mounting US college-level concern about his being unable to enter America as a visitor or tourist. ``I'm sure we'll get there,' John said, ``but it's just a matter of under what conditions. We won't play games with governments."

American media began to focus on John's immigration plight and became more sympathetic, although the major Establishment outlets continued to regard the Lennons as potential radicals bent on bringing down the United States. John was delighted by the US media's coverage of his apparent distress over growing student violence.

``The students are being conned,' he declared. ``It's like the school bully - he aggravates you and aggravates you until you hit him, and then they kill you like in the Berkeley riots. Establishment - it's just another name for evil. The monster doesn't care - the blue meanies are insane. We really care about life. Destruction is good enough for the Establishment. The only thing they can't control is the mind, and we have to fight for sanity and peace on that level. But the students have gotten conned into thinking you can change it with violence, and you can't, you know - that can only make it uglier and worse.''

But before John and Yoko plunged into the *War Is Over* campaign - which would unfold for Christmas 1969 - there was some unfinished business to attend to. And that involved John's Member of the British Empire Medal (which the Beatles each received in 1965). John had always been uncomfortable with being the recipient of this award. With the raging violence in Vietnam and another outrageous war in Biafra, he felt that the time and occasion was right for a renunciation of this accolade. Continuing to be part of this mockery of Establishment self-aggrandisement was too much for the liberal Lennon. The MBE was something which made John - an anti-monarchist and anti-honours sort of guy - sick. And so on November 26, John directed his chauffeur, Les, to drive up to Bournemouth where his Aunt Mimi lived to retrieve the MBE medal from the top of her TV set. While Les headed to Bournemouth, John, Yoko and Anthony Fawcett headed into the Apple offices to draft a rejection letter to the Queen.

After an hour's diligence, John produced a draft of a letter. It read: ``Your Majesty, I am returning this MBE in protest against Britain's involvement in the Nigeria-Biafra thing, against our support of America in Vietnam*, and against *Cold Turkey* slipping down the charts. With love, John Lennon of Bag.''

John arranged for the letter and the medal to be delivered to the tradesmen's entrance to Buckingham Palace in London (a working man's statement in itself) in his new six-door white Mercedes limousine (to add an appetizer of irony). A copy of the letter was also dispatched to the Prime Minister's residence at 10 Downing Street, while Beatles' publicist Derek Taylor organised a press conference for John to vent his feelings about the returning of the MBE and his outlook on the political status quo. Initially John declared: ``I have been planning this for over a year and now feels the right time to do it.''

Lennon was upfront about his rejection of the MBE: ``Of course my action was a publicity gimmick for peace. That's what I learned in The Beatles - the art and game of publicity. I always squirmed when I saw that phrase MBE on my letters. I didn't really belong to that sort of world. I think the Establishment bought The Beatles with it. Now I am giving it back, thank you very much. Investitures are a waste of time. It's mostly hypocritical snobbery and part of the class system. I only accepted it to help The Beatles make the big time. I know I sold my soul when I received it, but now I have helped to redeem it in the cause of peace.''

On the mention of his controversial song *Cold Turkey* in the rejection message: ``When we thought of that we were screaming with laughter, and so a few snobs and hypocrites got very upset about mentioning Cold Turkey (alongside) the problem of Biafra and Vietnam, but that saved it from being too serious ... You have to try and do everything with humour and keep smiling.'' He added, ``I don't think the Queen will be embarrassed'', to which a palace spokesman responded tartly, ``The Queen is above embarrassment''. Bertrand Russell**, philosopher, logician, mathematician, historian, socialist, pacifist and social theorist, a man widely regarded as one of the foremost thinkers of the 20th century, wrote to John saying he was pleased to see the Beatle condemn the British government's involvement in the wars in Biafra and Vietnam. He wrote: ``Whatever abuse you have suffered in the press because of this, I am confident that your remarks will have caused a very large number of people to think again about these wars.'' Bertrand Russell was an outstanding individual who served jail time repeatedly for his anti-war peace protest activities. He was a man whom Lennon was proud to regard as an intellectual anti-war mentor.

After the dust settled on the return of the MBE, John and Yoko focused on the launching of their *War Is Over* peace campaign. It was arranged for large roadside billboards to be mounted in 10 major world cities, including Paris, Rome, Berlin, Athens, Tokyo, New York, Toronto, Los Angeles, Montreal and Port-of-Spain in Trinidad. In addition, thousands of posters were delivered to suburbs. I worked with promoter John Brower glueing up *War Is Over* posters at strategic spots all over Toronto.

The *War Is Over* billboard/poster campaign was unveiled on December 15 at a special Peace for Christmas launch at London's Lyceum Theatre. John had invited George Harrison - who had been touring with Delaney and Bonnie as one of their ``Friends'' - but wouldn't receive a confirmation until the last minute. So John went ahead and recruited his Plastic Ono grouping from the Toronto Rock'n'Roll Revival (drummer Alan White, bassist Klaus Voormann and guitarist Eric Clapton) to join him for the gig, which would also feature Yoko and ultimately the complete Delaney and Bonnie Band, sometime-Beatles' keyboard player Billy Preston and Who drummer Keith Moon. George showing up at the last minute completed a spectacular and historic line-up, marking the first time in four years that two Beatles had performed together in public.

The all-star band plunged into a splendid version of *Cold Turkey*, John's ``new'' song, and then what has been described as a ``climactic 17-minute rendition'' of *Don't Worry Kyoko*. Up to this point Yoko had been on stage in a white bag but after the band launched into *Don't Worry Kyoko* she was up and into a fervent performance including shrill cries of ``You Killed Hanratty!''. The case of James Hanratty, executed in 1962 for a murder it was widely believed he did not commit, became a cause célèbre in the Lennon camp; it was viewed as an example of official ignorance.

The next day the Lennons were up early for the flight to Toronto where they were about to announce some of the most potentially meaningful events in their peace campaign. Meetings with communication prophets, magazine publishers, soft drug investigators and even prime ministers were looming as the Lennons became even more serious about their dedication to the peace cause.

*FOOTNOTE

The Vietnam War, which lasted from 1955 to 1975, was a communism vs democracy civil conflict that the United States and its allies, including Australia, became involved in. While Britain did not contribute troops, Prime Minister Harold Wilson gave verbal support to the American effort.

**FOOTNOTE

At the age of 84, Bertrand Russell added a five-paragraph prologue to a new edition of his autobiography which we respectfully reproduce herewith:

WHAT I HAVE LIVED FOR

``Three passions, simple but overwhelmingly strong, have governed my life: the longing for love, the search for knowledge, and unbearable pity for the suffering of mankind. These passions, like great winds, have blown me hither and thither, in a wayward course, over a deep ocean of anguish, reaching to the very verge of despair.

I have sought love, first, because it brings ecstasy - ecstasy so great that I would often have sacrificed all the rest of life for a few hours of this joy. I have sought it, next, because it relieves loneliness - that terrible loneliness in which one shivering consciousness looks over the rim of the world into the cold unfathomable lifeless abyss. I have sought it, finally, because in the union of love I have seen, in a mystic miniature, the prefiguring vision of the heaven that saints and poets have imagined. This is what I sought, and though it might seem too good for human life, this is what - at last - I have found.

``With equal passion I have sought knowledge. I have wished to understand the hearts of men. I have wished to know why the stars shine. And I have tried to apprehend the Pythagorean power by which number holds sway above the flux. A little of this, but not much, I have achieved.

``Love and knowledge, so far as they were possible, led upward toward the heavens. But always pity brought me back to earth. Echoes of cries of pain reverberate in my heart. Children in famine, victims tortured by oppressors, helpless old people a hated burden to their sons, and the whole world of loneliness, poverty, and pain make a mockery of what human life should be. I long to alleviate the evil, but I cannot, and I too suffer.

``This has been my life. I have found it worth living, and would gladly live it again if the chance were offered me.''

7. THE LENNONS ENCAMP TO CANADA FOR CHRISTMAS

``We are launching a campaign of peace persuasion. It's called *War Is Over If You Want It Happy Christmas from John and Yoko* and it's something which the public can and must understand for its own sake. To convince the people that peace is within their grasp, whenever they want it, we have to use conventional media.

"We were really treated well in Canada on our two visits this year (for the Montreal Bed-In and the Toronto Rock 'n'Roll Revival). The maturity of the people is amazing when you consider Canada is so young. The Immigration Department has been a lot nicer to us than any countries I could mention. Canada's attitudes with regard to Vietnam, China and NATO are very sensible. Everything points to Canada as being one of the key countries in the new race for survival.

"We've had the arms race and the space race and the cold war - the time has come for the peace race.''

(JOHN LENNON, speaking from London on December 15, 1969, just before to embarking for Toronto, Canada)

I'd never been so embarrassed in my life - and I need hardly tell you I've seen a few embarrassments along the ups and downs of this journey on the peace train. By now we had moved to the residence of Rompin' Ronnie Hawkins, the rockabilly legend who'd emigrated to Canada from Arkansas in 1959.

Of course I should have known it was a mistake to fly the white Rolls Royce flag. I should have realised it was crazy to expect Walter ``Heavy'' Andrews, Hawkins' security guy, to be able to maintain a low profile while picking up John and Yoko Lennon and entourage from Toronto Airport in the Hawk's immaculate white Roller. Jeez, get real mate! They were always going to attract attention, internationally recognised celebrities arriving in their black outfits and disappearing into a white Roller. The media hounds who hang around airports looking for leads were bound to pick up on an arrival like this, if they hadn't already been tipped off in advance by an airline staffer.

Now, less than 24 hours after they'd arrived in Canada, we were summoned by John and Yoko for an urgent meeting. They had unexpectedly called promoter John Brower and me in for a private chat in the quiet of their newly-acquired guest bedroom at the Hawkins house in Mississauga, on the western outskirts of Toronto. I instinctively knew it could be about only one matter - and it wasn't something you'd necessarily welcome in the middle of a peace campaign. It was all to do with the unfortunate punching out of an over-zealous newspaper photographer, ironically named Frank Lennon (no relation), by ``Heavy'' Andrews.

Brower and I were acutely aware of what had happened the day before. We'd actually watched it unfold. We were ensconced in the Roller on Mississauga Road outside Hawkins' 10-acre ranch just south of Streetsville. We'd already dropped off John and Yoko and their PA and made the necessary introductions at the front door of the Hawkins' homestead. Then, like guardians of the castle keep, we headed back out to the road to sort out an apparent affront to the Lennons' privacy. I watched in dismay as the insistent photographer's car, with reporter Marci McDonald aboard, which had tailed us from the airport, finally confronted Andrews. Heavy wasn't the sort of guy who would back off from anybody, certainly not a member of the fourth estate trying to invade the privacy of his employer and close friend, Ronnie Hawkins.

I was still haunted by memories of the Lennons' traumatic escape from the frenzied clutches of hundreds of fans who'd mobbed the corridors of the King Edward Hotel in downtown Toronto in late April. But this unmarked news car had followed us all the way from the airport despite our efforts to throw them off the trail. I assumed it was either the media or the Royal Canadian Mounted Police. Mind you, we'd met John, Yoko and Anthony Fawcett in Hawkins' recently acquired white Phantom Rolls-Royce, which was bound to draw attention. Ron had bought the Roller the year before for $36,000. As we came upon the Hawkins' estate it was obvious there was no turning back. Much as we wanted to keep the Lennons' location top secret, our cover had been blown. This led to a confrontation on the side of Mississauga Road, right outside the Hawk's property. John Brower provided his retrospective on that madhouse afternoon:

``I motioned for the following car - the press car being driven by Frank Lennon - to back off, which it did not. As we approached the gate at Ronnie's spread, Heavy stopped the Rolls and he and I jumped out and accosted Frank and Marci, who had jumped out too. Frank was snapping pictures. I started screaming at them to stop taking pictures and to piss off. They didn't back off and she told me this was public property and they could do what they wanted.

``At that point Heavy grabbed Frank in a choke hold and gave him a roundhouse to the jaw, sending (presumably false) teeth flying. He dropped his camera, which I grabbed and ripped the film out. Marci started screaming whereupon I grabbed her and hauled her into the ditch. We got back in our cars and (re-)entered Ronnie's driveway, The Toronto Star people got in their car and went to the nearest police station and reported the assault. Heavy and I were subsequently charged with assault with bodily harm, I went to court and was fined $55. The charge against Heavy was dropped. Anyway, I like to point out that that charge is the only thing on my Canadian criminal record."

Later on that day, the Lennons had accidentally stumbled upon TV news coverage of this unsavoury incident while surfing the box and were not impressed. "Boys, we just can't have this sort of thing going on when we're trying to sell the world on peace,' John said patiently. "We know you were only trying to prevent the media from going out and telling everybody where we are staying and what we're doing... that's all fine. But boys, we just can't be going about it like this. We can't be punching out photographers. We have to set a perfect example." Yoko nodded silently and I cringed! I looked askance at John Brower and we almost fell over each other as we hastened to apologise for what had unfolded in the heat of the moment.

Having lectured us on appropriate public behavior and protocols for peace campaigners, John and Yoko settled back into life at the Hawkins' homestead. They were experiencing their first blast of Canadian winter, which is often whiter than white - and yet another snowfall was forecast. When the mercury rose to near freezing point (sometimes it went down to 20 below overnight) we could dare to go outside and play in the snow. John and Yoko enjoyed tossing a few obligatory snowballs but the mechanized snow machines offered more heart-pounding thrills.

Despite such distractions, John had no choice but to immediately plunge into the mammoth task of signing 4500 lithographs. The Bag One lithos were part of a collection of 14 images John had drawn a few months earlier as a wedding present for Yoko. The set chronicled recent events in the life of the Lennons - their wedding ceremony in Gibraltar, their Amsterdam Bed-In honeymoon, their pursuit of peace and some erotica. Only 300 sets plus spares were printed and they were presented in a white vinyl portfolio bag, very rock'n'roll in style. In the late '60s John was fond of drawing, mainly in pen and ink. For a favoured few, he sometimes drew small doodles to

embellish his autograph (see pictured example). There was no shortage of opportunities.

Meanwhile in the streets of downtown Toronto - and other cities of the world - the launch of the *War Is Over* billboard campaign was off and running. Toronto could boast 30 roadside billboards and thousands of posters and handbills. I helped stick up many posters. Capitol Records of Canada took ads in the daily papers proclaiming the same message. The *War Is Over* billboards were also displayed in tourist traffic-heavy locations such as Times Square in New York, London's Shaftesbury Avenue and Sunset Strip in Hollywood. Some were printed white on black, others black on white.

On leaving London's Heathrow Airport, John had quipped to a curious press contingent that he didn't know the actual cost of producing the billboards, but joked about making US President Richard Nixon responsible. ``They cost less than the life of one man, and I am sending the bill for printing to President Nixon.''

For now, we were concerned about securing a suitable venue for John and Yoko to announce their Peace Festival plans. The Ontario Science Centre, which had opened a few weeks earlier, was considered the ideal location for the largest press conference held in Toronto. More than 100 members of the media turned out to hear John and Yoko, dressed all in black (photographers asked Yoko to remove her black felt hat, but she politely declined), face the music about their *War Is Over* campaign. And reveal a few surprises.

The basic thrust of this latest peace initiative was declared in John's opening statement to the media. ``Well, we've come back to Canada to announce plans for a big peace-and-music festival to be held at Mosport Park near Toronto on July third, fourth and fifth next year. We aim to make it the biggest music festival in history, and we're going to be asking everybody who's anybody to play. The whole idea of our new peace campaign is to be positive. You can't expect anybody to do anything for nothing. You must run things the way the Establishment does.

" The idea came from the Toronto people – mainly Ritchie Yorke and John Brower. They wanted to produce the biggest pop festival in history by the usual means, and then give a percentage of the gross to a new peace fund, which we're setting up. But it won't be the usual fund thing, and that's what we liked about the idea. We are forming a peace council that will administer the fund as it sees fit. If we decide, for example, that we want to give food to starving children in Biafra, we won't use the traditional means. We'll hire planes and take the stuff there ourselves. We're doing away with all the old methods because they haven't worked very well from what we can see. Anyway, now we'd be happy to answer your questions as best we can.''

Q. There are a lot of people around the world now trying to promote world peace. Why do you think you can succeed where they have so far failed?

John: That's like saying why bother keeping on Christianity because Jesus got killed. We don't think people have tried advertising before. Pretend peace is new then, because we've never had it before. So you start advertising it: sell, sell, sell! Whatever gimmicks or irrelevancies are going on during the advert, it's the drink or the car that they buy at the end of it, whether there's chicks in it, white horses or snow. The product sells, and we believe in selling, you know.

Q. Are there any similarities between where The Beatles were during the (early London) Cavern days and this *War Is Over* peace campaign now?

J: We do consider that we're now in the Cavern stage; you know, we haven't got out of Liverpool with this campaign. And we've got to break London and then America. I feel exactly the same as I did then about The Beatles as I do about peace and what we're doing now. But I don't care how long it takes, and what obstacles there are. We won't stop.

Q. Was there any one incident that got you into the *War Is Over* peace campaign?

J: Well, it built up over a number of years, but the thing that struck it off was a letter we got from a guy called Peter Watkins, who made a film called *The War Game*. It was a long letter stating what's happening – how the media is controlled, how it's all run, and it ended up: 'What are you going to do about it?'.

He said people in our position and his position have a responsibility to use the media for world peace. And we sat on the letter for three weeks and thought it over and figured we were doing our best with songs like *All You Need is Love*.

Finally we came up with the bed event and that was what sparked it off. It was like getting your call-up papers for peace. Then we did the bed event.

Q. Is it true that you were planning on going to Biafra a short while back?

J: Yeah. At the time, Yoko was pregnant and we decided not to go and she had a miscarriage. Then we thought and thought about it. But we're scared to go somewhere where it's happening. 'Cos we don't want to be dead saints or martyrs. I'm scared of going to Vietnam and Biafra, and, until I'm convinced that I can do better there than I can outside of it, I'll stay out of it. I'd go to Russia, but I'd think twice about China.

Yoko: I think we did a lot of good for Biafra when John returned his MBE.

J: Another thing we're doing with this Peace Festival idea is to try and set up a 'peace vote' for all the youth in the world, which would be like a petition, but it'd be a vote. You just vote for peace or war, and we'll set up a thing where all the youth votes, or anybody votes.

Q. How do you answer accusations that this kind of thing is bordering on naivete?

J: Let's see. If anybody thinks our campaign is naive, that's their opinion and that's OK. Let them do something else and if we like their ideas, we'll join in with them. But until then, we'll do it the way we are. We're artists, not politicians. Not newspapermen, not anything. We do it in the way that suits us best, and this is the way we work.

Publicity and things like that is our game. The Beatles' thing was that. And that was the trade I've learned. This is my trade, and I'm using it to the best of my ability.

Q. But what is the point of having a vote for peace?

J: Why do people have those Gallup polls? If we get a vote from around the world with millions and millions of kids that want peace, that's a nice Gallup poll. We can wave those figures around. That's all. It's a positive move; all we want is a yes.

Q. Will The Beatles play at this festival?

J: I'll try to hustle them out. Maybe I'll get one or two of them, or something like that. I got George on the other night for UNICEF in London. I can't speak for The Beatles because I'm only me. But if I can get them, if I can get Elvis ... I'll try. I'll try and get all of them.

Q. Do you think this peace festival could become something like that recent Rolling Stones' affair at Altamont in California, where some people died?

J: The Stones' concert was bad. I've heard a lot of things about that concert. I think it was just a bad scene. It won't be like that here. I think they created that either subconsciously or whatever, and that is the result of the image and the mood they create. I think if you create a peaceful scene, you stand a better chance. We have six months to prevent that sort of thing: the Stones' thing was done overnight.

Q. How soon can the world reach a state of peace?

J: As soon as people realise that they have the power. The power doesn't belong with (world leaders) Mr Trudeau, Mr Wilson or Mr Nixon. We are the power. The people are the power. And as soon as people are aware that they have the power, then they can do what they want. And if it's a case of they don't know what to do, let's advertise to them to tell them they have an option. They've all got a vote. Vote for peace, folks.

Q. Don't you think that your long hair and your clothes might put old people off in your pursuit of peace?

J: I understand that. Many people say, 'Why don't you get a butch haircut, and a tie and suit?'. The thing is that's what politicians do. We just try to be as natural as possible. Now, many members of the public are gullible to politicians, with the nice picture of the family, the dog and the whore on the side. Now, I could do that, but I don't think people would believe it. That's the politicians' way, but youth certainly doesn't believe it any more.

We have an intuition about 'leaving one gate open'. There's an old Chinese saying that 'the castle falls from within'. Say, for example America, no communists are going to over-run them. The place'll collapse from within. Always leave one door open. If you have every door shut in the castle, the enemy will attack from every side, and you stand a chance of losing. If you leave one door open, they'll concentrate there. Our door is our hair, or mentioning Cold Turkey on the MBE letter to the Queen, some kind of irrelevancy to distract, so that the attack doesn't hit us. And we try to be natural you know. (Pauses) If I feel like cutting it, I'll cut it.

Q. Have you ever thought of taking your ideas to someone like (car-making giant) Henry Ford?

J: When we get a bit more organised, we might. You see, what we didn't want to become was leaders. I believe in that Wilhelm Reich guy who said: 'Don't become a leader.' We don't want to be the people that everyone says, 'It was your fault we didn't get peace.' We want to be part of it. It's like people said that The Beatles were the movement; but we were only part of the movement. We were influenced as much as we influenced.

And John and Yoko refuse to be the leaders of the youth movement for peace. That's dictatorship. We want everybody to help us. And then, if it takes time for this kind of news to get through to Henry Ford or (Greek shipping magnate Aristotle) Onassis or anybody like that. When we get something functional happening and a few people that aren't John and Yoko, we can approach from that angle. We can then say we've got so much money, will you double it? Because we know they all do charity for whatever reason.

Q. Do you believe in God?

J: Yes, I believe that God is like a powerhouse, like where you keep electricity. Like a power station.

And that he's a supreme power, and that he's neither good nor bad, left, right, black or white. He just is. And we tap that source of power and make of it what we will. Just as electricity can kill people in a chair, or you can light a room with it. I think God is.

Q. Do you worry about being identified as a father figure?

J: I believe that leaders and father figures are the mistake of all the generations before us. And that all of us rely on Nixon or Jesus or whoever we rely on; it's lack of responsibility that you expect some body else to do it. He must help me or we kill him or we vote him out. I think that's the mistake, just having father figures. It's a sign of weakness; you must do the 'greasing' yourself.

I won't be a leader. Everybody is a leader. People thought The Beatles were leaders, but they weren't, and now people are finding that out.

Q. What in brief is your philosophy?

J: Peace, just no violence, and everybody grooving, if you don't mind the word. Of course we all have violence in us, but it must be chanelled or something. If I have long hair, I don't see why everybody else should have long hair. And if I want peace, I'll suggest peace to everyone. But I won't hustle them up for peace. If people want to be violent, let them not interfere with people who don't want violence. Let them kill each other if there has to be that.

Q. Are there any alternatives?

J: You either get tired fighting for peace, or you die.

Q. Do you see the peace grease as a substitute for the supposedly massive problem young people are having with drugs?

J: Well, the liquor problem is even worse. I think the drug problem is a hang-up and a drag, but if we hadn't had methedrine, and all the rest of it, the ones that are going to go through that trip would have been alcoholics. Everybody seems to need something in the way society is – because of the pressure. So it would have been alcohol or something. The problem isn't what they're on, it's what made them go on whatever they're on.

Q. The best antidote for drugtaking and liquor is hope, one would think. And you're giving young people hope.

J: The only time Yoko and I took heavy drugs was when we were without hope. And the only way we got out of it was with hope. And if we can sustain the hope, we don't need liquor, hard drugs or anything. But if we lose hope, what can you do? What is there to do?

Q. John, would you have achieved that state of hope without the success of The Beatles?

J: The Beatles had nothing to do with the hope. This is after ... I mean The Beatles made it four years ago and they stopped touring and they had all the money they wanted, and all the fame they wanted and they found out that they had nothing. And then we started on our various trips of LSD and the Maharishi* and all the rest of the things we did. And the old gag about money and power and fame is not the answer. We didn't have any hope just because we were famous.

You see, (actress) Marilyn Monroe (who died of a drug overdose) and all the other people, they had everything The Beatles had, but that's no answer. So John and Yoko had the same problems and fears and hopes and aspirations that any other couple on earth does, regardless of the position we were in and regardless of the money we had.

We had exactly the same paranoia as everybody else, the same petty thoughts, the same everything. We had no super answer that came through The Beatles or power. In that respect, The Beatles were irrelevant to what I'm talking about.

Q. Going back to where it started, how did you and Yoko initially find ground for this campaign?

J: Both Yoko and I were in different bags, as we call it. But both had a positive side - we (The Beatles) were singing *All You Need is Love* and Yoko was in Trafalgar Square, protesting for peace in a black bag. We met, then we had to decide what our common goal was. We had one thing in common - we were in love. But love is just a gift, and it doesn't answer everything and it's like a precious plant that you have to nurture and look after and all that.

So we had to find out what we wanted to do together - these two egos. What they had in common was love; we had to work on it. What goes with love, we thought, was peace. Now we were thinking of all this, and planning on getting married and not getting married and what we were going to do and how we were going to do it and rock'n'roll and avant garde and all that bit, and then we got that letter from (filmmaker) Peter Watkins. And it all started from there.

Q. Last time you were here (when you were) doing the Montreal Bed-In, you mentioned something about acorns?

J: We'll keep sending them (to world leaders) until everybody's planted one. King Hussein planted his, he's the only one I know about. We've had about 20 replies from here and there, but I don't know who, so it's no good asking me. We've had replies saying, 'Yes, thank you' and we guess they're (those who responded) sort of the peaceniks.

Q. Do you intend to go anywhere else in Canada besides Toronto?

J: We'll probably go down to Montreal to dedicate these radio stations to peace** in a few days.

Q. We're trying to arrange a meeting with the Prime Minister (Pierre Trudeau), as we tried when you were here last time. If we could arrange it, would you be interested in going to Ottawa (the seat of government)?

J: Yes, of course we would, but we don't want to hassle him and press him into things, because obviously - if our lives are anything to go by - his is a lot more delicate and pressurised. And I don't want to do all this 'they're gonna give him acorns, and they're gonna do this', because that spoils it. I'd rather not talk about it. If it's possible, of course we'd enjoy it.

Q. What about the Bag One lithographs? Can you confirm that you'll personally be signing them? From what we've heard, some of the lithographs are erotic and may have trouble passing through Customs.

J: Yeah, with lithographs, you've got to sign them. I have no idea (about Customs). That's the publisher's problem. He asked me to do some lithographs. I did them, and they can handle it themselves.

Q. Have you given any thought to the possibility of using the Peace Festival in the way they are using festivals in the States now, especially the Earth People's Park, using the proceeds from the festival to buy a piece of land, a thousand acres or something?

J: Any ideas like that, please bring them to us, all suggestions like that. The thing is only in the baby stage now. We've come here to think about it and to say that we're setting it up, we've got a place to do it, we hope it'll be well. The stage is gonna be a bed, and where the proceeds go and how we'll work that out will be worked out with the help we can get from Rabbi Feinberg and anybody else who's got more of an organised brain than we have. We're not organisers - that's the kind of help we need.

Any ideas like that we're open to. What to do with money if we get any money, and how to use it, we'd have to decide then. But all ideas are welcome so please approach us through John Brower and Ritchie Yorke. Any help that you have or want to give, you contact John Brower or Ritchie Yorke here, or Rabbi Feinberg, and channel it through them. They're John and Yoko in Canada, and they're in constant touch with us.

Q. Do you think the musical *Hair* is a source of entertainment that sells peace effectively?

J: The *Hair* thing probably did some good. I don't really know. I think it's all right, it was a nice reflection. Everything positive is nice. I like it. Just the effect it had on people was good, I think.

Q. Is there any significance to those black clothes you're wearing?

J: We just like them (the jumpsuits). We like black and white, and they're warm.

Q. Can we ask you a question about The Beatles? Do you ever expect to perform again? I know you had a bit of a hang-up in not wanting to perform as The Beatles.

J: It's like a few months ago, George didn't want to tour. Now he's just been on tour with Delaney and Bonnie and Eric Clapton. And I go off it and on it. And so there's four of us, you know, and I don't know how Ringo feels about it now. But I'm gonna try and sew him up for the Peace Festival in July.

Q. What about the future of The Beatles? Do you expect to remain a foursome?

J: I've no idea. If we are comfortable and enjoy being The Beatles, we'll do it. And when we don't, we won't. That's always been the case. The last four years, every time we've made a record, it's been a decision of whether to carry it on from there. The point is, in the old days, Paul and I would knock off an LP and write most of the songs and do it. Nowadays, there's three of us writing equally good songs, wanting that much space. The problem now, is, do you make a double album every time, which takes six months of your life, or do you make one album? We spend three or four months making one album, maybe get two or three tracks each, that's the problem. You know, it's just a physical problem, and whether we do it or not, I've no idea.

Q. Do you ever fear that your name coupled with the word 'peace' could be used for other means?

J: There is always a danger of that, but if anybody tries to use us, we have you people here, and if we find out, we'll say, 'that man used us'. Our only protection against being used is to tell you.

Q. Are there any circumstances in which you personally could support a war?

J: No. People sometimes raise the question of 'what about 1939 (when WWII began)?' I can only say, 'don't talk to me about'39, talk to me about 1930!'

Q. But the death of six million Jews in itself is not ... Yoko: It was the responsibility of everybody.

J: It was all our responsibility. It wasn't just the Germans. The Germans say, 'Oh it was Hitler'. And the world says, 'Oh it was the Germans', etc. etc. etc. It was all our responsibility then. I know for people that were there then and all that – I was only a child being bombed, and it was different. But I just don't believe it. I believe it was all our responsibility before it happened, you know. That's all I can say about it. I don't believe in killing.

Rabbi Feinberg (Interjecting at the press conference): John, you are now endowed with more influence over young people in the world than all the bishops and rabbis and priests put together. That is true.

Do you ever feel any sense of fright at the power you have?

John: It's an abstract power. If we have something specific we'd like to use the power for – say we wanted to plug a certain product that wasn't peace, and I contact any press I know and try to get it over - there's a good chance it won't work. So I haven't got the power that I can really get hold of and do something with.

Rabbi Feinberg: But you're using it now for peace, and I think the whole world should be very grateful to you and Yoko for doing it.

John: Well, thank you for that, you know.

A hearty round of applause underlined the fact that the media had been - in the main - extremely impressed by John and Yoko's performance at what went down in history as the Toronto Peace Festival Press Conference.

On the 20-mile journey back to the Hawkins' Mississauga property in Ron's white Roller, the Lennons had every reason to feel satisfied about how the media engagement had gone. ``Yeah well that went pretty well,'' John allowed to nobody in particular as we tooled westwards down Highway 401. Back at the Hawk's place, we relaxed with a cup of tea and a few puffs before John plunged into the time-consuming task of signing the Bag One lithographs. We hadn't really given them much thought until a small truck came up the driveway and its driver deposited several paper bundles at Hawkins' front door.

The publisher's representative, Ed Newman, had flown over from Paris to oversee the signing and it was a monumental exercise. Newman had to cope with a delicate agenda - getting the lithographs signed without offending John in any way. Consequently he was overprotective and precious about everything. For example, he arranged for special pictures to be taken of the signed lithographs but later neglected to respond to the photographer's invoice.

Pencil after pencil wore down as minutes stretched into hours which stretched into a couple of days and John just kept on signing. I doubt if he'd initially realised just how much effort it would take to complete the lithograph commitment. I assisted the flow in two particular ways - firstly in making sure that John had a constant supply of hash joints to enhance his diligence and, secondly, in providing suitably stimulating background music.

As it turned out, Ronnie Hawkins had recently completed recording a ``comeback'' album with the widely acknowledged ``godfather'' of rock 'n' roll, the eminent producer Jerry Wexler, with the famed rhythm section of David Hood, Roger Hawkins, Barry Beckett and Jimmy Johnson, augmented for these sessions by Duane "Skydog" Allman on slide guitar and the King Biscuit Boy (Richard Newell), a Hawkins protégé, blowing some serious harp. I had the great pleasure of providing liner notes for the album and I went to town on the assignment.

I put the advance acetate of the album, which Jerry Wexler had sent to us the week before, on repeat cycle on the turntable. The self-titled LP had been recorded in Muscle Shoals, Alabama, a few weeks earlier. With topnotch production, fine instrumentation and that laidback feeling of the American South, the album was a nice mix of the old days and the new. The repertoire included an impressive balance of familiar (the Clovers' *Down in the Alley,* Bo Diddley's *Who Do You Love*, Carl Perkins' *Match-*

box, Bob Dylan's *One Too Many Mornings*, the evergreen chestnut *Will the Circle Be Unbroken* and Ronnie's own remade hit version of Chuck Berry's *Thirty Days* which The Hawk did as *Forty Days*, along with two Gordon Lightfoot tunes, *Home From the Forest* and *Bitter Green*). We played it over and over while John signed the lithos; as the tracks rolled by, slowly but surely John warmed to it.

Although he confessed that he rarely listened to new albums in case he ``accidentally stole something from another singer or songwriter'', John grew more and more attached to Ron's Muscle Shoals album. He liked the combination of the old licks and rock'n' roll antics with a red-hot contemporary rhythm section. Later, as a special thank you to the Hawkins family for barging into their lives and disrupting their household for this unforgettable week, John recorded a special spoken-word endorsement for use by Atlantic Records to promote the disc and in particular the single, *Down in the Alley*.

Here's what John said: ``This is John Lennon here just muttering about Ronnie Hawkins. And how on our last trip to Canada, it was somehow arranged for us to stay at his home. We had a great time and I'd known Ronnie on record for ages *40 Days* and all that. But I didn't know anything about him. But he's turned out to be a great guy. And it just so happened as it were that he'd just made an al bum. He's about the only person who doesn't try and grease you, as they say. He played us the album well, he didn't play it because he was shy like most musicians, like all of us are shy. I hate playing my new record to other people but you have to do it because you have that need. I hope this isn't too long for a promo. Anyway I wasting there signing these 20 million lithographs and the album was going on. And I was listening to most of it and still signing when this track called *Down in the Alley* came on. And it really sort of buzzed me. And it sounded like now and then. And I like that. So let's hear it....''

Jerry Wexler, a rock legend who has seen virtually "everything that moves in the rhythm and the blues" (*Rhythm and the Blues* being the title of his outstanding autobiography, written with David Ritz), was for once lost for words when I arranged for John to phone him impromptu with words of praise about the Hawkins record. When I told him John had recorded an endorsement to use in promoting the Hawk album, Jerry could barely believe it, while Hawkins might well have thought that his chart future had been secured. I think we all did.

Later in the afternoons, as a break from the drudgery of scrawling ``John Lennon'' on litho after litho, John and Yoko would venture into the whiteness of the great Ontario outdoors to play with some of the winter ``toys''

Ronnie had organised to entertain his celebrity guests. There were Moto-Skis, basically a motorbike with skis attached to provide rapid transport over snow and ice. And there was an Amphicat, a large-wheeled jeep-like device. John preferred the relative sanity of the slower-moving Amphicat, while the rest of us let off steam and tension on the high-speed Moto-Skis.

Now I'm no speed freak and I'd never driven a vehicle other than a car before the Lennons came to stay at the Hawkins' place. The supposed thrill of riding a motorbike, for example, held no allure for me. But I can't deny that in just a matter of days I somehow managed to win an amazing reputation as a devil-driven driver of motorized ski machines. With a beginner's arrogance and attitude, I would take visitors for rides on the back of my Moto-Ski, tearing across the fields out back of the Hawk's 10-acre property and then plunging forth at high speed over the edge of a dip in the field. The machine would fly through the air for three or four yards and then hit the frozen ground with an almighty thud.

John's visiting UK rock writer friend Ray Connolly (of London daily The Evening Standard and later author of the book *Stardust,* which was made into a movie starring David Essex) apparently continued to talk in later life of his awe at venturing out as my unwitting pillion passenger back in December, 1969. I guess that in the heat of these historic tension-fueled moments, I just went over the top and past the sanity barrier. This is not something that I'm particularly proud of but apparently I melted the pistons on one Moto-Ski in just three days from my frenzied rides. Needless to say, the Moto-Ski manufacturers were quick to replace the machine I'd seized up. The publicity they were receiving in newscasts around the world only helped to boost their sales. John Lennon tooling around on a Moto-Ski - it was a marketing man's dream! You'd go for a quick burn around on the Moto-Ski and then return to try and get Elvis Presley's office on the phone to lure The King into joining our peace endeavours. I think I should mention that I've never set foot on a motorized vehicle (other than a car or a golf cart) since that week when the Lennons stayed with Ronnie Hawkins. It was a total one-off, a temporary release to let off steam. It worked at the time.

As dignitaries came and departed from the Hawkins' property (their ranks included human rights campaigner Dick Gregory, avant-garde magazine editor Ralph Ginzburg and various journalists and media people), John persevered through the task of signing the lithographs. We set him up at a table in the Hawkins' living room, within sight of the piano with its fancy paintwork, and augmented this with suitable stimulants and soundwaves.

The 19th-century piano - and the décor of the surrounding living room - had to be seen to be believed. It was as though an Arkansas family of hillbillies had brought in a classical European master to make his impressions upon the place. It was an attempt to import culture into the hills of Mississauga. The piano's wooden structure had been painted over and anointed with cherubic likenesses of the two young Hawkins sons - Ronnie Jr and Robin. They had been drawn in the pseudo-religious style of Michelangelo's Sistine Chapel artwork in the Vatican.

Ronnie used to joke that the Italian painter they employed - who was provided with food, drink and lodging, and the odd other benefit while he toiled - had stayed for so long in the late '60s that he started painting the ceilings as well. Sadly, they would be later painted over by a new, presumably less cultured, owner. But the painted piano ended up travelling with the Hawkins family to their new home on Stoney Lake near Lakefield in Ontario. A third cherub - representing daughter Leah, who presumably had complained about not being adorned on the keyboard in the same manner as her siblings - was added later by another artist. Much gilt surrounded the artwork. There was also a matching writing desk and small table but we chose a more conventional dining room table for John to sign his lithographs.

Some light relief was provided when a Capitol Records flunky - sent over from head office to ingratiate himself with the Lennons and to act as a gofer - was asked to remove and burn a bunch of paper sheets that separated the various lithographs. Next thing we heard alarmed cries of ``Fire, fire!'', and we raced outside into the snow to find that the incinerator barrel had flared up and was setting fire to a corner of Hawkins' garage where the Rolls-Royce was stored. The Hawk was still joking 40 years later about John Lennon running out with a toy watering can to help quell the soaring flames. Eventually we got the blaze under control and John resumed the litho signing.

*FOOTNOTE

Maharishi Mahesh Yogi, who was born in 1914 and died in 2008, led the transcendental meditation religious movement which attracted the attention of The Beatles in 1967, around the time of Brian Epstein's death when they were, according to Paul McCartney, seeking stability. The band went to India to study TM in 1968.

**FOOTNOTE

The *War Is Over* peace radio network, an idea first promulgated by Canadian broadcaster Geoff Stirling in league with Doug Pringle, ultimately attracted the interest of several hundred stations internationally. They were to join in an informal network of stations pushing peace and non-violence as a way of life among enlightened citizens.

8. MARSHALL MCLUHAN MEETS A WORD MAGICIAN

The next important event in the lives of the Lennons' peace initiatives on Canadian soil was a meeting with media and communications prophet Marshall McLuhan, the author of several internationally acclaimed books including *The Mechanical Bride, The Gutenberg Galaxy, Understanding Media* and *The Medium is the Massage.* The Canadian educator, philosopher and scholar - a professor of English literature, a literary critic, a rhetorician and a communications theorist - was universally known for having coined the terms ``the medium is the message'' and the ``global village''. He also possibly coined and certainly popularised the word ``surfing'', as in negotiating the web. Time magazine accoladed McLuhan as ``Canada's intellectual comet.''

Astute CBS television executives had lined up the filming of a ``meeting of the minds'' between McLuhan and the Lennons, which would be used as the final episode in the 1960s of the American news program *60 Minutes.* It was an exceptional editorial idea, the concept being that John and Yoko and McLuhan would not have any pre-interview dialogue until they met for the first time at the latter's office in the Department of Culture and Technology on the University of Toronto's downtown campus - in front of CBS cameras. It would be discourse unlimited and open verbal confrontation. John and Yoko approached the upcoming interview with confident positivity.

On the Saturday afternoon we drove through a near-blinding snowstorm into the centre of Toronto in the Hawkins Rolls, and John and Yoko swept into a video-recording space set up by CBS. The cameras whirred as the intriguing conversation unfolded, quite dramatically. McLuhan, the silver-haired multi-media prophet, immediately connected with the ever-curious Lennon.

McLuhan: Can you recall the occasion or the immediate reasons for your getting involved in music?

John: I heard Elvis Presley. And that was it. There were lots of other things going on but that was the conversion. I kind of dropped everything.

M: Ah. You felt you could do it at least as well as he could?

J: Yeah. But I thought that we better get a few people together, because maybe we couldn't make it alone. So we did a team job.

M: The British are still more team-oriented than the Americans in terms of performance. The star system doesn't play quite as well in England. The private star.

J: They have a reaction to that in England - treating their stars and entertainers like animals. We're not like the Americans, to be hyped by Hollywood. The attitude is be quiet, do a dance at the London Palladium, and stop talking about peace. That's what we get in London.

Prof McLuhan then outlined to the Lennons his theories about why rock festivals were becoming larger and larger:

M: Frustration creates bigness. And when people are frustrated, they feel the need to expand, to get more room and length. The man who gives up smoking gets so frustrated that he puts on huge amounts of weight, even when he doesn't eat anything. Frustration in organisations results in huge growth of cities, businesses, countries, territorial imperatives and so on. Frustration releases adrenalin into the system. Adrenalin creates much bigger muscles and bigger arms and legs, and has tremendous weight on the political body. This is why dinosaurs ended in sudden death, because as the environment (became) more and more hostile, more and more adrenalin was released into their bodies and they got bigger and bigger and then they collapsed. It could happen to America; it already happened to the British Empire. Adrenalin just gave out. In fact, your songs represented the end of that big adrenalin flow. As far as the UK was concerned, Beatles music was the end of the adrenalin. And the beginning of peace and contentment.

McLuhan then switched to a more familiar topic: communication.

M: Language is a form of organised stutter. Literally you chop your sounds up into bits in order to talk. Now, when you sing, you don't stutter, so singing is a way of stretching language into long, harmonious patterns and cycles. How do you think about language in songs?

J: Language and song is to me, apart from being pure vibrations, just like trying to describe a dream. And because we don't have telepathy or whatever it is, we try and describe the dream to each other, to verify to each other what we know, what we believe is inside each other. And the stuttering is right - because we can't say it. No matter how you say it, it's never how you want to say it.

M: The moment you sing, you feel you are communicating much more?
J: Yes, because the words are irrelevant.

M: Rowan and Martin (TV show hosts) say: ``We don't tell jokes, we just project a mood.'' You're concerned with projecting a mood and defining it. Putting down some pattern so that other people can find the pattern, participate, and ...

J: As soon as you find the pattern, you break it. Otherwise it gets boring. The Beatles' pattern is one that has to be scrapped. If it remains the same, it's a monument, or a museum, and one thing this age is about is no museums. The Beatles turned into a museum, so they have to be scrapped or deformed or changed.

M: They're in danger of becoming good taste?

J: They passed through that. They have to be thoroughly horse-whipped. (Big laughs). M: What do you think we're moving into in the way of new rhythms, new patterns?

J: Just complete freedom and non-expectation from audience or musician or performer. And then, when we've had that for a few hundred years, then we can talk about playing around with patterns and bars and music again. We must get away from the patterns we've had for these thousands of years. M: Well, this means very much in the way of decentralizing our world, doesn't it?

J: Yes. We must be one country and stick together. You don't have to have badges to say we're together. We're together if we're together, and no stamps or flags are going to make anybody together ...folks.

After 45 minutes of this intriguing dialogue, the professor and the world's most famous couple shook hands and we headed back to the Hawk's Roller and waited while the Lennons' assistant Anthony Fawcett exchanged phone numbers with one of McLuhan's daughters. He would later develop this liaison. As he waved goodbye, the professor informed John and Yoko that "these portals have been honoured by your presence". Then we drove off through great white sheets of snow towards the Hawkins' property.

McLuhan, a huge figure in the development of our understanding of modern media and technology, died in 1980 at the age of 69, just over three weeks after John Lennon was assassinated.

Back at the pseudo-Tudor Hawkins homestead, the stream of visitors would continue without relief. Media and peace messengers were forming a chain through the snow into the house. The morning after the Marshall McLuhan adventure, we picked up human rights campaigner Dick Gregory from the airport. He proved to be a breath of fresh air, embracing the Peace Festival discussions with passion and vigor. I found him a remarkable human being, full of compassion but very suspicious of the American Establishment. As well he might be, presenting as a genuine peace activist in a tumultuous time.

In 1995, at a civil rights rally marking the 30th anniversary of the 1965 Voting Rights Act, which prevented the practice of disallowing illiterate Americans (particularly of African heritage) the vote, Gregory called the United States ``the most dishonest, unGodly, unspiritual nation that ever existed in the history of the planet. As we talk now, America is 5 per cent of the world's population, consuming 96 per cent of the world's hard drugs''. That was a sobering observation.

Another welcome visitor was Rabbi Abraham Feinberg and his wife, Ruth, who continued to connect in a positive way with the Lennons. The rabbi - who'd gained a reputation for being quite unorthodox after making a trip in 1967 to North Vietnam with three other well-known clergymen - was a keen supporter of the Lennons' peace cause. He had written a controversial book, *Rabbi Feinberg's Hanoi Diary*, and he undertook an extensive tour of the US and Canada speaking out against the Vietnam War.

He encouraged John and Yoko in a number of significant ways. He had attended the Montreal Bed-In and had suggested a slight change in John's lyrics for *Give Peace a Chance*. Whereupon John had urged the rabbi to make his own album, *I Was So Much Older Then*, which was released in 1969. John and Yoko didn't have a lot of genuine friends within the ranks of the Establishment, and even though the rabbi was regarded as a radical in some circles, he reached across a significant divide to the Lennons.

After Ruth died in 1971, Rabbi Feinberg relocated to California for a new start. He died of cancer in Reno, Nevada in October 1986, but he had been a loyal supporter of the Lennons' peace cause. I had the pleasure of being invited to a lunch at the Forest Hill home of the Feinbergs after the Canadian *War Is Over* events.

On the afternoon after the *60 Minutes* discussion I sat with John and Yoko and watched an end-of-decade wrap of The Best of Ed Sullivan, which featured several Beatles appearances. Ronnie's wife Wanda Hawkins drew our attention to the TV coverage of the band. A surprised Lennon leapt out of his sofa seat and knelt close to the TV as a long shot cut to a close-up of Paul McCartney crooning, ``Yesterday, all my troubles seemed ...''

John laughed heartily. ``Boy,' he said to nobody in particular, ``was he shitting then!'' The screen changed to a rerun of The Beatles' first appearance on the Sullivan show and there was John - short-haired and obviously nervous - strumming his guitar and screaming into the mic. Yoko laughed as John returned to the sofa; ``Is that really my husband?'' she teased and John simply shrugged.

Then it cut to New York's Shea Stadium with John leading the rest of the band through a line of police security as they stumbled towards the stage amid cutaway scenes of crying teenyboppers.

``Yes, yes, yes,' John bubbled. ``I remember every moment of that. It was incredible.''

In the face of such frankness from the Lennons, one could only react in kind. I felt a near-desperate need to unburden myself of a lingering view to the Beatle, no matter how rocky and fragile his band's future might be. After days of nervous contemplation I finally had the chance to sit down in the Hawkins' living room, hash joint in one hand and wearing my heart on my sleeve. Behind the couch were stashed several of the Bag One lithographs which John had somehow screwed up in the signing process and he'd handed to me as some kind of peace offering. Unfortunately the stash slipped my mind and Ronnie ended up passing along my ``reject'' lithographs to a sibling and they now adorn a palatial place on Long Island. Big lesson learned there.

As the joint burned down, I began to unload my feelings about The Beatles to John. ``John, I want to say how honoured I feel to be involved with your *War Is Over* peace campaign. It's such a profound joy to me to be trying to do something about the state of the planet ... and as part of your team,' I stammered. ``I really enjoy working with you and I am absolutely blown away by how you embrace ideas that I manage to come up with occasionally - like Year One AP (for After Peace) and the International Peace Vote. That is incredibly encouraging to me. But there's another thing I have to tell you. It's something I feel very deeply about and I feel it's important that I talk to you about it.'' ``All right,' he said curiously, ``what is that?''

``I have to own up to the fact that I've always had issues with The Beatles' early music. To be honest, I wasn't a big fan at all of the band in its early days and I deliberately didn't attend the band's only concert ever in my home town of Brisbane in Australia. For me the problem was The Beatles recording covers of what I considered to be sacred R & B songs. I thought your cover versions were vastly inferior to the originals and it really bugged me that racist whitebread Australian radio stations would rush to play your covers while totally ignoring the originals. This happened time and time and time again. It really bugged me John, I gotta tell you.

"Brilliant songs like *You Really Got a Hold on Me* by the Miracles, *Please Mr Postman* by the Marvelettes, *Money* by Barrett Strong, *Twist and Shout* by the Isley Brothers, the Shirelles' *Baby It's You* and *Boys, Anna (Go to Him)* by Arthur Alexander, Chuck Berry's *Rock'n'roll Music* and *Chains* by the Cookies are just a handful of great records that were never heard by Australians until The Beatles covered them. I was fired from two Australian radio stations for daring to play the originals. One of those originals was *Fingertips* by Little Stevie Wonder in 1963, when he was the first artist to have a number one single and album on the US Billboard charts simultaneously. But I really didn't like your cover versions and I have to say it bothered me hugely that The Beatles were getting all this local radio exposure and so much acclaim from radio listeners who didn't know any better."

I paused to slow down my rapidly beating heart. I was unloading a whole cargo of built up bias against the proponents of the British sound, baggage which I had carried deeply for a long, long time. I didn't care a lot about the original output of bands like the Animals, the Rolling Stones, the Searchers, the Tremeloes, the Dreamers, the Walker Brothers and Manfred Mann. Some of their songs were OK but many were lightweight puff. Whereas the originals were religiously avoided. Under the directive of racist Australian radio, local music fans would not be hearing the original versions of great R & B classics.

After my anti-Beatles, pro-real R & B tirade, John rubbed his chin, took a large drag on the spliff and looked me straight in the eye. For a moment, I was really worried that I might have offended him. That was the last thing I wanted at this point, having been entranced by his message of peace on a poisoned planet, especially in his utterances of recent days.

"Hmmm,' he exhaled, after a long spell and with a wicked grin. "You know, to tell you the truth Ritchie, I didn't like our versions either. Or even our covering of those songs. It was all Paul's idea! I much prefer the originals than our versions."

Holy fucking hell, you could only laugh! But it was obvious that John shared my deep love of many rhythm and blues classics. Somehow they represented - for him and for me - a medium which could cut through adolescent abandonment issues and provide one with a renewed feeling of hope. Later that night he would mention that the Shirelles' original rendition of *Baby It's You* was among his all-time top 10 favourite discs.

During the Lennons' stay, the Hawkins household was often reduced to a shambles by the intensity of activity. It was full-on communication. Extra phone lines were installed so that John and Yoko could maintain contact with the world and hustle up more support, artistic and political, for the Peace Festival and the *War Is Over* campaign. Visitors were coming and going, calls were pouring in and blasting out, people were constantly hitting on John and Yoko for all manner of favours and connections. Ronnie's band, And Many Others, featuring the King Biscuit Boy and Kelly Jay, were rehearsing night and day 400 hundred yards away in another house on the property, hoping that John would drop by and check them out during his stay. He didn't. It wasn't that he wasn't interested - he was just so intensely locked into sync with what he and Yoko were doing.

The presence of John and Yoko in and around Toronto was having multiple effects, spiritual and otherwise. In addition to saturation media coverage, the *War Is Over* billboard and poster campaign was ingratiating itself into the heads of peace lovers and war makers alike. The Lennon's amusing antics for the peace cause was the number one topic of conversation at water coolers and coffee makers around the province.

And it carried out into bigger space as other committed and confirmed peaceniks joined the bandwagon. In the era before social networking, people climbed on the peace train through other media. Such as the skywriting of the *War Is Over* message by sympathetic ad crews. And multiple mentions of the message on radio and T V. John and Yoko's presence in Canada for that week in December would have enormous repercussions, both then and now.

Ronnie himself was careful not to get in John and Yoko's way and maintained a very laidback presence, only really talking when spoken to. That was unusual for the Hawk, who wasn't being his typical robust and rollicking self, cracking jokes and entertaining all and sundry. In fact, he was so out of character, even to John - who'd known him only a few days - that he asked Ron if anything was wrong.

``Everyone is always trying to talk to me or grease me or hustle me with something or other, but you hardly say a word,' John said. ``I was concerned that something wasn't right.''

``No no no, not at all,' said Ron. ``I just want you and Yoko to be able to do your thing without getting in your way. We just want to help make things easier for you.'' Ronnie's reluctance to bother the Lennons in any way continued right through their stay, even in the most provocative circumstances. One evening, Ronnie and Wanda were sitting in their wood-paneled and wide-windowed sunroom, gazing at gifts from the Canadian head office of EMI-Capitol Records - a giant silver Christmas tree complete with fake white doves, plus a cage containing two live white ``peace'' doves. The label was trying to get into the spirit of things.

Capitol Records, thanks to their astute A & R man Paul White, had played an early role in the breaking of The Beatles in the North American markets. And they'd profited handsomely from White's wisdom, making many millions of dollars off the back of The Beatles' catalogue.

One evening, as Ron and Wanda sat sipping coffees and no doubt pondering the unexpected career benefits of having John Lennon come to stay and the world media exposure that such an event guaranteed, they heard the unmistakable sound of dripping water coming from a corner of the room. Looking in its direction, they quickly noticed drops gushing from the ceiling. And not just a few drops. Instantly the couple shared a flash of realization: the bath in the en suite had overflowed. John and Yoko had turned on the taps to the bathtub and then gone missing. Presumably they had smoked one of their hash joints and nodded off. But it was one thing for the Hawkins to know about it, and another thing to take steps to arrest the problem. Neither Ron nor Wanda felt inclined to go knocking on their loaned master bedroom to wake up John and Yoko. They didn't have any desire to bother them with such a trifle as a flood from an overflowing bathtub. So they fetched buckets and sat and watched the water pouring down their sunroom walls from the en suite above. As the doves tweeted out a message of peace. It was quite a few minutes (and a few thousand dollars' damage, as it turned out) before the Lennons awoke and hurriedly turned off the taps.

To his credit, Ronnie in later years didn't mind owning up to this escapade and his unwillingness to disturb the Lennons - even when they were inadvertently damaging his house! Ultimately, the week with the Lennons was an enormous career boost for Hawkins. Unfortunately in the end, the Hawk's first class Muscle Shoals album did not take off as we had all hoped. Despite John Lennon's unique endorsement, radio station programmers all over the planet were perplexed by the thought of embracing a rock 'n' roll hero from the '50s.

The Canadian peace trip was nowhere near finished. One great milestone was to be achieved in the coming days. The historic birth of political pop was about to unfold.

9. THE TRUDEAU-LENNON GATHERING AND THE BEGINNING OF POLITICAL POP

``It was the best trip we've ever had. We got more done for peace this week than in our whole lives.''

John Lennon reflecting on his visit to Canada with Yoko in December 1969, which ushered in the new era of political pop after the historic Ottawa meeting between the Lennons and Canadian Prime Minister, Pierre Trudeau.

We were about to reach the climax of a very heady week of peace. Our excitement about what possibly could be achieved had caught us in its rapture, entranced us with its positivity. Any doubts we might have harboured had been blown off to the edges of the new road forward. We really were on a roll and it felt deeply inspiring.

Sitting on the end of John Lennon's king-size bed in a suite at the Chateau Laurier Hotel, in Ottawa, on a frigid Tuesday morning, a few days before Christmas in December 1969, I watched with quiet amusement as the most politically savvy member of The Beatles nervously prepared to climb out onto the stage of political pop. Yoko was dutifully assisting John to knot his black tie but he couldn't hide his rampaging bundle of nerves. John was having trouble restraining himself from pacing the bone-coloured carpet as he contemplated the possibilities of the forthcoming meeting.

By now I was working full-time for the Lennons, as their peace envoy. Two days after the couple touched down in Canada for this latest visit - and as a result of my lengthy absences from The Globe and Mail newsroom, despite filing regular pieces - I was called into the office of the features editor. A straight-talking Scot, he went for the jugular. "Ritchie, you can't be working for John Lennon... and for us. Things can't go on like this. You're going to have to make a decision about your future."

In my view, there wasn't much of a choice to make - to continue being a professional inkstained wretch or to become a full-time peacemaker. It took me all of two seconds to inform the features editor that as much as I'd appreciated my spell in the Establishment press, we would be parting company. I'd greatly enjoyed being the good old gray Globe's first full time rock writer (and indeed becoming the first writer ever to wear a coloured dress shirt in the notoriously super-conservative newsroom). But I knew the *War Is Over* peace campaign would have more to offer in the way of challenges and events of global significance.

It was decided that I would move over to the Karma Productions payroll. Karma was a company that had been formed by John Brower and partners in November to administer the affairs of the Toronto Peace Festival, and other Lennon-related ventures such as the International Peace Vote and setting up the International Peace Fund. John and Yoko were immediately receptive to the idea of my becoming their international peace envoy to assist them in spreading their anti-war ideas around the planet. When the idea of an international peace tour was first bandied around, the Lennons were keen. They knew that *War Is Over* needed to be spread internationally, local contacts needed to be established, plans had to be extended on an individual country-by-country basis. To make a difference, in Lennon's own words, we needed ``to get John and Yoko's in every country''. In this pre-internet period, establishing and maintaining international connections was exceedingly important. The opportunity to set up and get on board an international peace train was considerably tempting.

When Karma Productions offered to fund a peace tour of yours truly, the Lennons were in total support. They weren't asked to contribute money themselves, as Karma Productions was keen to maintain their goodwill and access to the world's most famous couple. This was early days in our peace initiative and we were still feeling our way, so to speak, while the Lennons were pleased to see any positive developments in the *War Is Over* peace campaign.

There could be no doubting that the occasion occupying our attention in the Ottawa hotel room was a highly positive development. John and Yoko were scheduled to present themselves at the office of the Prime Minister of Canada, Pierre Elliott Trudeau, later that morning. The scheduled get-together would make history as the first time a member of The Beatles had met the political leader of a country. Of course The Beatles had already interacted with just about every other kind of dignitary or celebrity in the world of entertainment and show business. But the domain of politics- up until the late '60s - had remained an uncharted field. However, I always instinctively knew that an intelligent, perceptive and sensitive individual such as Prime Minister Trudeau would present a very real opportunity for an unprecedented dialogue between a peace believer and a concerned politician.

Trudeau had opposed conscription during WWII, almost two decades before the anti-war demonstrations and flag-burning that came to signify the Vietnam War in the '60s. He first became a public advocate for change in 1949, when as a journalist (his qualification was in law) he supported the trade union during Quebec's asbestos strike, considered a turning point in the province's history.

I had been around a few tumultuous moments in Lennon's latter-day career, but I'd never seen John in the grip of such intense and restless energy as on the day he was to meet the young, charismatic PM. Forty years later, I can see and feel John's lips pursed almost grimly with granny glasses perched at the end of his nose, fiddling with the black taffeta tie which defined the cut of his black Pierre Cardin suit. I can even smell the omnipresent, pungent fumes of Continental tobacco as John fired up one Gitane (a robust brand of French cigarette) after another. His concern was admittedly contagious: some glimmers of it touched each of us playing at being cool in his hotel dressing room that morning. But John was metaphorically shitting himself. His nerves were all but strangling him.

Ronnie Hawkins sat quietly with Wanda, puffing cigar smoke into the already-chemically-tainted atmosphere. John Brower and I tried to generate small talk. In the background, Anthony Fawcett had managed to patch himself into an unrestricted direct phone line to Apple in London. Transatlantic long distance calls were difficult to organise in 1969 and Fawcett had urgent business (and other interests of a romantic nature) to maintain.

Fawcett was an up-and-coming art critic specialising in the avant garde when he first crossed paths with John and Yoko during their first exhibition together. He was subsequently offered a gig as the couple's personal assistant, replacing John's boyhood friend Peter Shotton. He worked closely with the Lennons through the launching of the *War Is Over* peace initiative, and left their employ in late 1971 when they departed for New York. His place was later filled by May Pang, who went on to share a Yoko-facilitated relationship with John starting in October 1973.

Fawcett was a humourous and horny little bounder, and had a penchant for pursuing members of the opposite sex at every opportunity. Restraint was a way of life he had yet to master. Yoko actually caught him in bed with a girl during the Lennons' stay at Ronnie Hawkins homestead in December 1969.

Six months down the track from the Montreal Bed-In and an historic live appearance as part of the North American debut of the Plastic Ono Band at the Toronto Rock'n' Roll Revival in September (the cause of the break-up of The Beatles), the Lennons had returned to Canada's French province. This time we had traveled on a specially chartered railway observation car attached to the rear of the daily Montreal Rapido train service. Peace Festival promoter John Brower recalls that it cost around $2000 to charter the separate carriage. It was money well spent - and more than worth that outlay to be in a position to guarantee John and Yoko's security and privacy. And to provide transportation for our eager little band of peace propaganda promoters which comprised John and Yoko, Fawcett, Ronnie and Wanda Hawkins, Brower, my then wife Annette Yorke (now Carter) and myself. The sight of the private observation car, redolent of the grand old days of rail travel, was also bound to impress the legion of media types who turned out to bid us farewell from Toronto.

The beginnings of this journey had been confirmed in a letter to Trudeau dated December 9. On Bag Productions Inc. stationery from their Tittenhurst Park private address, John and Yoko had written: ``Dear Prime Minister, as per our telephone conversations with your various aides we are pleased to inform you that we shall be arriving in Toronto next Tuesday and shall be staying there for at least a week. We look forward to the opportunity of meeting with you during that time and would be pleased if your office could try to arrange an appointment at your convenience. Pursuant to this we are asking Messrs John Brower, Richard Miller (originator of the Peace Festival concept) and Ritchie Yorke to contact your office and to look after the necessary arrangements. We look forward very much to seeing you. Love and peace. J & Y''

As we shuffled our luggage and famous charges into the observation car, little did any of the eager-beaver press corps pressing upon the platform at Union Station know about the motives for this out-of-town excursion. They had simply concluded that we were headed for Montreal to further spread the word – and to alert Quebec media to the expanding Peace Festival plans. They had no idea of a private meeting involving federal government officials that was scheduled to take place deep in the bowels of Bonaventure Station, Montreal, that evening. Nor were they aware that our private carriage would be coupled to an Ottawa-bound express early the next morning headed for an even more headline-capturing get-together. But they would be finding out a great deal more when the next afternoon's newspapers and radio and TV bulletins beamed out some surprising news.

Throughout the generally upbeat tone of the Montreal Bed-In some six months earlier, there had been whispers about the very real possibility of arranging a meeting between the Lennons and Canada's very clued-in Prime Minister. It was simply the logical next step in the Lennons' bid to secure Establishment political support for their peace initiatives. Too bad if the leaders of John's homeland, and of the United States, didn't possess the wisdom to see the benefits of communicating with prime spokespeople for the emerging generations.*

But even in the green-light atmosphere that we were absorbing from the seat of power, Ottawa, it was made very clear to us from the outset that the Prime Minister's Office did not want a circus. There could be absolutely no advance tip-offs to the media about the pending Lennon visit to Parliament Hill. Even a passing vague column mention would jeopardise, if not jettison, the meeting. So our lips were sealed and woe betide any of us who let the secret out of John and Yoko's Bag.

After a pleasant trip through a snowbound south-eastern Ontario, we slid into Montreal's main station in the late afternoon. Our observation car was uncoupled from the passenger train which had hauled us across Ontario and shunted into a quiet siding to avoid the possible crush of fans. Shortly afterwards, we headed into a function room at the Queen Elizabeth Hotel for a peace festival press conference which continued for 45 minutes. And then we returned to the solitude of the private carriage to await the arrival of distinguished Canadian lawyer Gerald Le Dain, the chairman of the Le Dain Commission into drug use.

Earlier, John had agreed to talk with the Commission's representatives generally about youth and marihuana use after he'd been convinced that it was genuinely looking at reforming the archaic laws about soft drug use. He wasn't prepared to be a stooge for anybody, certainly not in regards to such a hot and topical subject as drug laws. He had some very firm opinions on the subject and would be happy to tender them at an appropriate proceeding. Ultimately the Le Dain Commission was considered by John to be a worthy recipient of his thoughts and experiences, and proved to be so in time.

The Commission of Inquiry into the Non-Medical Use of Drugs had been set up by Pierre Trudeau's Liberal government and Le Dain, a distinguished Montreal lawyer (later to become a Supreme Court judge) was tapped to chair the four-year investigation. At the peak of its sittings, the Le Dain Commission employed 100 people including 30 full-time researchers. The researchers basically looked into four target areas: (1) the effects of the drugs, especially cannabis, (2) drug use, (3) treatment problems, and (4) the influence of the media on the phenomenon. It was one of the early legitimate attempts to investigate the negatives and positives of the burgeoning soft drug culture. It is an issue that continues to resonate until this day and still remains unresolved.

In December 1973, the Commission produced findings that marked a turning point in the official outlook on recreational drugs in general, but particularly marihuana. There was widespread disagreement within its ranks but all five members of the Commission supported the movement towards decriminalisation, especially marihuana. The founder of the Drug Policy Foundation in the US, Arnold Trebach, described the impact of the Le Dain report as ``stunning''. Le Dain's four lengthy reports are credited with marking a turning point in official attitudes to all recreational drugs.

After the publication of this work, Prime Minister Trudeau promised legislation that would decriminalise minor cases of marihuana possession, but politics being what they are, these were never kept and while the drug's use is broadly tolerated in that country, it remains illegal. It should be noted however that the present repressive right-wing Progressive Conservative government in Canada is totally opposed to any liberation of marihuana laws.

Gerald Le Dain was 44 years old when appointed chair of the Commission. But I doubt he was prepared for John Lennon's initial response to his entreaties in our private railroad carriage. The Lennon response amazed all of us, even though we were quite closely aware of John's keen sense of wit and occasion. He, after all, was the man who had started a (false) rumor that he and his fellow Beatles had (God forbid) smoked a marihuana joint in the washrooms at Buckingham Palace when they were there for the MBE presentation. Initially the Le Dain Commission's representatives had approached our camp with a request for a consultation with this particular member of The Beatles, because he was considered an articulate and enlightened spokesperson for youth culture, and therefore a credible commentator on the nuances of an emerging drug-slanted ethos around the world.

When Mr Le Dain and a colleague fronted to our railway carriage parked in a siding underneath the Bonaventure Hotel early that evening, John immediately asked the two legal entities a crucial question: ``Had they,' he politely enquired, ``ever actually smoked marihuana, the prime subject of the inquiry, the source of all this concern?'' Upon hearing their negative response, John immediately drew a line in the sand. He insisted that if they wanted to obtain his opinions about marihuana-smoking and the effects thereof, they needed to be in the loop, so to speak. They didn't have to be ``stout-hearted believers'' but they needed to know what the heck they were talking or writing about. How could one possibly come to a judgment about marihuana without actually trying it, queried John in apparent good faith?

Messrs Le Dain and partner reluctantly looked back at the Lennons and realised it was now or never. A gentle shrug of the shoulders indicated that this was a deal they could not and would not reject. Whereupon John, Yoko, Le Dain and his colleague retired to the Lennons private sleeping compartment for further research. They emerged some 45 minutes later, none the worse for wear. We gave them a knowing smile as they glided out of the observation car, hoping that their mission would help to bring some sanity to a patently ridiculous situation. There's a lot to be said for ``hands-on'' experience. As I have noted earlier, these were heady times.

The rest of the carriage-confined party spent a relatively quiet night doing some soft drug research of our own before turning in early, to be woken the next morning by the crunch and clatter of our by-now-beloved observation car being shunted back to the main line to be attached to the regular Ottawa service. In the early morning zoom of the express service, I reflected on the positive aspects of the Lennons traversing Canadian soil. All their visits to Canadian soil during 1969 had been of a pioneering nature: each time they'd turned up, we'd followed them out upon the untrodden snow of some metaphorical winter blizzard. Each event left a trail of fresh footprints.

All these energies and occasions were historic in their own way, but the memory which clings most clearly to me is John's acute nervousness at the prospect of meeting Prime Minister Trudeau. It was an incredible reaction from such a well-seasoned cultural trailblazer who had hobnobbed with the elite of rock'n'roll and could obviously hold his end up in any conversation. One only has to recall the quick quips and feisty one-liners that accompanied every press conference involving The Beatles. How many unwitting fools of the old-school Fleet Street had been skewered on the horns of the band's collective and scathing wit?

So over time I'd witnessed John and Yoko work their way through an assortment of different dilemmas and situations - not all of them agreeable - in the course of the *War Is Over If You Want It* peace campaign.

Given the clarity of hindsight, one presumes that John's concern centred around interaction with a big-league politician, no matter what persuasion. This was to be a direct connection into the other world of the of-

9. THE TRUDEAU-LENNON GATHERING AND THE BEGINNING OF POLITICAL POP

ten-despised Establishment. After all, less than a month earlier, John had snubbed his nose at that power centre by returning his MBE medal to the Queen. The music scene was bemused by this, but the powerbrokers were distinctly un-amused. They were insulted big time!

Pierre Trudeau, as John was about to discover, was cut from a wholly different cloth. His political progress was not in any way connected with - or measured by - the prevailing political agenda of this period. On a personal note, in my lifetime I have never been more impressed by a world leader. Pierre Trudeau was a man with a vision engaging a mission! A politician not ruled by poll results but by his humanitarian outlook.

In the last month of 1969, the Vietnam fiasco continued to horrify the public thanks to uncensored media coverage. The terrible truths of modern warfare invaded millions of American households during every news bulletin. There remains some doubt to this day as to whether the public was appropriately equipped to process that sort of shocking information. Perhaps that's why – post Vietnam war correspondents and photographers are no longer allowed unfettered access to battle regions. Now we live in the sheltered, politically safe cushioning of embedding media in a tightly controlled situation.

Disgraced US President Richard Nixon, who was in power at the height of the Vietnam War, reportedly detested Trudeau. When the surreptitious tapes which Nixon made of conversations he had with staff during his presidency (and which brought about his downfall during the scandal known as Watergate) were transcribed, it was revealed that Tricky Dicky had crudely dismissed the Canadian leader as ``that asshole Trudeau'' due to differences over American policy in Vietnam. One will always admire Trudeau's immediate response: ``I've been called worse things by better people,' the PM shrugged with typical frankness.

And so on an icy but brilliantly sunny Tuesday morning, just 10 days from the end of the'60s, we found ourselves clustered in John and Yoko's Ottawa hotel dressing room attempting to calm John's nerves and make him a little more comfortable about the prospects of the forthcoming get-together with the PM, which we all instinctively knew would go well. How could it not? Two of the sharpest, most probing intellects on the planet interacting in a frank, open exploration of the status quo. It was a mission from the universe, we thought.

Yoko, quite naturally, was doing her best to ease this attack of nerves but it was tough going, a real challenge. John was quite seriously enmeshed in his anxiety. No questions were asked but you couldn't help but speculate privately on why this meeting in particular was causing the collywobbles. Perhaps John had done some due diligence and discovered that Pierre Trudeau hadn't been a soppy whatever-you-say-kinda-guy in his previous dealings with show business dignitaries.**

However on that late-1969 morning it was too late to slow down the grind of the protocol machinery. At precisely 10.30am the media-at-large was notified that John and Yoko Lennon would be meeting with Canadian Prime Minister. Twenty-five minutes later, they pulled up outside Parliament House, Ottawa for the encounter in a limousine driven by the man who would later become Canada's Ambassador to the United Nations, Allan Rock.

The Lennon/Trudeau meeting was originally scheduled to run for 15 minutes. But it ended up expanding to 51 minutes before the world's most famous couple emerged from Mr Trudeau's inner sanctum. One couldn't help but notice John's relief as the pressure eased.

As it turned out, it had been an intensely agreeable meeting of minds. There had been a profusion of points of fruitful discussion and opportunities for the Lennons to expand upon their peace philosophy. And explain what led them to pursue such a potentially thankless task as uniting human beings. Trudeau was most encouraging of the Lennons' anti-war aspirations. He didn't for a moment dismiss the sincerity of their endeavours. He complimented them on the *War Is Over* campaign and openly encouraged the Lennons to continue standing up for peace, indicating his government's support for the Peace Festival which John and Yoko had unveiled a few days earlier at at the huge Ontario Science Centre. The Prime Minister all but formally offered government support for the organisation of the festival.

John was equally enthusiastic about the Canadian leader's open-mindedness. ``If there were more leaders like Mr Trudeau,' John affirmed into a battery of microphones and camera lenses moments after the meeting concluded and the Prime Minister's door closed, ``the world would have peace. You people in Canada don't realise how lucky you are!" Added Yoko, in her tender Japanese-accented voice: ``We're just enthralled meeting Mr Trudeau - he is a beautiful person. It gives us great incentive seeing people like him in the Establishment."

Later John detailed for me the flow of the meeting: how Trudeau had talked about how important it was for him - and people like him - to keep in close contact with young people at large, and was most interested in hearing in some depth about the issues that mattered to young people. They were and are the future! Mr Trudeau also emphasized that he would like to meet again in less formal circumstances for further discussions.

The three had found much of mutual interest. In short, John's fears had not been realised. The meeting had proceeded incredibly smoothly and painlessly.

``The political climate in Canada is completely different from any other country,' John declared to me later that fateful day. ``The politicians here at least want to hear what young people think. They'll talk, and that is the important first step.'' While their conversation had mainly been concerned with generalisations, John noted that, ``We achieved something like communication ... talk is the state of any communication''.

John and Yoko were on a serious high in the aftermath of the interaction with Trudeau. Not surprisingly, some of the crustier outposts of Canadian media with a right-wing persuasion were less than overwhelmed by the Lennon's *War Is Over* crusade. British media, in particular the parochial tabloids, had earlier railed against the Lennons' perceived naivety in campaigning for peace. Even in Canada, and despite the official nod the prime ministerial meeting had given the Lennons' peace efforts, there would be the odd grumpiness in the newspaper opinion pages and random discontent in editorials. Thundered Medicine Hat News circa Christmas Eve, 1969:

``Most Canadians cannot help but react with skepticism to Lennon's current crusade. His goal of world peace is an admirable one, of course, but his methods of realizing this ideal are naïve. An end to war between nations - to official violence - cannot be achieved by buying full page ads in the New York Times or by bleating *Give Peace a Chance* in the streets of Toronto. These are exercises in futility. Theatrics that don't resolve anything. Every sane person on Earth wants peace, but most of us are sophisticated enough to know that only our leaders can end war.''

The Medicine Hat editorial also called into question John Lennon's motivation in taking part in the peace initiative, suggesting that the musician, songwriter and peace activist had his eye on a future political career: ``These rumors (of Lennon as a latent politician wooing tomorrow's electorate) have persisted because Lennon has long been the most politically conscious of the four Beatles members. He has deliberately identified himself with the Now Generation - in fact he helped to mould it - and often speaks his mind on such gut issues as pot, peace and pollution. And developing an authoritative image, it must be remembered, is a prerequisite for any aspiring politician. When seen in this context, therefore, Lennon's Canadian peace offensive gradually becomes less an exercise in wayward idealism and more a shrewd attempt to manufacture credentials.''

Nonetheless, the Lennons worked the Ottawa window of opportunity. After the Trudeau get-together, they were escorted to the Ministry of Health for lengthy discussions with the Health Minister, John Munro, and his senior aides. The drug issue was raised once again and with the media in attendance, the Health Department officials showed no desire to cover it up. John and Yoko didn't back off from defending soft drugs, while condemning so-called "hard" drugs. Health Minister Munro requested John's advice on how he should best deal with the generation gap:

``Often when I talk to people, I can't even get to open my mouth before I'm battered with placards and posters and catchphrases.'' John's response was characteristic. ``Get your own posters and fire them back!''

After the Ottawa meetings, the Lennons were scheduled to fly back to Ronnie Hawkins' country estate in Mississauga on the fringes of Toronto, to wind up their Canadian trip and to tie the final knots. But when our party arrived at Ottawa Airport, John Brower realised that he'd not brought along his credit card. ``So I was able to get the Lennons back for going on the (fashion retailer) Le Chateau shopping spree buying black jumpsuits on my tab,' Brower later privately gloated, ``by discovering I had 'forgotten' my wallet at the hotel so John paid for all the plane tickets back to Toronto on an Apple Records Amex card.'' As we prepared to board the Apple-funded flight at Ottawa Airport, a now-relaxed John joked about the extent of his nervousness earlier in the day.

As we boarded the plane, I wondered about some of the faces and people that were accompanying us on the flight to Toronto. Hadn't I seen some of these visages before? Recently? Who were these people? Historian and author Jon Wiener would later provide some answers to these questions with his relentless pursuit of Freedom of Information documents. We were being tailed – as peace pursuers by representatives of spy agencies such as the CIA, FBI and RCMP.

But our flight companions weren't all conducting surveillance. Along with these mysterious regulars was former Canadian Prime Minister Lester Pearson (1963-68) and his wife. It was highly ironic that the man regarded as the Godfather of Canadian peacekeeping - and the winner of the Nobel Peace Prize in 1957 - would be sharing the flight with the Lennons. Politely, we asked the cabin steward to pass along John and Yoko's greetings, which were warmly received. It was a serendipitous conclusion to a wonderful first encounter between a political leader and an integral figure from the youth culture.

The next day, Christmas Eve, the Lennons set forth once again in Ronnie

Hawkins' white Rolls-Royce through the volley of snow flurries to what is now known as Lester B. Pearson Airport for the flight home. After returning to London and reflecting on his most recent Canadian odyssey, John observed with conviction: ``It was the best trip we ever had. We got more done for peace this week than in our whole lives.'' This was a huge and revealing statement which I know John meant. Much had been accomplished. We didn't know it, but John Lennon would never return to Canadian soil.

*FOOTNOTE

It was no great surprise that other political leaders had declined the opportunity of a meeting with The Beatles' most outspoken and controversial member. The Queen was apparently miffed over the MBE incident.

Britain's Labour Prime Minister Harold Wilson regarded John Lennon as an undignified and unprincipled radical. Newly elected US President Richard Nixon clearly viewed Lennon as a huge threat to keeping the lid on mounting counter-culture protests against the Vietnam war.

After the release of Freedom of Information documents concerning America's Federal Bureau of Investigation and Royal Canadian Mounted Police (RCMP), the extent of these organisations' surveillance of John and Yoko Lennon, myself and Peace Festival promoter John Brower during the *War Is Over If You Want It* campaign became clear, as reported by the Canadian Press wire services dated July 23, 2007 under the heading "RCMP security branch briefed FBI on John and Yoko's peace festival plans".

OTTAWA (CP) - The suspicions of a Delaware radio station manager prompted RCMP spies to share information with their American counterparts about Beatle John Lennon's plans for a peace festival near Toronto.

Declassified records show the Mounties sent confidential correspondence to the Federal Bureau of Investigation concerning efforts by Lennon and wife Yoko Ono to assemble a star-studded line-up of performers for the July 1970 event at Mosport Park (Ontario, about 100km [60 miles] east of Toronto).

"The Mosport Peace Festival was initiated by John Lennon (of Beatle fame) and his wife, while visiting Canada during December 1969," says the April 1970 letter to a liaison officer at the US Embassy in Ottawa from the RCMP's J.E.M. Barrette, Director of Security and Intelligence.

The RCMP correspondence, portions of which remain secret, found its way into what would soon become an extensive FBI file on Lennon.

In the months before The Beatles formally parted ways in 1970, Lennon devoted much of his energy to promoting global harmony. Ritchie Yorke, a Globe and Mail music writer who left his job to work for John and Yoko's peace campaign, recalls helping persuade broadcasters to air the messages.

"We tried to spread the word about that around (to) American radio stations, and quite a few responded very positively to it."But not Edward Marzoa, manager of WJWL-AM in Georgetown, Delaware.

When approached by the Canadians associated with the Peace Station Network, he asked listeners whether his station should air their five-minute peace-oriented programs. "The response was overwhelmingly against such programming," says Marzoa's March 1970 note to the RCMP.

"The purpose of this letter is not to solicit any program recommendation from your organisation. It is rather, to ascertain if the Royal Canadian Mounted Police has any information which may shed some light on the Peace Station Network," Marzoa wrote. "I would like to know who the officers are; what their purposes are; how they are financed; and why the Canadian base. I have my suspicions."

The RCMP dispatched a polite reply to Marzoa, advising him to contact the FBI, "as government policy requires us to liaise with the Federal Bureau of Investigation in matters related to enquiries of this nature." The Mounties were indeed aware of what Marzoa was on about. RCMP Security Service records recently obtained by The Canadian Press from Library and Archives Canada reveal the Mounties' security branch was actively monitoring plans for the Mosport peace festival.

The RCMP advised US officials the radio programming was intended to help promote the planned Mosport event. The Mounties noted the venue had been vetoed by the Ontario Municipal Board and "at the present time it is not certain whether the 'festival' will proceed at some other location." The ambitious musical event collapsed under the weight of organisational disputes.

Lennon's rabble-rousing activism of the early 1970s drew the attention of the FBI, which like the RCMP spied on many left-wing individuals and groups suspected of subversion. A memo to the FBI director, noting enclosure of the RCMP correspondence, carries the subject line, "New Left - Foreign influence - Canada." The FBI records were released under the US Freedom of Information Act in response to a request from California history professor Jon Wiener, who waged a long legal fight for disclosure.

**FOOTNOTE

A classic example took place some years later, in 1978. Hollywood superstar actor Marlon Brando set up a meeting with the Canadian prime minister in an attempt to obtain funding for a film about native people. To support his case, the renowned actor explained that he felt Canada and the US had a common indigenous tradition. Whereupon Mr Trudeau noted, a trifle acidly, ``Ah, there are differences in the way we treated our native people. You hunted them down and murdered them. We starved them to death.'' After that meeting, the actor admitted to the PM's communications director: "That's the most frightened I've ever been in my life. He (Trudeau) is the most intimidating person I've ever met."

10. DUELLING WITH THE DEVIL IN DENMARK

The son of a butcher who had migrated to Manhattan from Budapest, Allen Klein - who died in July, 2009 - was a mean and ugly piece of work. But for a brief window of 21 months at the end of the '60s, he would be the big boss man of The Beatles' business, the master of Apple Records' destiny, the diviner of pop music history. The peace man allied with the profits man sounds bizarre - and it was.

Klein had been introduced to the New York music biz by a fellow New York City college student named Don Kirshner, who would later play a key role in the evolution of the Tin Pan Alley songwriting scene - and ultimately, America's musical answer to The Beatles in the form of the Monkees. He was the manager of pop singer Connie Francis and was also connected with the up-and-coming American-Italian crooner Bobby Darin.

Kirshner (who died early in 2011) introduced Klein to Darin at a party, where the audacious failed accountant offered the singer who'd revived *Mack the Knife*, the Kurt Weill/Bertolt Brecht chestnut from the 1929 German production of *The Threepenny Opera*, a guaranteed payment of $100,000. All Klein required to complete the deal was Darin's permission for his company to have the right and opportunity to audit his record and songwriting royalties. And that became Klein's credo - "no dough, no go". If he couldn't come up with amounts owing to the artist, then he also received nothing. It was a compelling sales pitch which would ultimately reach, and delight, the ears of the majority of The Beatles. It was this connection with Bobby Darin - coupled with the Connie Francis association and also a relationship with the brilliant soul/gospel pioneer Sam Cooke - that provided Klein an entrance into the enticing world of contemporary music, at a time when there was no shortage of record companies and music publishers which specialized in short-changing their talent signings. Virtually any official audit of record sales would reveal shortcomings in the amount of royalties labels accorded their artists. It was the shabby way in which record companies ordinarily conducted business in the late '50s and early '60s.

If nothing else, Klein was a hustler of epic proportions. He prided himself on being able to figure out complex financial transactions in his head without the benefit of pen and paper or, indeed, calculators. In a sense, he was a cold-hearted human calculator. He eagerly proclaimed his business agenda and profit-hungry motives through a biblical desk plaque adorning his work space. It was based on the 23rd Psalm, and it was right to the point: "Yea, though I walk through the valley of the shadow of death, I shall fear no evil, for I am the biggest bastard in the valley." Not a philosophy everybody would want to embrace, no matter what their ambition or objective. But it fitted Klein to a T.

By the latter '60s, Klein had slithered out from his New York office and ventured across the Atlantic to secure some of the juicier pickings in the burgeoning British music scene. He became involved with the London-born producer and entrepreneur, Michael Peter Hayes, aka Mickie Most, who'd enjoyed recording success in South Africa (from where his wife Christina hailed). He was actually a member of a South African-based band called Mickie Most and the Playboys, which scored 11 No. 1s in that then-bastion of white supremacy. They were all covers of US hits, often by coloured artists. Most was the archetype South African covers merchant.

Mickie Most specialised in putting British beat groups such as the Nashville Teens, the Yardbirds, Jeff Beck, the Animals et al with commercial R&B songs originally recorded by Afro-American artists but little known outside the US due to racist radio programming policies around the world. He also became partners with Peter Grant, the legendary and larger-than-life protector of guitarist Jimmy Page, in an association that would lead to the formation of Led Zeppelin. And therein, the biggest rock band of the sizzling '70s.

In a sense it was almost inevitable that Klein would desire an entry portal into the camps of Britain's most successful pop groups, The Rolling Stones and The Beatles. Initially he gained access to the Stones' early catalogue of songs through a shrewd deal he made with the band's then manager, Andrew Loog-Oldham. Oldham sold Klein to the members of the Stones as a music hustling guy who operated outside the law. His anarchistic tendencies apparently appealed to an ever dollar-driven Mick Jagger. Mick was suitably sucked in. Keith Richards would later describe the legal action which Klein and the Stones fought in 1971 as "the price of an education". But that was only the start of this story.

Even more significantly, a few months down the management track, Jagger urged John Lennon to become involved with Klein, a piece of advice that may well have been motivated by professional jealousy. There had long been envy between the Stones and The Beatles camps. Jagger was always a pretty shrewd piece of work, and he likely figured out that Klein would be quick to climb inside The Beatles' engine room through a ladder built upon Lennon's obvious insecurities. And the wanton burn up of

Beatles' revenues by leeches and layabouts attracted to Apple.

After the death of manager Brian Epstein in August, 1967, The Beatles' business activities had been run with what could only be described as a laissez-faire arrangement. There was very little accounting of activities, let alone outgoing expenses. The idealistic Apple organisation, where creative people would be nurtured and supported, was a wonderful philanthropic concept but unworkable within the mindscape of human beings and their foibles. The wonderful oneness of Apple had soon disintegrated into a pork-barrel of goodies for those fortunate enough to be employed at the trough. The Beatles' money was spent in incredible amounts by selfish individuals who lapped up the spoils of the band's outstanding creative output and subsequent profits. I personally witnessed one Apple staffer - in the days when intercontinental phone calls cost a fortune - calling his girlfriend at the Apple New York office and leaving the line open for the entire business day to provide constant access for the occasional transatlantic chat-up conversation!

By early 1969, the respective Beatles were acutely aware of their dwindling finances and the perilous profit-and-loss picture of Apple Inc. Something had to be urgently done to ease the bleeding. The band was seriously missing Epstein's influence. They'd realised that their strength was not in management, and began to look around for an appropriate candidate to fill Epstein's shoes. The name of Lord Beeching came up. But Paul McCartney was pushing for Lee Eastman, the father of his new wife, New York City photographer Linda. The other Beatles were suspicious of Macca's move, as they felt Paul's interests would be preferred over theirs.

Allen Klein chose to get in touch with John Lennon after reading the Beatle's plaintive comment that the band would be "broke within six months" if the situation did not change. Klein's compelling claim was that his involvement would be limited by money he earned for them that he would share only in the proceeds of increased business which he had personally generated. This proved to be a persuasive argument but Paul - although appearing in a publicity photo of the Klein signing - never actually signed the management contract. It was this demonstration of independence - not the presence of Yoko Ono - which hastened the demise of pop's favourite group. This is a fact that cannot be over-emphasized in a climate of perennial anti Yoko sentiment. Get a grip, folks!

It's difficult to deny that Klein played Lennon perfectly in the beginning. He was savvy to the lyrics of John's songs and also stressed, to John's delight, that Yoko's original music was significant as well. And he didn't resist reminding Lennon that they even shared the loss of a mother.

(Klein's mother died of cancer when he was under a year old, and was at the age of four dispatched to a Hebrew orphanage to spend his next eight years. He reportedly hated every moment, which might explain how he became such a hard case in so many ways.)

Because Apple Records had been oozing money and whittling away a big chunk of Beatles' profits, George Harrison and Ringo Starr were not opposed to the idea of having some sort of administrator appointed to oversee the management of their initially idealistic record label. They wanted to keep Apple alive, as did John, but they had grown increasingly disenchanted at the expenses of their philanthropic outpourings and staff abuse of the label's good-vibes image. Klein seemed a worthy candidate for the gig. From the outset, Paul McCartney was aggressively opposed to this, because he was touting Lee Eastman.

On May 22, 1969, Apple issued a press statement: "Allen Klein is to receive 20 per cent of The Beatles' income through Apple Corps. Klein has now been officially appointed as The Beatles' business manager ..." Later George Harrison noted: "Apple was Paul's idea and once he started going he was very active in there and then it got very chaotic. Then, once we all started doing something about Apple, obviously, Paul didn't have as much say in the matter and then, because he wanted Lee Eastman, his in-laws, to run it and we didn't, it soon became a problem. That's a personal problem that he will have to get over. The reality is that he's out-voted and we are a partnership."

To which Paul responded: "The thing is, I'm not signed to Allen Klein because I don't like him and I don't think he is the man for me, however the other three like him. The truth is, he only has three-quarters of The Beatles and he doesn't have The Beatles. He is definitely the manager of John, George and Ringo, but I have ... told him that he doesn't manage me." Ironically, within weeks of The Beatles signing with Klein, Mick Jagger raced into the band's dressing room with the news that the Klein honeymoon was over. "Don't sign man'cos we're suing him,' declared a distraught Jagger. But it was too late by then. And one can't help but wonder about his private agenda and motives.

After Klein was installed at Apple, Nat Weiss, The Beatles' New York attorney (and North American partner of their late manager Brian Epstein) observed: "I had lunch with Klein and his cronies just prior to his takeover of Apple. I knew Klein was going to succeed. His timing was so good. Klein is a creature of instinct, who likes to intimidate you, just to see how far he can go."

During the course of the Klein era, John had countered: "Apple is as safe as houses and has never been in better shape. We've been losing a lot of money but the company is based on The Beatles' royalties, and all the rest is just wrapping. The talk about The Beatles having to go on the road again to raise money was not really serious. We don't need cash that much. We have a vast income from royalties and now that Klein is looking after our affairs, things are really working well. Klein and Apple were bound to meet sooner or later."

That observation was undoubtedly true. But by the time the *War Is Over* peace campaign was rearing its idealistic head, John and Yoko had grown a tad disenchanted with Klein. Money was not the whole box and dice. At the very least, they were doubting his motives and questioning his claims. It was clear that Klein viewed anything to do with John and Yoko and their interest in the *War Is Over* effort as an affront to his over-riding agenda - to pull together one last spectacular North American tour by The Beatles. The pursuit of peace was getting in the way of generating profits.

After the Plastic Ono Band's appearance at the Toronto Rock'n'roll Revival on September 13, 1969, John had informed the other members of The Beatles and Klein that the group was finished. But Klein beseeched him to keep it quiet, at least while he renegotiated their existing record contract with EMI and explored possibilities with a major sponsor for a final Beatles concert tour of North America. This ultimately enabled Paul to come out with his "quitting The Beatles" announcement in March, 1970, which totally pissed off John. It was all about the timing.

But back to 1969. The conflict between John and Yoko's peace endeavours and Klein's Beatles tour agenda was bound to create tension in the camp. There were animated discussions back and forth between concert promoter John Brower and myself, and John and Yoko. After several negative Klein discussions, around December, 1969, John and Yoko asked me to compile a no-holds-barred dossier on Klein. If, as they noted, he was so universally despised and therefore a liability to the peace campaign, maybe they should be thinking of giving him the flick. And so I was instructed to set forth on putting together a collection of significant music figures' written appraisals and opinions of Klein.

I approached this task with some trepidation: I was apprehensive about being seen as attacking Klein in his own domain. But in the enthusiasm of my youth, I was quick to rally to the peace cause and cheerfully and passionately take on whatever task John and Yoko willed to me. So I urgently contacted a bunch of industry VIPs and requested their written, totally confidential comments about the suitability of Klein acting on John Lennon's artistic behalf. Among the contacts were such distinguished names as Atlantic Records' co-founder Ahmet Ertegun, Atlantic's senior vice-president Jerry Wexler, Mort Nasatir (then head of Billboard Publications), 4Neil Bogart (the former chief of Buddah Records who had then launched the Casablanca imprint) and Rolling Stone founder and publisher Jann Wenner.

Not one of them was complimentary about Klein - much to the contrary. Apparently the power players felt his involvement with any aspect of The Beatles belittled their artistic standing in the community. To most, Klein was nothing more than a money-grubber. I could hardly deny that the compilation of this report represented an attack on the Klein castle. So in approaching the task, I also sought to obtain some behind-the-scenes intelligence on the state of the opposition. I arranged for Ronnie Hawkins, a man with fairly serious Family connections, to make some enquiries on our behalf through Morris Levy, his old label chief at Roulette Records, in New York. We wanted to know just how big a threat Allen Klein might be if we got on the wrong side of him.

The information which returned to our camp was distressing. To be perfectly candid, Hawkins' security advisor and bodyguard, "Heavy" Andrews, called me and offered us a supply of plastic explosive to take on our forthcoming trip to Denmark to meet the Lennons, as insurance against any possibly unfriendly behavior from people we might encounter. I was absolutely horrified at the prospect - the thought of carrying plastic explosive on a peace mission for any reason was simply too outrageous to contemplate.

But when we were informed by these same New York sources that no less a personage than founding member of the Rolling Stones Brian Jones, who died on July 3, 1969, had been allegedly eliminated for a token payment of $US10,000, we took the intelligence seriously. In fact, it frightened the shit out of us all. A sense of paranoia crept into proceedings. We were informed that Jones, who was found floating dead in a swimming pool in mysterious circumstances, had been "rubbed out" and the manner of his demise indicated we were all small fry in the overall scheme of things. And that we should be really careful about whom we might offend in our crusade for peace. That information has remained steadfast in our minds.

John and Yoko insisted over the phone from Europe that they wanted us to present this Klein dossier in person. And so, on a frozen January afternoon in the second week of the new decade, I ended up sharing a airport-bound limousine with John Brower yet again as we tooled off into a frozen rural Denmark. We were headed for a remote farmhouse rented by Yoko's former husband Tony Cox in the snowy wilds of northern Jutland. We'd flown into Aarlborg from Copenhagen the previous day after an overnight flight from Toronto. It was to here that we had been urgently summoned by John and Yoko to discuss the Klein issue. When we discovered that the German military had parachuted on to this same airport 30 years earlier, we were taken aback. We also learned that Aarlborg can lay claim to be the first city in the world to be captured by paratroopers. With a population of 122,000, it was the fourth-largest city in Denmark in 2009.

The reason we found ourselves blasting through a blizzard from Aarlborg into the Jutland countryside was that Tony Cox had holed up in the farmhouse with his girlfriend Melinde and Yoko's daughter Kyoko Chan Cox, born August 8, 1963. Yoko and Cox had divorced a year earlier and it was early days in a bitter custody contest which would drag on for years. John and Yoko had finally tracked Kyoko and her father to this out-of-the-way location. It seemed like an interminable journey as the car sped through a veil of snowflakes. Finally, we slid to a halt in the drive outside the modest dwelling. Another black limousine sat idling in the snow, smoke curling into the cold from its exhaust.

It would be an unforgettable afternoon, a collision of cultures and consciousness. We knocked at the door and were soon confronted with one of the most unforgettable surprises of our lives. In addition to Tony Cox and his lady friend and Allen Klein, we were welcomed by an almost unrecognisable John, Yoko and Kyoko - minus their long hair. Their dark locks of a fortnight ago had been hacked off to a mere inch long. The Lennons didn't look anything like the couple we'd seen off at Toronto Airport two days before Christmas.

Yoko reflected in 2010: ``I didn't mind when I had my hair cut. I thought it was nice. But when John started getting his hair cut off, I began to cry. I was really crying. John looked good with or without the hair. But I just knew that I'd become used to that long hair and the bearded look – it was a daddy look. So John was my daddy, OK, even though he was a young guy!''

It turned out that a hairdresser had been brought from Aarlborg expressly to conduct the shearing ceremony; later that night, in a restaurant back at our hotel, the "stylist" would present her account for Brower to pay. He found that particular bill a bit hard to swallow, but he coughed up. "It was very much a period farmhouse,' Brower recalled. "It was very simply furnished - no antiques, or stuff like that. It was pretty basic. But there were cameras everywhere, all over the place. And in those days, cameras were chunky, bulky things. They were everywhere but I don't know if they were filming or not. Didn't even think to ask at the time, because our minds were on other things." In my memory, the interior of the farmhouse was all about varnished pine. John, Yoko, Brower, Klein and I sat around a pine kitchen table while Melinde and Kyoko fiddled off to the side. There was a tartan sofa, again constructed of pine.

Tony Cox was definitely eccentric. Some years later he would unburden himself to People magazine in the following manner: "I grew up with the whole scene - I was a beat, then I was a beatnik, then I was a hippie. I went through the whole drug trip. I was taking acid when you could get acid for free. I took my first mescaline and acid before one word had been written about it. I took a lot of acid thinking this was going to improve my mind, and it took me years to discover the opposite was true. All drugs are a very bad scene."

A year later, Yoko would obtain permanent custody of Kyoko but Cox absconded with her. He and Melinde (who became his second wife), along with Kyoko, joined a wacko religious cult group known as Church of the Living Word or The Walk. Obviously there was a lot going on behind the scenes. Yoko and her daughter would not reunite until 1998. Cox remained bitter about Yoko's relationship with John and at the time of writing, was reportedly working on a film in development, *Yoko Ono: Money Can't Buy Me Love*. One can reliably expect that this proposed film will not be complimentary to Yoko.

Back there outside Aarlborg 40 years ago, Brower and I weren't quite sure what to make of the situation. But there was no way back. Here we were in the middle of nowhere providing a dossier on a man who professed to be "the biggest bastard in the valley". God knows what he might resort to, or contemplate, once my report was tabled. It was a very sobering reality.

Lennon himself would later write in Rolling Stone that we'd turned up in Denmark with "lots of dirt on Klein". But as John Brower would note in a subsequent unpublished letter to the magazine: "John asked us to compile a report on Klein - his possible gangster connections, his standing in the North American music industry, the pure paradox of (the peace-loving) Lennon being involved with Klein. We had no desire at all to prepare such a report and did so very reluctantly, only after John had virtually begged us to do so. The reason for our reluctance (as Peace Festival organisers) to do business with Klein stemmed from the fact that our sources close to the Canadian government informed us that it would give no support to an event in which Mr Klein had any involvement." In effect, Klein was a persona non grata in the eyes of Canadian authorities.

We were caught between a rock and a very hard place. I sat in frozen dismay as John read through the report I'd compiled. Some excerpts:

What follows is an unbiased account of Allen Klein, as compiled from sources as designated. Jann Wenner - Editor of Rolling Stone magazine, Mr Wenner believes that Mr Klein is very harmful to John and Yoko's peace campaign. He says that nobody decries The Beatles wanting someone to manage their financial affairs, but, he says, surely there are dozens of people better than Klein. Mr Wenner claims that Mr Klein's method of operation is as follows ... if he is getting a contract, he sends in some Mafia heavies to dissuade the opposition. Mr Wenner says that Mr Klein's association with the Mafia is well known, and that there is no doubt of it. As for the Rolling Stones' Altamont fiasco, Mr Wenner says he is not sure if Mr Klein would accept full responsibility for it. However, acting as he does on behalf of the Stones, he must accept some of the blame, according to Mr Wenner.

Mr Wenner feels it is extremely detrimental to John and Yoko (more so than The Beatles collectively) to be involved with Mr Klein. He says the underground press and radio in the US view Mr Klein with great hostility, because he stands for everything that they're against. Mr Wenner is surprised that John and Yoko are apparently not aware of Mr Klein's reputation and methods of operation. He feels strongly that John and Yoko - for the good of their peace beliefs - should end their association with Mr Klein as soon as possible. Mr Wenner is also surprised that the Lennons have anything to do with Lee Solters' publicity firm, a regular business associate of Klein. It is, he claims, an old-line hype publicity outfit, viewed with disdain by the hip underground press contingent in the US. He has suggested a couple of other - in his estimation - more appropriate publicity companies.

In general, Mr Wenner feels that John and Yoko are being hurt by their involvement with Mr Klein. They may make more money (through record royalties et al) this way, Mr Wenner concludes, "but the price they pay in travelling that road doesn't justify the means". He has offered to talk further about Mr Klein's reputation with the Lennons at their convenience. Hoodlum associations, links with the Mafia. This sort of information is difficult and dangerous to obtain, especially when it comes to specific cases of jobs done.

But after checking with Mr Morris Levy, president of Roulette Records, and an admitted cohort of the (Mafia), we found that Mr Klein had links in the past on small levels - cash up front for small tasks performed. In other words, Mr Klein had apparently utilised their services. But even among crooks and thieves, there is apparently some honour. In Mr Klein's case, this is apparently not true. Mr Levy despises him, apparently because he is not honest about his lack of scruples.

Morris Levy remains something of an enigma. He was closely associated with the Genovese Family in New York and his views on Allen Klein must carry considerable weight. Later on in the '70s, perhaps coincidentally, John Lennon would be involved in a legal dispute with Morris Levy. When The Beatles released their last recorded album *Abbey Road*, John Lennon offered his personal tribute to Chuck Berry a tad too openly. Levy - as owner of the copyright for Chuck Berry's *You Can't Catch Me* - claimed that the *Abbey Road* album opener, *Come Together*, was too similar to his tune.

Levy managed to extract an out-of-court settlement promise that Lennon - in return for the alleged creative borrowings -would record three of his Big Seven Music Corp copyrights (Levy owned the publishing on a slew of great early rock classics such as *Why Do Fools Fall in Love*) for a planned forthcoming covers album of rock gems. These would be produced by Phil Spector (who in 2009 began an 18-year sentence for murdering a girl whom he picked up and took home from a Hollywood nightclub. Spector's reputation suffered quite a beating during the course of two trials before his eventual conviction).

In 1974, Spector was an Allen Klein associate - a hot young producer known for his eccentricity, although there was no suggestion then of his later depravity. Klein introduced the producer to The Beatles. This led to his remixing and adapting the tracks for the *Let It Be* album, which caused Paul McCartney much ongoing grief. Macca objected to the "sweetening" of tracks with strings, echo and the like; he was particularly opposed to Spector's interference on his own composition and the album's title track, *Let It Be*, as well as *The Long and Winding Road*.

But why couldn't McCartney find the time to travel the two miles to *Abbey Road* Studios to take a listen to what Spector might be doing to his beloved songs? This has always been suspect to me. Spector is a unique human being. He would work on early post-Beatles projects such as John's *Imagine* album and George Harrison's All Things Must Pass triple album project. But during the recording of Lennon's 1974 album Rock'n' Roll, things got a bit crazy with Spector and the release of the album was delayed. The producer disappeared with the tapes, citing unpaid session costs.

This prompted an impatient Levy - who'd managed to obtain a cassette copy of the developing album - to rush out the unfinished version as a mail order special release entitled Roots. The album is now a coveted collectors' item, since only 1270 copies were sold. Lawsuits flew back and forth; after years of legal manoeuvring, Lennon's copyright claim prevailed.

Levy might have worked from the wrong side of the law but that didn't prevent him from influencing and inspiring music industry successors such as Tommy Mottola, one-time CEO of Sony Music and husband of singer Mariah Carey, who was an investment partner of Levy and regarded him as a "personal hero". Levy was a legend in music biz circles for his support of original rock'n'roll DJ Alan Freed. Freed, the subject of the memorable 1978 movie *American Hot Wax*, had formed a high school band named The Sultans of Swing, a moniker later immortalized by Dire Straits in their debut hit from 1977. Freed had observed in 1956: ``Rock 'n' roll is really swing with a modern name. It began on the levees and plantations, took in folk songs, and features blues and rhythm. It's the rhythm that gets to the kids they're starved of music they can dance to, after all those years of crooners.''

The pioneer of pop launched a radio career in Ohio - Youngstown, Akron, Cleveland - and ultimately New York City, where for a time he prospered. Suffice to say that after being tried in 1962 for accepting commercial bribes (in essence, pay for programming play), for which he received a token $300 fine and a six-month suspended sentence, Freed - the son of a Welsh mother and Lithuanian father - was a broken man. The person who popularised the term rock'n'roll and pioneered the genre on radio with his Moondog Matinee show in Cleveland was now shunned by the industry he loved.

He moved from the heights of New York, where he had been the audio architect of Manhattan's, and indeed the world's, rock'n'roll airwaves, to the lows of small town radio stations in Santa Monica, California, and Miami, Florida, dying broken and penniless at the age of 43 of uremia and cirrhosis brought on by alcoholism. He literally drank himself to death. He had promoted and protected Afro-American musicians' right to be heard by all races. It's one of the saddest stories in early rock, even more tragic than that of R&B vocalist Johnny Ace (his biggest hit being *Pledging My Love*), who shot himself playing Russian roulette with a loaded revolver between sets backstage in Texas in 1954, aged 25.

John Lennon was a passionate fan of Freed's contribution to the R&B genre, as is this writer. Pity indeed, that certain other high-profile proponents and beneficiaries of the payola years were not so harshly dealt with as Freed. Notwithstanding Morris Levy's contribution to Freed's career, Levy will be best remembered by the masses as a TV character on which he was based - Herman "Hesh" Rabkin, the racehorse-owning rich man from upstate New York featured in *The Sopranos* series. Morris

Levy was a larger-than-life character and I feel enriched to have known him, to have shared dinner with him and his attentive wife, Ruth, and to have visited their East 77th Street townhouse in Manhattan. They were a friendly and very social couple, keen to welcome an aspiring rock culture commentator to their den. Especially in the company of the ever-loquacious Ronnie Hawkins, who had been signed to Levy's Roulette label in 1959. Levy was most keen to spill the beans about Allen Klein when I talked to him on John Lennon's behalf for the ``Tell All Dossier'' in late 1969. "It's a pleasure to help you,' he generously responded to my phone request. "I don't like seeing an artist like John Lennon put through this sort of shit. Klein is just an accountant who flunked his exams. He would do absolutely anything for money and he doesn't care how he does it. He has no conscience at all. That's all right, but you should at least be honest about it. Klein isn't. I wouldn't trust that bastard one inch.'' Both Klein and his promo henchman, Pete Bennett - described by Morris as a ``punk'' - at one time worked for Levy.

There were some indications, I noted in my report to John and Yoko, that Klein was "preparing for a major leap into the big league of the Family''. He apparently had visions of a monstrous deal with a giant soft drink company for a world Beatles tour - a deal which would apparently involve negotiating with the owners rather than the executives of the company. There was scuttlebutt around that some sectors of the corporation had questionable criminal-related connections.

Levy ominously warned us that "Mr Klein will take any action; I repeat any action, to see that his wishes are carried out. Be very careful in any associations with him or around him''. In the current decade, I have learnt through sources including Levy that Klein went very close to being jailed for fraud and embezzlement in recent years. One of his former associates, who did not wish to be named, stated that Klein was "totally unscrupulous and without any redeeming features''.

So in Denmark in 1970, I was with the Lennons and the man they had charged me with dishing the dirt on. Brower and I sat in silence as John scanned our report, occasionally uttering a negative or non-committal comment. Klein, seated on the other side of the pine table, fixed me with a withering stare that would have frightened the crap out of a grizzly bear. Clearly, I had crossed him in a most reprehensible manner. Brower decided to avail himself of the prevailing drug opportunities but I, for once, declined. There was enough heavy trippy shit going on for me to absorb without adding the effects of majoun, an intoxicating honey-marihuana spread served on toast, which Brower accepted without reservation. I was more concerned with how Allen Klein was going to cope with the tabling of our dossier.

"We were pretty traumatised,' Brower recently admitted. "We had this dossier of all this unflattering stuff on Klein. And we went out there to the farmhouse and found Lennon with his hair cut off and his family and stepdaughter all culted out by Tony Cox and his friend Dr Don Hamrick. The Lennons had been staying there for two weeks and they had been effectively programmed. I've discovered all this stuff about Hamrick who was the leader of a fucking weirdo cult encouraging communication between aliens and people on earth. It was all multi-dimensional stuff. Hamrick was hiding out because a girl had died up there at his clinic in Peterborough in Canada."

John Lennon kept on reading. "Well this all sounds like a bunch of crap to me,' he finally muttered, which certainly melted some of the ice which had descended around the group. "This is all a bunch of hearsay. I don't give a crap about this." And he tossed over the dossier to Klein himself, who began to read it.

I have rarely been a central player in such a potentially embarrassing scenario. " You guys,' John said, looking intently at Brower and myself, "are going to HAVE to work with Allen'cos he looks after our management now. And Allen, you're just going to have to work with John and Ritchie because we want to do this Peace Festival and look into all of these other ideas they've come up with. They've got some great stuff on the table and we want to explore it further." John was nothing if not fair to all comers. And all participants above and below the reach of the peace campaign.

The following few minutes brought new meaning to the word `uncomfortable.' A short time later, we entered our respective chauffeured vehicles - Brower and me in one and Klein in the other - and tooled back along snow-blown roads to Aarlborg to a well-deserved over-potent cocktail and dinner. Despite the abundance of alcohol, it was a very sobering discussion.

Back in Manhattan a few days later, John Brower and associates met Klein. They spent three hours talking to him. Klein made it clear that he wanted to forget all about the plans for the Toronto Peace Festival and he was anxious for Brower to commit to a planned mid-year Beatles 1970 proposed concert performance in Toronto for $2 million, against 75 per cent of the gate. Feeling he had no choice or breathing space, Brower agreed to the proposed deal and duly informed John, who "freaked out and said he knew nothing about a Beatles' tour". John had long since tired of touring and was only interested in distancing himself from the

Beatles template. But Klein had other plans, and felt that if he could come up with an attractive enough touring offer, he could get the reluctant Beatles back on the road again for one last go round.

There was never any shortage of promoters willing to put up whatever was required to lure the world's biggest pop band back to the boards. John's talk of tearing up the future of The Beatles gave no joy to Klein's bottom-line aspirations. But sitting around that Jutland farmhouse kitchen table in the early days of the soon-to-be-soaring '70s, listening to a newly-shorn John and Yoko dispensing their thoughts for world peace, any thoughts of a Beatles tour seemed like a pipe dream.

We'd seen evidence enough in recent days of the smouldering dislike between John and Paul to know that these two '60s counter-culture heroes would not be gracing the same stage together in the foreseeable future. But Klein kept on hoping against hope that he would be able to change their outlook and even overcome Paul's tenacious rejection of all that he offered and represented. At this point, John and Paul were scarcely on speaking terms - there was a distinct and obvious dissension that divided them into separate camps.

"In the course of our experiences with him,' Brower recalled, "there were three different John Lennons. The guy who played the Rock'n'roll Revival was the white-suited rock'n'roller who fronted the Plastic Ono Band. That Christmas in 1969, I saw the black-suited peacemaker and preacher going to meet with the Prime Minister, Pierre Trudeau. And then in Aarlborg, Denmark, I saw the complete programmed wacko, with his hair cut off and pounding on the table about 'Adolf Hitler being right' and that you've got to control people." (I was outside having a smoke when this took place - Cox did not allow any smoking of anything inside his house.) While at the same time he was being surrounded by complete mania and professional manipulation. There was no denying that John Lennon was the kind of person who was easily manipulated or he was easily convinced to jump on somebody's bandwagon.

In my experience, it wasn't so much that John was flaky or gullible. It's just that he was – perhaps too ready to listen to almost anybody's opinion or outlook on virtually any subject. We joked about it, but it was a constant fear that somebody else would present themselves in front of John and steal our thunder and appropriate the agenda. John did tend to run hot and cold on favourite projects and it was important to keep his concentration on the subject at hand. John was always approachable, which was a blessing and a bane. The wrong people could get in front of him and present a persuasive approach that he would – possibly too willingly – listen through. Said Brower: "When he finally arrived in America, self-obsessed political activists Jerry Rubin and Abbie Hoffman hit on him right away. They manipulated him right into the situation of getting White Panthers leader John Sinclair out of prison (the anti-racist activist had been jailed for 10 years on a minor drug offence). No wonder the US establishment was flabbergasted - a couple of hustlers like Rubin and Hoffman succeeded in getting John to be their frontman, and he went for it!"

Lennon never denied his attraction to radical causes. "I got off the boat, only it was an airplane and landed in New York, and the first people who got in touch with me were Jerry Rubin and Abbie Hoffman,' John admitted in 1975. "It's as simple as that. It's those two famous guys from America - and the next thing you know, I'm doing John Sinclair benefits and one thing and another. I'm pretty movable, as an artist, you know. They almost greeted me off the plane and the next minute I'm involved, you know."

Allen Klein did not last out the year with the Lennons. An embittered John wrote a special song for Klein - the vituperative blast of *Steel and Glass* (" Your mother left you when you were small, but you're gonna wish you weren't born at all ...") in his *Walls and Bridges* album of 1974. If you had dared to try and screw John Lennon, you'd best beware of his vicious and inspirational wit!

Early in the '70s, Paul McCartney sued the other Beatles in what he described as "a divorce". He stated that he chose to legally dissolve The Beatles as a business unit rather than allow Klein to milk and diminish their artistic legacy. Klein's ongoing career was less than spectacular. He had struck while his iron was hot with the Stones and The Beatles - master scores to be sure - but despite the ownership of more than 2000 vital copyrights (including such gems as *Satisfaction, The Last Time, 96 Tears* and *The Twist*), Klein ultimately served a two-month prison sentence in 1979 for avoiding tax on illegal sales of George Harrison's *The Concert for Bangladesh* charity album. Klein had also screwed up the accounting process on tabulating royalties on this well-intentioned effort to the point where the profits did not reach the victims until a decade later.

Shame really, but flogging off charity albums? Hardly the right way to proceed. But that was the way the ever-greedy Klein worked - he never slacked off from chasing any opportunity to squeeze a buck out of an unfortunate artist, often using the Ponzi scheme (a fraudulent investment operation that pays returns to separate investors from their own money or money paid by subsequent investors, rather than from any actual profit earned).

I was especially interested in obtaining Yoko's long-haul perspective on Allen Klein's involvement in the Lennon lives to include in this book. Midway through 2010, she described Klein as "`a very fascinating person. The kind of person that the American business world produced. The way the thinking was going on in the business world was very different to the creative side. Even now you can see the effect of that kind of thinking. In Klein's case, he thought of some brilliant ideas and he established himself upon those ideas. He went to various recording artists and said, `Listen, I'm going to find some money for you - money that you didn't get before but you should have gotten', or something like that. 'If I find that money, I want a percentage of it.' Since those artists didn't know they had this money, so of course they were pleased to find out about it. That's how Allen Klein established himself initially, and I think that was brilliant."

11. THE WORLD PEACE TOUR BEGINS

My new job as a peace envoy for the Lennons necessitated a lot of travel. I discussed it with my partner and she agreed that opportunity was clearly knocking on our door. She shared my belief that we could hardly decline the chance to be part of something that potentially might mean a lot in terms of my career prospects and might even help to change the world's attitude to violence.

So I waved goodbye and set off on this five-week odyssey to spread the *War Is Over* words. My partner wasn't particularly impressed when increasing tensions between John Brower and Allen Klein's office led to the need for the preparation of a dossier on Klein's unsavoury reputation and suitability to be representing a declared peacenik such as John Lennon. And for the delivery of that dossier in person to the wilds of northern Denmark. I departed on that crucial mission with John Brower on January 9, returning to Toronto on January 15. It would be an unforgettable half a dozen days.

After a two-day turnaround and quick repack of my suitcase, I was departing on the International Peace Tour on Saturday the 17th. It meant that in January, 1970, I set foot in eight countries, all up. The following month, another 10 countries. I became the peace man in motion, riding the peace train from nation to nation. It was a heady experience to be sure, but at the time, we felt that this was our destiny - to use the dynamics of rock'n'roll superstardom to spread a message of peace to the world. We felt, rightly or wrongly, the end would always justify the means.

So on January 17, 1970, as the Australasia-bound Air New Zealand jet tore down the San Francisco runway en route to Sydney, I realised I would be returning to my homeland of Australia for the first time since leaving with distinctly mixed feelings four years earlier. In April, 1966, I'd sailed out of Sydney Heads with my new bride on a five-week maritime odyssey to England. At the time of departure, I despised The Beatles for ``stealing'' so many of the great R&B records that I'd loved but never heard on racist Australian radio. US hits by coloured artists were rarely welcome on Oz airwaves but cover versions by British performers were greeted with open playlists. Now I was returning as the international peace envoy for John Lennon's *War Is Over* campaign. You could almost believe that I'd joined the opposition.

11. THE WORLD PEACE TOUR BEGINS

Who would ever have imagined this?

I'd been such a passionate fan of great R&B records such as the Marvelettes' *Please Mr Postman, You've Really Got a Hold On Me* by the Miracles and Barrett Strong's *Money,* that I'd become the first Australian member of Britain's Tamla-Motown Appreciation Society. (Not forgetting other non-Motown covers by The Beatles, including the Isley Brothers' *Twist and Shout,* Arthur Alexander's Anna *(Go to Him),* the Cookies' *Chains,* the Shirelles' *Baby It's You* and *Boys* and Chuck Berry's *Roll Over Beethoven.*) But these original tracks were never programmed on Australian radio, at least not until The Beatles turned up with their woefully inferior covers. I had big issues with that but I'd learned to put them aside by the time I arrived back in my musically color-conscious homeland.

After clearing Customs and Immigration in Sydney, I grabbed a cab into the city to check into the hotel and catch up with my travelling companion, who had arrived separately the day before. Ronnie Hawkins, better known as The Hawk in rockabilly circles, had flown out from Toronto with several Canadian friends who were pursuing an international party agenda. The Hawk had already connected with another rockabilly hero from the South, Roy Orbison. Being white, bespectacled and no great threat to young Australian womanhood, Roy had found glowing support for his music on local radio and consequently he was touring Down Under again, playing a series of upmarket club shows.

Ronnie too was being embraced by the gatekeepers of Oz radio. A single from his self-titled Muscle Shoals-produced album - a rollicking revival of the Clovers' *Down in the Alley* with outstanding virtuoso performances by Duane ``Skydog'' Allman on wailing guitar and King Biscuit Boy on probing harmonica - was quickly moving up the Oz charts. And why not? It was an unknown song locally: the Clovers had struggled even to get their Leiber and Stoller humour-filled shuffle *Love Potion No. 9* on the radio Down Under. Of that stable, only the Coasters were able to stir up even a modicum of airplay in Australia with *Poison Ivy* (later covered by Billy Thorpe, of whom more shortly) and *Along Came Jones,* fringe hits in the Oz market. (The latter was a hit for Ray Stevens in Australia in 1969.)

With Ronnie's breaking hit, it wasn't long before the Sydney rock'n'roll brigade began to descend upon us with rampant invitations to various delicatessens of excess. One of our first visits was to a harbourside soiree organised by a sharply-focused Canadian entrepreneur named Jack Cowin. He was a good mate of several members of our party crew and he had something quite substantial, it would later be seen, to offer any of us who might be interested.

Turned out Jack was in the process of launching the Australian franchises of Kentucky Fried Chicken and Burger King (a name changed to Hungry Jacks Down Under because of brand name ownership - some cheeky Aussie had earlier sneaked in and trademarked the Burger King name for the Oz territory, which would have meant a royalty payment of 2c for every burger sold ad infinitum) in the Australian market.

Born in Windsor, Ontario, the border city with Detroit, Jack had visited Down Under in 1968 and couldn't believe the difficulties he experienced in trying to organise a simple meal. Later Jack would tell an Aussie journalist: ``The advantage was that I had lived in North America where this fast food industry had started to develop. I was able to see that a limited menu, fast service and the ability to process people quickly was something that the public were attracted to. But it hadn't arrived in Australia yet.''

That less-than-satisfying eating out drama prompted the 26-year-old Cowin to relocate his wife and two young children from Canada to Australia. Finding local investors wasn't as easy as one might think, but after being promised $30,000 from about 30 supporters, Cowin set up Australia's first KFC outlet in Perth in 1969. He followed up with the first Hungry Jacks outlet two years later.

Jack was more than ready to share the ownership of his infant fast food empire with visiting Canadians. And so when we arrived Down Under in early 1970, opportunity in the fast food game loomed big time! Really big, big time! For a meagre outlay of only $5000 per share, an investor could have a piece of the expanding empire of the American fast food giants. God, with a few spare dollars, you could hardly go wrong!

Jack was a true believer and his faith had been boosted by some earlier business associations in Canada. ``A good friend of mine was Harrison McCain who, with a mere hundred thousand dollars in 1957, was able to build the largest potato-processing business in the world - a seven-billion-dollar company,' Cowin said. ``I became involved with the Channel Ten TV business in Australia through a man called Izzy Asper who started out with a defunct TV equipment business in North Dakota which launched Canwest. If it hadn't been for venture capitalists prepared to back an entrepreneur, I'd probably be shovelling snow somewhere in Canada about now.''

Ronnie and his friends were sorely tempted by the sheer raw attraction of Jack Cowin's offer - to flog a US-inspired and proven product seemed like a surefire fortune-maker for any smalltime investor. But I felt I owed

11. THE WORLD PEACE TOUR BEGINS

it to Ron to offer a piece of what I (mistakenly it would turn out) believed to be informed local intelligence. I took Ron aside at the Sydney pre-launch party - between puffs on some powerful joints of class grass - and assured him that no matter how attractive it looked like from the outside, Australians would never bite on this American fast-food fad. Never in a million years! It could never work Down Under, I told him. Not in a million years!

``Why, they've already got their own form of fast food down there - why would they want American junk food bathed in grease?'' I insisted. ``Aussies already have salad rolls, pies-and-peas, hot Chiko rolls, tropical hamburgers with pineapple and beetroot - why would they possibly want American mass-produced beef patties served with artificial cheese on plastic buns? Americans may be happy with that shit but Aussies ain't gonna go for it, mate. It'll never work down here. These people know better.''

Ronnie was sufficiently impressed with my ardor on the subject that he abandoned any plans he might have had to invest in the launch of these fast food giants Down Under. We've shared many a laugh about it since, but I suspect that Ronnie hangs on to some lingering regrets. I have no choice but to admit that those proffered $5000 shares have subsequently earned considerably more than $1 million apiece. So much for my insider's expert advice!

And Jack Cowin has gone on to become one of Australia's most successful transplanted Canadians, worth a third of a billion dollars. He owns 300 Hungry Jacks outlets, 50 KFC stores and his family has the majority interest in Domino's Pizza, a leading pizza chain. Jack Cowin has the fast food game outside of McDonald's wrapped up Down Under, and good on him. He also owns a very profitable and highly-regarded winery and has an interest in the Aussie experience, the Sydney Harbour Bridge Climb. Jesus, how good is that for a transplanted Canuck?

In Australia, Jack is regarded as ``the father of fast food''. And yours truly had the temerity to suggest that Jack's enterprises might be universally profitable but would never work in Australia! The monetary pile was clearly not to be my career route. Not in this life anyway. My return to Australia was a clear demonstration of the futility of pursuing the corporate-dollar connection. This I can clearly see now. Back then, it wasn't so apparent.

Also surfacing on the local media front during our visit Down Under was an out-of-left-field report that peacemakers supreme John and Yoko Lennon were coming to Australia to appear at a rock festival. Just a few short months after the momentous US impact of the Woodstock Festival, Australia was set to have its own Pilgrimage for Pop. Promoters Emle Stonewall Productions had wisely decided to restrict the show to local talent - much of it not yet signed up by record companies. And there was a strong focus on non-Top 40 acts. Most of the artists came from the alternative region of rock music, the sort of material being programmed by so-called ``underground'' FM stations in North America.

With the federal government Down Under providing monopolistic protection to existing AM band license-holders, Australians were still a long way from being permitted the audio benefits and expanded programming vision of commercial FM radio (it wouldn't be allowed Down Under until 1980). But Pilgrimage for Pop promoters were to be commended on the impressive array of Aussie artists secured - Billy Thorpe and the Aztecs, Tamam Shud, Jeff St John and Copperwine, Wendy Saddington, Doug Parkinson In Focus, Tully, Levi Smiths Clefs, Stevie Wright and Rachette and Max Merritt and the Meteors.

This would be an extremely important occasion for Billy Thorpe, who had been an Aussie rock hero of the mid-'60s and continued to make meaningful music until his untimely death in 2007. But contractual problems saw him disappear from the scene in 1967/68 while he tried to sort out his future. Pilgrimage for Pop at Ourimbah provided Thorpie with an opportunity to re-emerge with a new look, a new band featuring seminal guitarist Lobby Loyde and a career direction which would ultimately see him signed to the hot Macon, Georgia-based indie label, Capricorn Records. He toured North America several times and landed a platinum album with *Children of the Sun* in 1976.

Looking back, it can clearly be seen that Thorpie broke out of his then-Melbourne base through his strong performance at the Ourimbah festival. Later in 1970, he released a career-redefining album entitled *The Hoax is Over,* which confirmed the extent of his musical evolution. Another significant performer was Stevie Wright, who played his first show outside the band which had made him - The Easybeats. He debuted a new line-up called Rachette which was a short-lived entity but led to Stevie's securing a show-stopping role two years later in an Aussie stage version of *Jesus Christ Superstar.*

But as the festival show date crept closer, a feeling apparently emerged that an international big-name act was needed to boost the event and confirm its credibility. Somebody trotted out the names John and Yoko. The world's most famous couple had a notable track record for appearing in a solo context at exotic events - witness their turning out at the previous September's Toronto Rock'n'Roll Revival. Why, figured the Sydney promoters, wouldn't they want to commit to a 35 hour trip from London to whip Down Under to join the cast of the Pilgrimage for Pop?

Well, I was in the perfect position to be aware of several reasons why the Lennons would NOT be journeying to Australia for any sort of pop festival event! Firstly, they remained in Jutland, Denmark, trying to sort out custody of Yoko's daughter Kyoko. That was one consuming personal drama they were dealing with. Then there was the hair issue. An international media uproar had exploded a few days earlier when it was revealed that the Lennons had cut off their trademark long hair. In addition, there was the now-pressing legal issue of the Bag One lithographs. On January 16, 1970, the London Art Gallery's exhibition of the supposedly erotic Bag One lithograph series was closed by Scotland Yard. Eight of the 14 prints were confiscated by the bobbies as evidence of pornography.

Unbelievable! Privately - and later publicly - John was pontificating with plenty of honesty: ``I certainly don't regard those drawings as pornographic or obscene. Dropping boiling oil on Vietnamese peasants is what I call obscene!'' Amen to that. Who could deny the righteous truth of John's heartfelt comments? This distressing scenario had unfolded in London the week before, so no, John and Yoko would not be coming to Australia to perform or speak at the first rock festival in that country. That particular task would be left to yours truly!

The publicity fires had been stoked by an article in the Sydney Sun newspaper quoting festival organiser Maureen Phillips claiming it was ``almost certain'' that John and Yoko would be appearing. It later turned out that organisers had been trying in vain to reach Lennon through the Apple offices in London. But of course he was in Denmark with no phone or other form of communication. Then the promoters discovered that the person they considered to be the next best thing - John and Yoko's personal peace envoy - was already in Sydney ensconced in a hotel proffering comments to the media about the Lennons' *War Is Over* campaign. So they swooped. And they pitched to a set of sympathetic ears.

Next thing I knew I had agreed to appear and take part in the Pilgrimage for Pop as John and Yoko's official representative. Not that I would be singing or performing - I would merely do my best to pass along the gist of the Lennons' outlook on peace and the compelling need for a safer, saner and more just world. Spreading the *War Is Over* message. My travelling companion, Ronnie Hawkins, might have been in a position to perform at the festival, but he just wasn't interested. He had confirmed plans to renew an old friendship with his fellow rocker and rockabilly pioneer, Roy Orbison. Besides, the Hawk harboured a serious paranoia about small aircraft, fueled no doubt by the 1959 deaths of some other rocker friends, Buddy Holly, Ritchie Valens and the Big Bopper, in an accident after a concert in Clear Lake, Iowa. Being nine years younger and notably more naive, I harboured no such fears. Mind you, if I'd seen in advance the bush airstrip adjacent to the festival site, where we were supposed to land, I might have felt a whole lot differently.

Ourimbah (an Aboriginal word with two meanings - "Oorin" meaning "belt of manhood", a pouch in which a stone axe was carried on hunting expeditions, and "Oorinbah", which is the bora ring or ceremonial ground where the initiation ceremony of conferring the "belt of manhood" took place) is less than an hour's drive north of Sydney. But in a move probably designed to impress the assembled fans, organisers had decided to charter an aircraft to fly me to the site to deliver my opening ``peace blessing'' to the audience.

As I left the hotel, Ronnie gave me a look of dismay and wished me well. At Mascot Airport, I discovered my airborne guardian was in fact a Qantas airline pilot doing a bit of freelance work. He was agreeable enough and it wasn't long before we were lined up on the runway in among a string of large jets awaiting take-off clearance. That positioning was a tad intimidating, but the best was yet to come. About 10 minutes after we departed Mascot we began to descend into the middle of a dark green forest. Feeling panic-stricken, but not yet ready to declare it, I glanced at the pilot, who was relatively unconcerned.

As the plane lost altitude, my eyes discerned a tiny strip of brown amid the green blanket. We flew over the brown strip to check it out and then turned around and came back at it, this time cutting the engine back and slowing down. The wheels spun just above the treetops and then we descended to the brown dirt and after a couple of bumps, the pilot expertly brought the plane's speed down to where it could be safely turned around and we headed back towards the one-room shack which functioned as the airstrip's office space.

Festival organisers had driven over to the strip in a Land Rover to collect me. We duly tooled a short way to the backstage compound where I was welcomed by the promoters and asked to stand by to open the festival. With the typical nonchalance of a 26-year-old, I shrugged and lit another Old Port cigarillo. Various people came up to shake my hand and offer salutations but it wasn't long before the festival emcee, Adrian Rawlins, was introducing me to the crowd of about 6000. I strode out to the microphone in my black Le Chateau jumpsuit which John had given me, adorned with a black and yellow Rolling Stones button which had been bestowed on me by that band's producer, the late Jimmy Miller (and what a lovely chap he was). I looked the picture.

I was accorded a warm welcome, which was not entirely unexpected since I had travelling with me a lot of Lennon goodwill and largesse. I trotted out with an ad-lib spiel about peace and how John and Yoko perceived it. And how they would prefer that music fans around the world would accept the notion of peace and goodwill as an antidote to violence, the sort of mindless military ignorance going on in Vietnam and elsewhere. It was the good old time-for-a-change rap which always has validity with clear-thinking and open-minded youngsters. At Ourimbah, it found a ready and accepting audience. There was a hearty round of applause when I wound up my five-minute peace-boosting message with the catchcry, ``In the end folks, it's all up to you ... *War Is Over If You Want It*!'' With that, I retreated to the side of the stage.

The show moved on and after countless questions from backstage people about what John and Yoko had done, would be doing and might want to do, I felt it was time to withdraw. On the way back to the Land Rover I was accosted by a feral-looking young man. He said he was a passionate supporter of John Lennon's message and wanted me to take him a very personal present - two extra-special marihuana joints for the Lennons to celebrate their connection with the peace movement. This sort of random offering was not entirely novel to me in working with the Lennons so I stuffed the smokes in the top pocket of what had once been John's jumpsuit and clambered into the vehicle. Wisely as it turned out, I decided to stash the weed for a later buzz.

Back at the airstrip, our pilot was similarly keen to return to Sydney. So we climbed back on board the Cessna and prepared to head aloft. All went well and we zoomed across the outstretched forest and suburbs south to the city. As we started to lose altitude approaching the Sydney Harbor Bridge, the pilot asked me if I'd ever flown a plane. I said, "No, I haven't", and as we descended, he presented me with the opportunity. So here was our little aircraft with yours truly at the dual controls, hurtling downwards over the Harbour Bridge and heading towards Mascot. I flew the plane right up to a couple of hundred yards from the touchdown at Mascot International and what an unforgettable thrill that was. Turned out, I discovered after landing, that because of the badge I was wearing on my black jumpsuit, our pilot had actually thought I was a member of the Rolling Stones! So no wonder he had been so generous with letting me take over the controls for a few unforgettable minutes.

And so I bade him a grateful farewell and caught a cab back to my hotel. Upon entering our room, I discovered Ronnie Hawkins was still out partying with Roy Orbison. Just then I remembered the joints I'd been given backstage at the festival. I pulled one of them out and lit it up by an open window.

Now let me freely admit that I'd smoked the odd joint - reefer smoking is virtually de rigueur in my line of work - but nothing even remotely resembling the effects of this one. A few tokes in and I started to feel very, very strange. So weird that I had to head for the bathroom. I sat on the toilet aghast as the walls were literally coming at me. Back and forth, back and forth ... it was really quite frightening to be losing control in this manner.

Just then, Ronnie returned to the hotel room and to his amazement, found me in a state of shock.

``Boy, you should have seen Ritchie's face,' he still jokes to this day to anybody willing to listen. ``He was whiter than Casper's* backside!"

The rest of our brief stay Down Under was nowhere near as daunting as surviving the effects of the obviously laced joint. My round of peace interviews proceeded in a positive fashion and Ronnie's revival of *Down in the Alley* kept moving up the charts. It had soared to No. 9 as we flew out of Mascot en route to Tokyo, Japan, where a whole other world was awaiting your intrepid peace campaigners as we ventured inside the mysterious veil of the Orient.

*FOOTNOTE Cartoon character Casper the Friendly Ghost

12. TOKYO PIRATE RADIO INVADES AMERICA'S VIETNAM

Student protest and anti-militarism were peaking when we arrived in Tokyo as the next port of call on the international peace tour. We expected more of the anti-war feeling that then encompassed the world but were not prepared for the extent of the frustration being experienced by Japanese students and peaceniks of all persuasions. Here the anti-Establishment rage was obviously ramped up.

Excited about the prospects of where she might be able to lead us or connect us in the land of her birth, Yoko had given us the name of a longtime friend and associate, a journalist from one of the major daily papers, whom she felt would assist the *War Is Over* cause. And help us he did, in an absolutely unforgettable way. I called him shortly after we checked in at the Tokyo Palace Hotel. While the Hawk undertook interviews for his new album, I took time out for an introductory tea with Yoko's friend, who shall remain nameless to protect his identity.

In the course of our initial get-together, he produced two extremely graphic battlefront pictures from the Vietnamese war zone. They showed US soldiers callously flaunting body parts of Vietnamese peasants and/or revolutionaries. Yoko's friend explained that these pictures demonstrated what we peaceniks were up against. After viewing them, I was aghast. They were powerfully graphic images which spoke volumes of the instruments of modern warfare and the disregard for human life that all war entailed. An attitude check, so to speak.

Having gained my trust, Yoko's friend asked me if I might be willing to spread the peace message and broadcast some anti-war messages on John and Yoko's behalf to the battlefields of Vietnam. I enthusiastically agreed. He said he knew of a ``underground'' pirate radio station which broadcast into the war zone from suburban Tokyo and arranged for a car to pick me up the next morning.

Japan, as we would discover, has a fascinating history of student protest which had started in 1960 when the New Left gained prominence. This was the beginning of widespread student protest not driven by a communist agenda. Japanese youth were virulently opposed to the renewal of the Security Treaty with the US because they felt this would inevitably draw Japan into foreign military campaigns instigated by American foreign policy agendas.

Another reason for the New Left's opposition was the election in 1957 of Nobusuke Kishi, former Vice-Minister of Munitions, as Prime Minister. It was felt he represented a radical pro-military change from Japan's post-war concept of democracy and demilitarization. When he had departed Tokyo in early 1960 to sign the Security Treaty, there was a protest at the airport involving 7000 students, members of Zengakuren (All-Japan Federation of Student Self Government Associations). This group focused on domestic agitation. They invaded the Prime Minister's Diet Compound four times in 1960, and twice succeeded in burning police cars and other symbols of state authority.

After the treaty with the US was signed, the demonstrations were stepped up. On June 15, 1960, a massive demonstration took place in which 236 students and 570 police were injured and one female student was killed. Zengakuren was unable to overturn the treaty, but was able to force the Prime Minister from office, which was viewed as a considerable achievement in the circumstances.

It was a clear but cold morning in Tokyo when we set out for the secret radio station. I had convinced Ronnie Hawkins to join me on the excursion, telling him we were headed for another of the customary album-promo radio interviews. ``We might have a bit of peace propaganda work on the side,' I joked with Ronnie. The white-gloved driver took about 15 minutes to drop us off at our destination, an undistinguished factory building in suburban Tokyo. We were warmly greeted in the entrance hall and then ushered through to the back of the building. There a young man who had introduced himself as the station program manager pushed his arms against the wall. To our surprise, the entire wall rotated and we were shuffled into a back section not visible from the front of the building.

It was an armoury and a well-stocked one at that. Stacked in neat wire boxes were various weapons of war - hand grenades, semi-automatic weapons, bazookas, rocket launchers, the whole damn array of modern instruments of warfare. In my naivete, I simply shrugged this scenario off as a case of the local lads doing what they felt had to be done to fight the forces of oppression.

The experience, however, would be a fitting prelude to Robin Williams' feelgood movie, *Good Morning Vietnam*, which was released in 1987 but set in Saigon in 1967. The real-life disc jockey Adrian Cronauer, played by Williams, is a unique character who annoys his Army superiors with what they term his ``irreverent tendency''. But sadly, the film does not present a strong anti-war imprint. It would have been an incredible opportunity to make a powerful statement for peace and non-violence. Pity that Hollywood doesn't embrace such a message of positivity more often.

In real life, I had no such reluctance. Storming up to the microphone in the small studio amid the armoury, I let fly with a barrage of protestation. Informing the listening audience (which I was assured consisted primarily of serving US military on Vietnamese soil) that I had come to talk to them on behalf of John and Yoko Lennon, I proceeded to lash out at their belief systems and the basic underpinnings of their invasion philosophy. ``Hey there guys, this is crazy. What are you doing over there?,' I thundered. ``Put down your weapons, throw away those bullets. This whole business is crazy, totally fucking crazy!

``Why on earth would you want to kill somebody you haven't even met? What is that shit? I'm here to tell you that a lot of special people such as John and Yoko Lennon and many others really want to see you guys take control of your own destiny. Don't be pawns in this insane military madness! What have the Vietnamese peasants done to you to warrant such an extreme use of force against them and their villages?

``Come on guys - this crap doesn't have to continue. Stand up for your rights. Refuse to fight this unjust and totally wrong war. Just tell your officers that you don't want to be involved in such a stupid and unwarranted conflict. Lay down your weapons. And refuse to fight. What are they going to do to you for refusing to fight? They can hardly shoot you, can they? Stand up to and rebel against this crazy invasion.

``Remember what John Lennon said - no cause is worth dying for and no cause is worth killing someone else for. Think about that - I beg you. You're in the frontline of the battle against freedom. Surely the Vietnamese have the right to decide their own fate without American military intervention. Why be part of something which will go down in history as one of the most stupid and pointless wars in the 20th century, a period which has seen a process of crimes against humanity? Why would you want to be part of that? Put down your goddamn weapons and rethink what the hell you're doing!

``If John and Yoko were here with me right now, they'd be saying the same thing to you. Put down those goddam guns and forget about killing people out there in the fields of Vietnam.''

The pirate program director looked at me with a mixture of surprise and delight. He obviously hadn't expected such an aggressive anti-war broadcast to burst from my heart and soul. But I knew that - as Marshall McLuhan had informed John in Toronto just a few weeks earlier - the medium truly is the message and we have to use what we have to get our message across. It's as simple as that boiled-down raison d'etre - you're either part of the solution or part of the problem. I honestly believed that I could cast some shards of doubt and reconsideration in the minds of those American military invaders occupying the Vietnam nation. And make them wonder about what they were doing.

The Hawk meanwhile was clearly horrified. In fact, he was absolutely mortified. At the pirate radio station, he'd seen a different side to his travelling companion - a side that was more than willing to attack the status quo, stir hornets and stoke up the fires of discontent. I saw it as a splendid opportunity to spread the Lennons' anti-war message and I went for it.

In the car on the way back to our hotel, Ronnie went nuts. ``Holy fucking Christ, what are you doing?'', he demanded. ``What are you doing saying stuff like that on the radio? Don't you know they'll be able to track down that radio signal and they'll be able to track us down. We're inviting the thunder of the gods for stirring up the pot like that. You must be going crazy. We better be thinking of getting out of town before they track down our ASSES!''

Clearly the Hawk was not happy. And being a good ol' Southern boy who'd done his stint in the military, he figured we had somehow invoked the wrath of the big boss man. I didn't give a shit about that but Ronnie certainly did. He made note of the fact that he was a bit older and wiser than yours truly and I should be listening closely to his advice. As a consequence, Ronnie couldn't wait to get back to the airport and on the main drag out of town and away from this country. The old Southern redneck in him was extremely distressed that we might have offended our hosts in the Japanese government.

Meanwhile back in London, John Lennon was battling with another set of demons. The series of Bag One lithographs, signed at the Hawkins' spread in December, was viewed as revolutionary and obscene by the forces of repression. (Lithography is a process whereby the original images are transferred to a flat plate made of stone or metal. In the case of limited editions, these plates are destroyed after a predetermined number of copies have been printed. Each copy is then personally signed by the artist involved.)

Each suite (or set) of lithographs - there were 300 suites and 45 sets of artist's proofs - were ultimately pulled on BFK Rives paper at the Bank Street Atelier Ltd in New York. Each lithograph was 23"x 30" unframed. A unique carrying case in white leather, hand-stitched by Italian craftsmen, was created by fashion designer Ted Lapidus.

The Bag One sets which John had diligently signed over a marathon three-day session at the Hawkins' household ultimately went on display at the London Art Gallery on January 15. The next day police from Scotland Yard confiscated eight of the 14 drawings for possible prosecution on grounds of obscenity. The gallery was shut down for several hours while this censorship took place. Since many of the drawings showed John making love to Yoko in various positions, he was asked why there appeared to be a focus on cunnilingus. John simply smiled and said: ``Because I like it.''

Even more appropriate was John's comment about obscenity. ``I don't call drawings of people making love obscene - I consider dropping burning oil on peasants in Vietnam to be obscene!'' Amen! Eleven days after the bust John and Yoko were back in the studio writing, recording and mixing a new song, all in one day, with Phil Spector as co-producer, called *Instant Karma!*

It wasn't until three months later, April 27, that the lithographs were declared ``not obscene'' and returned. This after lawyers in John and Yoko's defense introduced testimony from other artists about the creative merits of the works and noted that Picasso had worked with similar subject matter. The individual lithographs and complete sets have become extremely valuable collectors' items.

There had been plans for a second suite of Lennon lithographs, based on the I Ching, but this never came to fruition. And so the ``Bag One'' lithographs represent the only example of this type of visual art created by John Lennon, although he often doodled self-portraits of Yoko and himself when autographing an item for a particular friend or associate.

The one other thing that separated Tokyo - and Japan - from the rest of the world was, surprisingly, marihuana. Despite being constantly in the company of local music industry people (notorious stoners) and attending bars and nightclubs, not once in the course of a four-day Japanese stay did we encounter a single puff of the allegedly deadly weed. And I have to admit I was not shy in asking the "can-we-score-a-smoke" question. I even journeyed back to one Japanese girl's suburban apartment late at night because she thought a nearby friend might have something, to no avail.

Later we would discover that the students-on-dope generation which had been spawned elsewhere was barely known in the Land of the Rising Sun. According to the recollection of Koji Takazawa, one of the leaders of Zenkyoto, an alliance of Japanese student groups: ``The simplest way for people to get marihuana was in pet stores. There were hemp seeds in the imported packets of birdseed, so students bought the birdseed and grew their own marihuana. In Europe and all over the world, the student movement was growing at that time and in Japan, the students didn't want to lag behind.''

But unfortunately a season of violence erupted. Prompted by governments invading and persecuting other countries, the more radical Japanese student groups turned to terrorism in the early '70s. The huge cultural divide between old-school Japanese and the emerging student generation was a significant factor. Prominent in the headlines of the period was the formation of the Red Army Faction, which was responsible for a number of regrettable violent actions - the hijacking of a Japan Airlines flight to North Korea in March, 1970, the hijacking of another Japan Airlines flight to Libya in 1973 and the attack at Lod Airport in Israel in which 26 people were killed.

Of special significance was the resistance campaign the Red Army Faction mounted against the construction of Tokyo's Narita Airport, first announced in 1966. There was a deep fear that the new facility would be used as a staging centre for US military flights and attacks against Vietnam. Militant students joined with displaced farmers in mounting an intensive campaign which featured specially constructed forts, towers, tunnels and underground bunkers in the airport construction zone. It was completed in 1978, but not before the deaths of two students and four riot police - three police were murdered by the Red Army Faction with bamboo spears. This was certainly not a happy scenario. And suggested lessons that the human race needed to learn, hopefully sooner rather than later! On that note, the Hawk and I headed for our next port of call, Hong Kong.

While the pirate radio broadcasts were a distinct positive in our efforts to spread the *War Is Over* word, some whispers of negativity were starting to reach us out on the road from Toronto base camp. Several phone conversations with John Brower revealed hints of organisational mayhem. It was difficult to get to the bottom of these reports from so far distant, but it was troubling to note that something that had started out so right was beginning to have too many signs of things going wrong.

13. A GONG IN HONG KONG

JOHN LENNON, ON BEING ASKED IF HE WANTED TO TAKE HIS *War Is Over* PEACE MESSAGE TO COMMUNIST TERRITORIES:

``Sure, but you must start with two people. Like in your own village, and our village happens to be the West. Of course we want to go to Russia and China and elsewhere. But we have to decide how to go and what to go as, because they probably don't know much about us there. Do we just get on a train and arrive in Moscow (or Peking) or do we take the Peace Festival there? I think that might be a good way. But the whole world is still quite large and we have to get a good team going here first, and then when we're a bit organised, we can go over there. I'd like to go somewhere over there, so as to stop that question (of also taking the message of peace to the communists) arising again in Year One AP (for After Peace).''

Over the millennia we'd had BC, AD and now the infinite implications of AP (for After Peace) but to tell the truth, we were more than ready for a little R&R. After the enormous risks associated with the controversial pirate radio broadcasts out of Tokyo and into Vietnam, I had naively expected that the glitter of Hong Kong might be a bit of an anticlimax as our International Peace Tour tumbled on to its third Pacific Rim destination.

In Hong Kong, more than anywhere else, it was easy to see the elevation of status that John's patronage had bestowed upon the revitalised career of Ronnie Hawkins. Ron - who was fiercely proud of his white Rolls - was suitably impressed when the local Warner/Atlantic Records rep appeared at the airport in an impeccable, new, large white Mercedes sedan, whipped us through a warren of back alleys and side streets to avoid the downtown gridlock and dropped us off at the Miramar Hotel inside 15 minutes.

Positivity beamed in all its glory at our press conference the next morning in the plush Mandarin Room of the Miramar, and we basked in its glow. Ron and I responded with warmth and enthusiasm as we fielded questions about the peace campaign from the assembled Hong Kong media, which was almost reverential towards us. There was absolutely no trace of the usual cynicism, sarcasm and mockery sadly evident in so many of

John and Yoko's *War Is Over* media events, particularly in Britain.

As a performer feeds off audience reaction, so we too were stimulated and ultimately inspired by the degree to which this band of media hands applauded and supported the essential *War Is Over* message. It was the perfect setting for a message of peace - the white light glaze of TV technology illuminating an environment implying ancient splendor. Dark-panelled walls framed rustic paintings, antique brass-handled Chinese furniture and the soft pastel tones of Oriental carpets. The Hawk and I, tuning in to the irony of the scene, edged our way to the microphones to welcome our guests to the *War Is Over* peace show, Hong Kong style.

Even Ray Charles* could see, as the Hawk later remarked, tongue in cheek, that these local media people were ripe and ready to receive our message about the philosophy of peace. We were only beginning to realise how extensively our own enthusiasm was mirrored by the Hong Kong media when out of the silken darkness behind the blast of the TV lights came the BIG query ... the inevitable question which would within hours thrust us into the very heartland of hostile enemy territory, where peace and protest were regarded rather differently.

Afterwards, we would ruminate that perhaps Sybil Wong had carried out her self-appointed task of getting the local media onside a little too efficiently. Sybil was Ronnie Hawkins' contact from way back - she and the Hawk had attended the University of Arkansas at Fayetteville together and were obviously firm friends. You could almost call them kissin' cousins. Back at home in Hong Kong, she had climbed up the corporate ladder, ultimately becoming the Asian editor of Reader's Digest.

"Of course, we all agree that world peace is a wonderful concept," came the voice from out of the blackness of the interview room, "and we totally agree it's wonderful that John and Yoko are using their media power to crusade against war and violence. I think I can speak for most of us in saying that we're totally with you," the voice continued, to a quick round of applause, "but since you've come all the way to Hong Kong on behalf of the Lennons to spread their philosophy of peace and love, shouldn't you be also taking this fantastic message to the other side - the Red Chinese?" A further burst of spontaneous clapping broke out.

"The communists are the ones who should be made aware of these ideas. A quarter of the world's population are living beyond our border and you should do something about reaching them with this message. The communists are the people who should be exposed to John and Yoko's *War Is Over* message. Why don't you do something about getting it out to them?"

In the onslaught of silence that followed the well-reasoned and timely suggestion, I struggled to find an appropriate response. Momentarily thrown off balance by the sharp-edged logic of the proposal, I nodded and agreed that " Yes indeed, reaching all of the people behind the Communist Curtain - Chinese and otherwise - is a top priority for John and Yoko."

I quickly reflected upon the Lennons' attitude to provocative peace campaign ideas ("as usual with anything to do with peace, we say yes and hope it will work out" was John's oft-expressed response to taking on board exciting new ideas and innovative non-violent concepts). Eventually I realised the abiding wisdom of the idea and how its successful execution might delight the Lennons, who were dealing with their own demons back at home base, Tittenhurst Park on the outskirts of London. The apparent crumbling of Peace Festival plans, the slow but painful dissolution of The Beatles and their own experience with the lingering tragedy of miscarriage a year earlier, were among John and Yoko's sources of pain at that time.

I jumped into this pool of uncertainty with both feet and my *War Is Over* placard.

"Of course," I heard myself muttering, "We'd love to get our message to the Red Chinese, but how can we do that? How can we get it together?" "Well," chimed in another journo, not missing a beat or the heat. "It's all pretty simple. Why don't you just drive out to the Red China border at Lokmachau and show your *War Is Over* banners for the Chinese to see? Take it right out there to the people."

"Plus," tossed in Sybil Wong, sensing the muted rumblings of a meganews event in the making right here in the Mandarin Room, "we could easily make up a copy of the *War Is Over* message in the Chinese language so that you could demonstrate the message in both languages, English and Chinese."

"Great idea," I grinned, without further ado, "let's get it rolling." I would have to admit that ever the eager peace protester, I didn't give a single thought to the possible consequences. "We should try and take the *War Is Over If You Want It* peace message to everybody in the world," I foolishly insisted. "John and Yoko have always wanted to spread their *War Is Over* campaign behind all the curtains - Iron, Bamboo or whatever," I said as the reporters scribbled in their notebooks. "I'm absolutely certain they'd be totally blown away by the opportunity of getting it to the attention of Red China. This is a fabulous chance to do precisely that, and we'd be crazy not to take advantage of it."

As the formidable issue of pooling film footage and factual accounts was being sorted out in heated Chinese (the central issue being which journos would go and who would be left behind), Sybil slipped off into the hotel kitchens and spread out on the huge wooden counter a piece of white cardboard. Upon its roughly 3ft x 2½ft dimensions, she inscribed the *War Is Over* universal peace message in Mandarin. Local media were not opposed to proffering any kind of political statement to Hong Kong's Communist neighbour. The only remaining detail still to be decided was our mode of transport. Ron and I, it must be shamefully admitted, had become all too accustomed to the limo lifestyle in recent times. But we realised that it would be absurd to try to pull off a protest demonstration at the Red Chinese border in the superb white Merc which had been tooling us around town, even if its owner had been crazy enough to loan it to us. So we settled on a volunteered vehicle, a less than luxurious battered old cream Volkswagen Kombie van, for the journey.

The Chinese owner/driver's name was Charlie and he'd been appointed pool photographer for a clutch of the daily papers to be represented at the event. He seemed a logical chauffeur candidate, we initially thought, not knowing that his driving talents bordered on the berserk. At least he was familiar with the region, we reasoned. Ron suggested a spot of lunch might be in order before starting out on our peace mission. But our freshly formed compact of six - aside from ourselves and Sybil Wong, two reporter/photographers and Charlie the chauffeur/freelancer - wanted to hit the road pronto. There was no time to lose.

We were crammed in the Kombie van as tight as could be, Ron would later relate to a bemused John and Yoko over dinner in London, just like a "gnat's ass stretched over a freight train, and that's tight". The Mirimar doorman had grinned broadly as the noisy engine fired and we set off surrounded by a cloud of noxious fumes into a sea of certain uncertainty. I instinctively knew there would be no half measures on this little venture. Even in our one-way bilingual mode, our team couldn't hear enough about John and Yoko and their dedication to the peace movement as we hurtled down a narrow highway.

We sped off at a frantic, fearsome rate ... incessant near-misses as we tore down tiny laneways separating huge blocks of untidy multi-storey tenements, myriad blind corners, flocks of dogs, cats and chickens scurrying from the bombast of our path, scorching past the high-rise housing, roaring through the most densely populated few acres in the world. And somehow managing not to kill anybody or anything.

Then the journey became serious. Charlie, our cheerful chauffeur, was only a few revs short of lunacy when he got loose on the single-lane ribbon of bitumen designated as the highway to Lokmachau and mainland China. If there weren't any vehicles within sight ahead, he simply shoved his foot flat to the floor and gleefully hung on to the steering wheel following the white line. I was not alone in my alarm. Charlie's ferocious driving didn't seem to bother his countrymen and women, but it was freaking the Hawk, who was no stranger to high speeds and cheap thrills.

"Jeeeeeesussss Chriiiist," bellowed Ron, a survivor of 10 men's share of auto anarchy, "this motherfucker is absolutely doggone crazy!!! He'd scare the shit out of Stirling Moss or Mario Andretti, and that's a fact."

Swerving to avoid mashing a market gardener pushing his produce across the narrow road, Charlie turned around to Ron and asked, "What's wrong man?"

"Fuck boys," yelled Ron, "I know none of you can wait to get into the fucking Guinness Book of Records, but you're gonna have to slow down a piece because my fucking nerves can't take it anymore. Fuck, you got me so goddamn worked up with that crazy driving that my poor little asshole is pinching buttonholes into the back seat, or what's left of it. Slow down a bit there boys ... I don't reckon anybody's going to be taking those one billion Chinese peasants anywhere in the next half hour. If you can't slow down, you're gonna have to let me off because my fucking heart can't stand no more."

Ron's comments, followed by copious translation from Sybil, were the cause of a bout of boisterous laughter which only abated when we all but slid off the road in a scream of hurtling gravel, trying to avoid a rumbling truck too far into our side of the road on a blind corner.

The Hawk and I had set forth on this adventure suitably dressed for the occasion, as our particular tastes (or lack of) dictated. Ronnie was decked out in a bluish gray suit over a navy blue turtleneck rising out of a pair of serious black cowboy boots, topped off by the inevitable beat-up straw hat and a stogie clamped between the teeth. For myself, I continued to be loyal to the Lennon *War Is Over* "uniform" of basic black (a black long-zippered jersey jumpsuit John had given me to take on our peace tour as a positive omen, centred with a maroon suede and snakeskin belt) which was visibly feeling the effects of the constant clouds of roadside dust which filled the van. As fashionable as our gear might have been along Oxford St in London, it was not the appropriate attire in which to avoid attention in the rice paddies of the New Territories.

Now, as we tooled towards Lokmachau at gut-wrenching speed, my instincts told me that - mode of motivation aside - we were indeed on the right track to delivering a significant peace statement.

Ronnie didn't agree. There was no question, the Hawk proclaimed, that the border guards were going to deny us access to the large strip of No-Man's-Land, the buffer zone which divided Britain's adopted peninsula of private enterprise from the vast Chinese mainland.

"Are we going to flash our peace signs to the border guards?" Ron taunted. "Boys," he bellowed from the back seat, "let me tell you something. I've been around Army people long enough to know that they're never gonna let a bunch of hotheads and fucking hippies like us through that border into No-Man's-Land to stir up any goddamn trouble with those millions of Chinese peasants. Get real! Are you all fucking crazy? One thing's for fucking certain - the dudes at the very first border post are gonna kick our asses and send us back where we came from. The guards aren't totally insane, though I'd reckon any length of service out in this neighbourhood would just about drive a man half crazy. So I'd reckon you'd be well advised to put away your cameras and tape recorders boys, 'cos we ain't gonna be making no headlines out here today." He sat back and inhaled deeply on his stogie.

"Stop worrying, you crazy guys," Charlie yelled over the whining grind of the Kombie's pistons working at full capacity up a small hill, suddenly acquiring a previously unrevealed English language fluency, "everything's gonna be fucking fine. You'll soon see I've been out here before," Charlie continued shouting, slamming on the brakes to avoid ramming the van up the backside end of a lorryload of wooden crates, "and I know how we can get through there without being stopped by the bloody border guards. Don't worry about a thing. We'll get our pictures and our story and it's gonna be all over the front pages everywhere. It's gonna be easy - you'll see."

As we croaked up to the crest of a range, to a chorus of gusty cheers, an unforgettable panorama of the Lokmachau border station stretched out in the distance. The moderate elevation provided us with almost a bird's-eye view of our destination ... the several winding ribbons of impenetrable barbed wire fencing, the compound of small border huts and semi-circular structures, the incision of a substantial river, and way off in the distance, a range of mountains behind which, presumably, lay a quarter of the planet's population. We were in view of a nation that the United States insisted did not exist. We felt like the Crusaders in sight of our personal Jerusalem.

Ron was freaking out as the border gates approached. He passed over a joint and looked at me with deepening despair, relit the charred end of his stogie, sat back in the mutilated seat and took his last shot. "All right boys," he said, "you do whatever you fucking well want, but don't ever say I didn't give you plenty of warning if you end up getting your goddamn balls blown off. You can count my country ass out of this fucking insane exercise."

Charlie, always eager to take his eye off the road ahead, felt a need to respond to Ron's doom and gloom. "Don't worry man, it'll be all right," he yelled. "I've been out here dozens of times to take pictures and nobody ever hassled me. Don't worry so much man."

The border post itself, now zooming into tighter focus, could reasonably be described as foreboding and formidable. Border stations - even between friendly nations - are seldom warm and inviting facilities, and the Lokmachau outpost was no exception. Behind the vast coils of imposing barbed wire and three small border inspection booths were two large dormitory-styled huts along with a scattering of smaller structures. Away from the cluster of border buildings, the fences of barbed wire snaked their way interminably into the distance along flat riverside rice paddies which followed the waterway as far as the eye could see.

About a mile back from the border post, a substantial hill overlooking a bend in the river commanded observation of the entire river plain and, not surprisingly, it was capped by a large building which appeared to be some kind of police or military barracks. From our close vantage point, it was obvious that the prime location for any kind of peace protest would be at the top of the barracks hill.

The Red Chinese border inspectors seemed in no hurry to expedite clearance for anybody, and continued waving their arms at the groups of clamouring peasants gathered around the gate. Eventually a couple of small trucks were waved through the crossing and we moved closer to the mayhem. The Lokmachau border post was grimy but functional, a tiny bracket of bureaucracy preserving communist law and order in the wilderness.

"Don't worry about anything," Sybil soothed, "these boys seem to have everything under control. They've been to this border crossing before and they know what we have to do." A pang of apprehension surged through my gut and Ron appeared absolutely horrified. But we were too far gone to turn around. It was at best a calculated gamble, astutely reasoned but not leaving much margin for error - let alone catastrophe.

Charlie kangaroo-hopped the Kombie van up to the booth and a uniform slowly sauntered towards us. Charlie - accorded his own centre stage at last - leaned out brandishing his Hong Kong Police Press ID card and mumbled a few words in Chinese. The soldier nodded. Then, without extending the courtesy of awaiting the official's reply, Charlie sank his boot into the gas pedal. Spraying a torrent of gravel among the milling peasants near the booth, Charlie directed his missile flat out into No-Man's-Land and we tore on to communist territory in an Oriental Bonnie and Clyde-styled manouvre. The Hawk shot me a withering look of grim resignation and I cringed. Even our companions demonstrated a singular lack of desire to look back on the response to our illegal entry. Imagining the momentary hail of rifle fire, I slid even further into the seat. But the lone sound - beyond our own thudding heartbeats - was the strained whine of the Kombie engine still toiling in second gear as we tore along a narrow road dividing the barren treeless landscape. I snuck a look back at the border station where at least six unformed officials waved and gesticulated in our direction. They seemed quite agitated but since they weren't yet shooting at us, we took a collective breath of relief.

Ever adept with the timely one-liner, the Hawk sat back and mumbled to nobody in particular: "Well, that little kamikaze run sure proves beyond any shadow of a doubt that you motherfuckers are totally fucking crazy. We're never gonna get out of this little episode alive. I can just see us spending the rest of our lives in a fucking communist labour camp eating nothing but fucking fishheads and rice!"

Nobody seemed sure whether to laugh or cry, to shout or scream. It was that strange calm that settles like a fog in the aftermath of calamities. With nothing more to lose, I tossed in an ill-considered quip of my own. "Shit," I yelled over the VW whine, "it's a bloody pity we didn't have a bit more time back at the border crossing because I wanted to get a Communist China stamp in my fucking passport and also check out the duty-free." Nobody laughed but me.

Christ, maybe this is a firing squad offence in fucking Red China, I found myself stupidly pondering in a burst of paranoia. Finally the old van wheezed its long-suffering engine and our entourage to the summit of the hill. We slid on the gravel of a large parking area extending around the two-storey barracks building and skidded to a halt under a puny and windswept pine tree which overlooked a vast plain of rice paddy fields.

Surely the barracks had been alerted to our illegal intrusion and looming arrival at the top of the hill? Where the hell were they? How come nobody was trying to shoot us? It was the perfect occasion to get cracking with our anti-war protest. We had what's now termed a window of opportunity and wasted no time in springing into action. So far Lady Luck had been with us. Perhaps if we remained peace-positive, she would hang in for a few more vital seconds.

I seized our two *War Is Over If You Want It* banners from the rear of the van and leapt out, pulling Ron behind me. Supercharged by the thrill of panic and desperation and several shades in between, the Hawk and I brandished aloft our peace signs in English and Mandarin. We stumbled through a variety of demonstration poses as the motor drives whirred in a photographic frenzy.

It must have been the fastest peace demonstration shoot in the history of the camera. And among the most stressful, as we all awaited the clunk of boots and the clang of weapons which must soon emerge from the doorway of the barracks.

And so we hung suspended in limbo, some sort of perennial suspense. The Hawk would reveal years later the intense paralysis of anguish he'd experienced in the lead-up to this hilltop *War Is Over* declaration on behalf of John and Yoko. "Even if I lived to be 90 - and there's not much chance of that considering what I've put my body through over the years - I'll never forget that goddamn trip out to Lokmachau at the Hong Kong border,' Ron would regale his closest friends over the crackle of a roaring log fire in the vast living room of his converted farmhouse home on the northern shore of Stony Lake near Peterborough in Ontario, Canada.

"We tore out to the Red Chinese border with Stirling Moss on amphetamines at the wheel of a clapped-out van with a bunch of these fucking lunatic Hong Kong journalists and photographers hellbent on leading Ritchie Yorke astray. And they did a pretty good fucking job on that score, even though it's never been too goddamn hard to lead that crazy bloody Kangaroo Kid astray. They were all eager as beavers, all completely fucking nuts, all imagining glory while they were chasing a typhoon to get an exclusive story - or at least stirring up enough goddam trouble to start a typhoon.

I've seen a million ugly scenes in all those years on the road playing those little old dives that used to book us all over the States and Canada, but it didn't take me long to see that this little episode with the crazy Chinese journalists plus Ritchie Yorke would take the fucking cake! There we were," Ron related, "making a fucking illegal entry into a hostile foreign country which the United States of America and the fucking United Nations didn't even recognize or admit its existence. Breaking into a place that doesn't even exist, a country that my passport totally ignores and has no dealings with - now that is what I personally consider to be totally fucking insane.

"What happens if they decided to keep us there? The United States says Communist China does not exist, so you can be sure as a hen going down on a June bug that our asses wouldn't exist either. Big chance we'd have of getting back home. It'd be worse than the American prisoners of war in North Vietnam. Talk about fucking hopeless! When that little Charlie dude drove straight through the border gates without even stopping, just waving his goddamn press card out the window like Walter Cronkite, I figured, 'Oh fuck, here we go again, doing our fucking darndest to get ourselves erased'."

In all probability, less than two full minutes had elapsed since we'd done the deed realigned the gravel under the tree, leapt out with our *War Is Over* signs and snapped a hundred shots and then stashed the banners into the back of the van, well out of the sight of prying eyes.

As the Hawk and I turned around to take in the panorama of this forbidden country, we found ourselves silently and suddenly surrounded by a ring of at least two dozen unsmiling soldiers. I hadn't even heard their approach, but there was no doubting their intentions. The guards were literally armed to the teeth - about half were what even I could detect as automatic weapons. Between them they clearly had enough firepower to blow away a battalion. But I didn't think they planned to shoot us, not yet anyway. They were menacing but they had a method; they apparently spoke no English; and did not seem to be armed with the knowledge that we were peace-demonstrating illegal aliens.

I had no problems with Ron taking command of our official response. The Chinese-speaking media had apparently indicated that Ronnie Hawkins was the reason we were up here on the hill. The surliest of the soldiers - and evidently the squad leader - approached the Hawk and me. Unexpectedly, he revealed a working acquaintance with the English language. He might reasonably have been described as "pretty fucking angry". It was easy to see we were some considerable distance from digging our way out of this mess.

"There we were," Ron later related, "surrounded by at least 20 Kamikaze warriors armed to the teeth and about as friendly as Vietnamese clap. Some of them were stroking their automatic weapons as they sized us up. But this guy who spoke a bit of English was the nastiest, meanest motherfucker of them all and he was very, very distressed about us being there. I called him the general. In the end, it all came down to pure luck and bullshit.

"I pulled out one of my little publicity pictures and told the general and his commandos who I was - a famous rock'n'roll singer playing tourist. Nobody was impressed. They couldn't give a shit. Their faces were locked into a permanent lack of expression - not a twitch, not an itch. So I try to crack a few harmless little jokes to loosen up the atmosphere. I'm usually pretty darn good at that. But not this time with this fucking audience of unhappy assholes - not one of the motherfuckers gave up even a hint of a smirk.

"They were dead-set deadpan like they were under strict orders or something,' Ronnie continued. "Apart from the general, most of them only looked about 15 to 16 years old, and they had in their ranks a few really surly motherfuckers. I could tell they were just dying for us to try something so that they could launch into a practice round-up. The Chinese journos tried to pretend they were tourists too, because they'd realised there was going to be some really serious trouble if these trigger-twitching commandos got wind of any media involvement in this little circus of ours."

This was without question the longest 10 minutes I had ever experienced. Ron just kept playing that good ol' Southern boy routine of naught but nooky and nonsense. He was, the Hawk made out, a harmless fool and self-confessed idiot. He made light of our tiny little transgression and indiscretion in somehow forgetting to check-in at the border crossing gate and piloting our old wreck up the hill to the barrack's parking lot across No-Man's-Land.

"Well, I'll be darned," the Hawk guffawed, "you'd never read about it ... how we made that mistake and drove straight through the crossing and up this goddamn hill trying to get a better view. No wonder you people got annoyed at us for being so stupid. Well, one thing's for fucking sure - we'll all know better next time."

It seemed hard to believe but they were buying it. With a shrug to his troop, the general turned back towards us, spat on the gravel and pointed to our beloved VW van and then in the direction of the highway to Hong Kong. The general and his boys seemed as pleased to see the back of us as we were to depart their encampment. We didn't object when Charlie tried to set a new downhill speed record, leaving behind a military Jeep that had suddenly appeared from within the bowels of the barracks. The Jeep tried to follow us down the incline. Our immensely relieved detachment of peace protesters remained silent until Charlie slipped through the border gate. All on board except Ron waved to the grim-looking crossing guards we had flaunted and then, safely back on British** soil, we let out an almighty roar of delirious delight and excitement.

We had fucking well won the day! Not only had we survived, but we had in our possession rolls of film proclaiming the success of our innocent little peace-loving invasion of Communist China. We could hardly believe such a huge demonstration had gone so smoothly. Surely this was going to capture some of those keenly-contested editorial column inches in tomorrow's papers. There must be some potential front pages in all of this.

One of the Chinese snappers eagerly offered to shout a couple of rounds of celebratory libations at the next village bar we passed, but the sullenly silent Hawk wasn't having any further deviation. "No sir, count me out boys, there's just no fucking way," Ron growled in a tone that discouraged debate. "Forget about stopping any fucking place near here. Let's just get our lucky country asses back to the goddamn hotel and civilization as quick as this little old garbage can will get us there. I'll give you a hundred dollar bill if you can get me back to my room in under half an hour. You can bet your last goddamn dollar that we're being followed right now after that little incident with the military."

Many years later, Ron would reflect: "I still don't think those goddam journalists realise just how fucking lucky we all were that afternoon. That's about as close as you can get to being blown away without it actually happening. It was like being on Death Row with your number coming up the next morning. Anything could have happened up there on that goddamn barracks hill. And since the United States didn't even recognize Red China until years later, we could easily have been there for a long spell.

"America would not have been keen to negotiate our release with a country that didn't exist. I'm absolutely fucking sure that we would never have gotten back if the general and his platoon had suspected what was really going on - that it was all a peace publicity event which was bound to be highly fucking embarrassing for the Lokmachau military guard in the coming days. If one of those commandos had been looking out the window and saw us waving those fucking peace signs, we'd have all been history. Nothing surer.

"And despite what the President might have thought, we went there and found out that mainland China certainly did exist. For certain. And we left the follow-up diplomatic work to Tricky Dicky Nixon and that bunch of ping pong players. We were there first, but we were fucking lucky to survive it. I didn't want to be a fucking martyr for anybody or anything," Ron declared emphatically in the early '90s. "Not even my old friends John and Yoko. John often used to say to me he didn't want to be a leader, didn't want to end up being a martyr. And I reckon he wouldn't have wanted me to be one either.

"Seriously though, none of us should ever forget how fucking stupid we were to stir up a hornet's nest like that. It was really stupid to just barge through the border barrier and burn around in No-Man's-Land. I heard later from Sybil Wong the border guards were so pissed off about what we did that they shot and killed the next week some poor Chinese peasant motherfucker who just walked through the crossing without getting permission. That's how fucking annoyed we made them, and that's an indication of how fucking lucky we were. Don't ever forget it."

*FOOTNOTE

Ray Charles was a brilliant blind singer/pianist, (1930-2004), who pioneered the soul genre and was signed to the Atlantic label.

**FOOTNOTE

Britain gained control of the island of Hong Kong in 1942 and it remained a centre for trade and western business as mainland China became a communist state. Hong Kong was returned to China in 1997.

14. PEACE HITS THE HEADLINES IN HONG KONG

Back in the metropolis of Hong Kong, things were looking up. A succession of encouraging editorial calls by our Lokmachau-linked comrades increased our positivity that our peace protest would be accorded priority coverage come the morning dailies. The photo snappers and their instantly converted editors had also moved into follow-up mode seeking agreement for a further round of Red China-related picture stories on the morrow. I knew Ron wouldn't be keen to co-operate, but he was out of it by now from a bout with his Napoleon brandy.

We were awoken early, shortly after 6am, by an excited and vigorous rapping on our door, which was none too eagerly received. "What the fuck is all this racket?," I muttered irritably to Ron who hauled the bedspread over his head. But the knocking continued, even more aggressively than before, and we heard the muffled voice of one of the hotel bellboys in a state of severe excitement. "Mr Yorke, Mr Hawkins, please hurry up and open your door. I have some very exciting publicity material demanding your immediate attention," insisted the bellboy. ``I have many, many newspapers with your picture on the cover."

What appeared from behind the door kicked me into instant waking gear. We had of course expected fairly substantial coverage of our little foray into No-Man's-Land but even I - well and truly familiar with the power of the Lennon name in the press - was in no way prepared for the barrage of saturation exposure which the giggling bellboy proceeded to lay up and down my unmade bed, one front page after another. ``Shit," cried out Ron, rubbing the sleep from his tormented eyes, "this is totally un-fucking-believable. Get John and Yoko on the fucking telephone right now!"

The results were nine Hong Kong front pages, including several lead features. It was by any definition a promotional coup and the reality of its impact was just beginning to sink in. Even the reticent Ron was blown away by the manner in which Hong Kong media had cottoned on to our protest initiative in terms of both placement and positioning. The extent of the coverage was simply overwhelming, especially to a laidback country boy from Arkansas who later acted like he'd uncovered Aladdin's Cave. "We just couldn't believe pulling nine fucking front pages, including to our absolute astonishment - the goddam official Communist Party daily," Ron would boast.

And our now historic *War Is Over If You Want It* banners - fresh from their tumultuous triumph at Lokmachau the previous day - would be destined for quite an airing throughout this news follow-up day.

Follow-up was to be the operative word for Saturday, January 31, 1970. We'd hardly managed to down our first coffee of the morning when the phone started to jangle and it rocked away all day long as I took any opportunity to encourage Hong Kong's communist cousins to ponder peace.

Ever-anxious to oblige a sympathetic media, I eventually agreed to pursue a suggestion by one of our Lokmachau photographer comrades to mount a low-key *War Is Over* banner demonstration in front of the two best-known Communist China landmarks in the heart of the crown colony of Hong Kong - the Red China Bank and the Communist China department store.

The Hawk was horrified. "We'd already made our point in no fucking uncertain manner at the border," the Hawk later recalled, "and pushed our goddamn luck to the limit. We'd stirred up a hornet's nest with that outrageous stunt. For Ritchie to agree to go back to those Red China buildings in Hong Kong to rub in some more War -Is -Over salt was absolutely fucking crazy and I told him so. We'd already pulled off a miracle and then Ritchie wants to follow-up with more pissing off of the communist regime just to get a few more pictures. He was totally out of his fucking mind.

"I didn't let nobody take my goddamn picture next to pictures of Chairman Mao. But I had to hang around and keep an eye on things, just in case that crazy Australian went completely berserk."

Back at the hotel, Ron found confirming evidence that we were under surveillance. ``We discovered that our room had been thoroughly checked over by person(s) unknown. All our possessions - our clothes and bags - had been gone through with a fine tooth comb,' Ronnie complained. ``I kind of suspected that this might happen and I'd deliberately left a couple of traps to find out if our room had been messed with while we were absent. I wanted to know for sure if we were under surveillance because it sure as shit felt like we were. It happened again later that afternoon when we went out to suburban Hong Kong to do a TV show with a bunch of local up-and-coming acts including martial arts expert Bruce Lee. Bruce was just starting out then and he was a really nice guy ... you'd never have guessed that he was about to become a world-famous movie star. Back at the hotel, I found that our room had been searched once again and I was getting really fucking worried. Something sinister was building up around us and I didn't like it one bit," Ron said.

By then our oft-invaded room at the Miramar was beginning to resemble

John and Yoko's memorable suite 1724 at Montreal's Queen Elizabeth Hotel where the second Bed-In for Peace had taken place the previous May. In Memory of the Montreal campaign, I'd plastered an impressive array of front page tearsheets around our walls, highlighted by our two Lokmachau banners. Our boudoir had evolved into some sort of mobile campaign office for the *War Is Over* movement.

But it couldn't be denied that the creeping mildew of a siege mentality was also on the rise. After the rush of break-ins, the Hawk was convinced that our room was bugged, which served to discourage conversation at a time when its familiar comfort would have been welcome. The next incoming call would be sobering.

One of our fellow Lokmachau photographers was shocked to discover that the proofsheet and negatives detailing our border protest had disappeared overnight from the newspaper's locked picture library. He was equally surprised to discover that his editor - gung-ho only hours earlier about keeping *War Is Over* alive and warm no matter how or what - had suddenly gone cold on the story. He was stonewalling any ongoing *War Is Over* story ideas or photo ops. It appeared that a fatwa had been declared upon the *War Is Over* campaign among Hong Kong editors. This story, came the instructions from above, was officially dead. And the pictures were missing in action. When two other photographers from the Lokmachau mission also called to report a similar raiding of their photographic libraries, the Hawk and I could only conclude that there was a considerable method behind this apparent madness. There had been systematic removal of pictorial evidence of our border incursion.

Or as some might conclude, a cover-up had occurred.

Our opposition, whichever side it happened to be on, had formidable influence. To have the authority to seize news pictures from newspaper files in a matter of hours demonstrates an all-but-invincible enemy. Eventually, I would find that the only surviving copies of pictures of the Lokmachau peace protest were the personal prints the photographers had secretly organised for their own files and had taken home with them the same night - and of course the newsprint reproductions of the published shots. It was almost as if the Lokmachau event had never taken place.

The Hawk's fear-laced paranoia was now proving to be on the money. We really had stumbled into a mother of a hornet's nest with our odyssey into the New Territories. According to Ron's subsequent recollection of events: "Later I found out from certain private contacts I have in Hong Kong that we really had pissed off the authorities in a big way - they became super worried about the possible repercussions of our border caper if the communists chose to be officially offended about it. There was not a lot of contact between the two countries at that time, and anything was possible. The Hong Kong authorities (and their American supporters) feared that the consequences of our illegal invasion to organise a publicity stunt might lead to an international incident, an official complaint from Peking, something very serious."

Continued Ron: "I later found out that Red China provides almost all the fresh water supplies for the state of Hong Kong, but these can be cut off at short notice at the whim of the communist authorities. The Hong Kong authorities were acutely concerned that we could really fuck things up between the two countries if we pissed off the touchy Red Chinese sensibilities. So they weren't going to risk their water supplies and their future existence just to satisfy the desires of a couple of fucking peaceniks flogging an anti-war message on behalf of the goddam Beatles. We were dead meat. We went from the top of the pole with the delivery of the morning papers, to the fucking basement by the time the sun went down."

Later Ron admitted that in a mysterious phone call he'd received through Sybil Wong that we'd been "strongly advised to lay low and pretend we were dead, or leave town". It would not be long before the Hawk chose the latter, safer course. We were not entirely unfamiliar with the unsavoury experience of undergoing professional surveillance since Ron and I had escorted the Lennons to the Canadian capital of Ottawa to meet Prime Minister Pierre Trudeau a few short weeks ago. We'd journeyed to Ottawa via Montreal - scene of the previous May's Bed In for Peace - where we'd scheduled a *War Is Over*/Peace Festival press conference. Around about the time we spent several hours discussing soft drug culture and the possibilities of legalization with key members of Canada's Le Dain Drug Commission in Montreal, we'd noticed certain vaguely familiar faces in all-weather coats would inevitably turn up wherever we went. It could have been a coincidence, couldn't it? Subsequent Freedom-of-Information discoveries would show that our suspicions of being tailed were on the money.

But this was Hong Kong and a very different scenario. We were strangers in a strange land and we had, in all probability, committed a cardinal sin. It was time to get out of Dodge for the Hawk. Too much weird shit going on. Pushing our luck big time. "Shit, it couldn't end too fucking soon for me," the Hawk would later relate to his inner circle. "We sure left a big fucking mark in Hong Kong but the time had come to leave town before someone tried to make a martyr out of my ass. So I moved the motherfuckin' itinerary forward a couple of days and grabbed the first flight out to Bangkok where I figured I could hustle up some goodtime gals and forget my fucking worries for a few days. I sure needed to relax away from that goddam crazy Australian and his insane promotion ideas. I like the fucking publicity he whipped up but I couldn't handle the risks a moment longer."

It would not be until later that final evening at the Miramar, after a heavy session of cramming countless clippings into the newly acquired "Hong Kong Kitbag" in preparation for the morning's departure, that I finally found relief through connecting by phone with the Lennons in their white bedroom at Tittenhurst Park. John and Yoko's attention had been drawn to our Communist China border exploits through initial wire service coverage in the UK dailies (transmission of which mysteriously shut down after the first photo op report) and their reactions sounded quite ecstatic. Usually very positive people in any matters related to their peace campaign, they were pretty much over the moon about the international implications of the wire service blanketing of world media.

"It's fantastic, Ritchie," chortled John with a hearty laugh. "That's just the right sort of thing we need to get this grease into a worldwide perspective. China's the largest fucking country in the world - we've simply got to have them involved in the *War Is Over* campaign."

"That's really quite amazing that you were able to pull this off, Ritchie," piped in Yoko, with a customary sense of practicality. "But did you manage to get us lots of copies of the newspaper coverage, all those front pages you were telling us about?" Glancing over at the bulging Hong Kong Kitbag on the end of my bed, I replied in the affirmative. "I'll mail you a full set of clips from the airport tomorrow morning by airmail, and I'll be bringing heaps of copies with me for your files. We'll be arriving in London seven countries from now in 12 days, and I can't wait to see you both again. There's lots to talk about, judging from what we've been seeing. The Peace Tour has been going really well, but I don't think we're ever going to top this little caper in Hong Kong."

John laughed enthusiastically. " Yeah, Ritchie. I'd reckon you're definitely right about that," he chuckled. "In fact, if what we've been through is any kind of a guide, you can expect a welcoming committee of fucking spies and undercover agents in every place you visit from now on. Be cool and careful boys. You and Ronnie are doing an incredible job but be a bit careful. How is Ronnie anyway?" John asked. "Let me pass on my congratulations to that old Arkansas legend."

Now it was my turn to laugh. "I only wish I could let you do that John, but he's done a runner on me," I cracked. "He bailed out of here yesterday and headed for Bangkok and left me to round up all the promo stuff. He found the suspense and the local intentions too intense for his liking."

I was pleased with the turn of phrase but John glided past its implication and moved on to another, much less upbeat and contentious issue. "Ritchie, have you been hearing much in the way of news from the Peace Festival organisers back in Canada?" he asked, the very question I had been nervously dreading. As far back as Tokyo the previous weekend, I'd heard by phone of a gathering cloud of doubt - some extending to actual newspaper reports - of the relative state of chaos in the festival organisation team in Toronto. Clearly the ship had sprung a leak or two, but my urgent enquiries to promoter John Brower had only brought a response that there'd been a couple of minor hassles - mainly with John and Yoko's chosen advisers, members of what Rolling Stone magazine later described as a "psychic cult living at a place in California called Harbinger Springs" which "believed and preached that they ... were in contact with supernatural beings from another planet who would arrive on Earth to save us from our own self-destruction" - but that everything was moving along according to plan.

I found this information less than reassuring, and sensed that the Lennons shared this apprehension. But there was little I could do about any apparent decay in the foundations of the Peace Festival when I was so far away from the roots of the problem. I was basically helpless but I tried to hide that. Certainly John and Yoko were in the process of a very real re-evaluation of their support and endorsement of this planned largest music festival in human history. The situation had gotten a little too shaky for the instigators of this utopian vision. Perhaps sensing the isolation of my present situation, John returned to the encouragement mode. "Of course, no matter what's going on in Canada, we know that you and Ronnie are really doing a fantastic job for us around the world, and we're very grateful for that. If only everybody else was as together and as committed as you guys.

"But I can't deny that Yoko and I are getting rather concerned about what's happening and what's not happening and what should be done about it. For now, we're laying low and finishing off a video edit. But see what you can find out from your sources in Toronto, see if you can sort out the truth from the bullshit. See if you can make any sense out of all this strangeness that seems to be descending on the festival. Things seem to be getting a bit out of hand and we just can't risk having our name associated with it if it's starting to fall apart." I stressed that I could readily understand their predicament.

After hanging up, I pondered the situation across the Pacific. Surely John

Brower and his latest team of companions could not have achieved communication breakdown, a state of play hinted at by John and Yoko.

I danced on the threshold of depression. Only the arrival of former chauffeur Charlie with a farewell treat - a little chunk of opiated black hashish which we promptly smoked in a wooden pipe managed to keep dear old Mistress Doubt from getting a grip on the entire stage. Charlie was still in a state of bewilderment over the events of recent days.

John would later write in Rolling Stone in his appraisal of the collapse of plans for the Peace Festival: ``Meanwhile, Ritchie Yorke was doing some nice things round the world with Ronnie Hawkins...'' It was an apt description of the state-of-play in the peace campaign circa March 1970. It was a very positive time in our pursuit of peace as we were coming out of Asia, Europe-bound.

The headline-making event has not lost its shine over time, at least in Yoko's eyes. ``We thought your taking the *War Is Over* message to the Red Chinese border was great,' she affirmed in mid 2010. "The main thing is that YOU did it (and not us). That was fine and it was beautiful. If John and I had done it - and demonstrated at the Red China border - the American government might have been suspicious that we were Commies or something. It was so good that you did it on our behalf. That was really great.''

15. BANGING THE PEACE DRUM IN BANGKOK

Still shell-shocked from our escapade at the Red China border, Ronnie Hawkins was super keen to head out of town – to anywhere! So while I gathered up tear sheets of the newspaper coverage of our Hong Kong exploits, Ron flew on to Bangkok. I followed the next evening with an unexpected detour.

The pilot commanding the Cathay Pacific flight to Bangkok announced over the public address system that inclement weather conditions had forced an unexpected overnight rerouting stopover in Manila. Saying a relieved-to-have-survived farewell to that splendid urban harbour panorama of Hong Kong was one thing. To be spending a surprise night in the Marcos stronghold of Manila was a development which required the rapid despatch of a couple of double cognacs. I'd had more than enough surprises in the past week of traveling the *War Is Over* Peace Tour road. I was looking for a little piece of peace to preserve my sanity.

In Bangkok meanwhile, at the elegant Erawan Hotel, a slightly older and infinitely wiser globe-trotting rockabilly legend toting his new album endorsed by John Lennon was relaying his new Oriental outlook to a reporter from the local daily, The Bangkok Post. "Now don't get me wrong," Ronnie cautioned, "I'm not on this peace thing myself, except for the country boy who's been singing rock'n'roll for the past 18 years, and this is the first vacation I've had in that whole time."

Expanding on this redefining of his role in the World Peace Tour, Ronnie said, "As a matter of fact, I didn't even know John Lennon, except through his music, just as he knew me. So now I'm travelling with Ritchie Yorke, one of the top new pop journalists and a member of John's peace campaign, promoting my new rock'n'roll record and hustling around."

Glancing over the piece with Ron in the Thai capital the next afternoon, I was thoroughly amused by the account of his none-too-subtle withdrawal from the *War Is Over* firing line, his calculated distancing of himself from the heat and heart of the peace campaign. It was a survival-slanted sidestep for which I could scarcely blame him. Although he was moving down to the back of the peace bus, the shrewd self-promoter in the Hawk couldn't prevent him squeezing one last little stream of Asian publicity juice from our recent escapade.

"We were the ones, you remember," he couldn't help but drop on the Post reporter, "who crashed through the Communist China border holding up John and Yoko's sign, *War Is Over*, written in Chinese letters." Horrified by the alarming developments in recent days, Ron nonetheless couldn't stop from bragging in celebration of the fact that he had survived and lived to tell the tale, which would only add to his legend.

The Thai capital was a whole other world after the formality of Tokyo and Hong Kong. Ronnie particularly enjoyed the relaxed moral attitudes that prevailed. ``Bangkok's the place though. I reckon a man could do just about anything in Bangkok - but I didn't, because we didn't have no time.''

Outside our hotel, he was surprised to bump casually into a former Miss Canada beauty pageant winner. At the bar, he entered a conversation with a Thai local who informed him that for $10 he could organise for Ron to go somewhere and see a man making out with a woman. ``Ah told him that for $10, I could probably find a girl and do it myself!''

The long Air France flight from Bangkok to Rome via New Delhi, Tehran and Tel Aviv was uneventful and accomplished with a couple of shots from Ronnie's latest bottle of cognac. And a return visit or two. I was beginning to understand what Ron meant when he suggested that a shot of brandy could rapidly lift one's energy levels.

We were met at Rome Airport by the wildly enthusiastic representatives of Ronnie's record label. As we relaxed in the marble corridors of the Rome Hilton, I was able to persuade the normally hotel-bound Ronnie to take a few steps out of the routine for a visit on the morrow to the famed Coliseum. Normally Ron fended off any one-on-one tourist experiences with an explanation that he didn't need to go out seeing things which he could just as easily look up in an encyclopaedia back home. It's another example of that Southern redneck outlook that Ron has never been able to shake, even in the more enlightened company of Canadians.

And so later on as we ventured down into the ghostly depths of the Coliseum - where the Hawk claimed to be communing with his gladiatorial predecessors - and we puffed on a hash spliff and dreamed of other scenes. It would be one of the highlights of the European leg of the international peace tour. We held a press conference at the Rome Hilton which attracted a fair complement of media types, most of them bilingual and able to comprehend our exhortations of peace and love and Ronnie Hawkins' new album.

After a fabulous three-course meal at a stunning Italian restaurant Roma-style, where the chef's special was cow's intestine stuffed with a delicious pork sausage, we were driven out to the Appian Way, the ancient Roman highway which linked the capital with the wonders of Naples and the province of Campania.

Again Ronnie wandered out on ``Shanks's pony'', stumbled around the ancient ruins and was caught up in the omnipresent vibe of imperial Rome. Its accoutrements had special appeal to Southern Americans of the Caucasian race.

After a day-and-a-half of confronting the spectacle of Rome's past, we were all-too-quickly returned to the airport for the early afternoon flight to Paris. At Orly Airport, we were greeted by the promo reps of Atlantic Records' distributor and they took motorized enthusiasm to another level. They were totally crazy behind the wheel, even for a veteran speed and hot rod freak such as Hawkins.

``Jeez, these boys were doggone crazy,' Ronnie would later allow. ``I was so scared as they tore around some of those roundabouts that my asshole was pinching buttonholes in the backseat of the car!'' I won't deny that it was a pretty scary experience.

But the Parisian media's support and stellar encouragement more than compensated for the over-exuberance of the local drivers. Our press conference was marked by a positive endorsement of the message we were sending, which we found inspirational. After dinner that night at a classy Left Bank cafe, we didn't rebel against the apparently traditional habit of dropping our drawers as an acknowledgement of the chef's superior talents.

Next day we were up early and Orly Airport-bound again for the short flight to Amsterdam, where we were booked to stay at the Hilton, the same hostelry where John and Yoko had their first Bed-In for peace some 10 months earlier. We were unable to rent the same rooms as the Lennons but we managed to maintain a notably peaceful profile in another suite.

As I wrote a piece for Rolling Stone magazine about the Hawk and I breaching the Red China border with John's peace message, Ronnie entertained a coterie of Dutch journos, broadcasters and well-credentialed others. In attendance were several media members who'd rolled up to John and Yoko's first Bed-In for Peace. Not surprisingly, they were fiercely positive about the prospects for peace through the auspices of the Lennons' headline-grabbing capabilities.

Next day we made the short flight to Copenhagen where we were again met with a chorus of media support for our peaceful aims. Parked in our hotel overlooking the Tivoli Gardens, we postulated about peace and appreciated the open-mindedness of Scandinavians. Of course I had visited Denmark the previous month on the mission to meet John and Yoko, along with Yoko's daughter Kyoko. And then we departed for Stockholm, the last of our European stopovers before we reached London and reconnected with the Lennons.

It was no great surprise in Sweden to be greeted by Canadian-like weather with temperatures of minus 12 Celsius and blowing snow. After our press conference, Ronnie linked up with one of the young and willing female journalists who provided a VIP escort on our cruise around Stockholm's nightlife. She took us to see a couple of local Swedish acts - an early incarnation of what would become Abba (which I thought was pop-awful, and for that matter, still feel that way) - and a new-album-launch performance by a robust Hawkins lookalike, the Dutch/Swedish singer/ songwriter Cornelis Vreeswijk.

His new studio album, *Cornelis Sjunger Taube*, had just been released. A protest singer with a biting and abrasive style, Cornelis was the exact opposite of Abba. His music was not disposable pap. His angry political music provided what has been described as ``a deliberate break from what Cornelis would later attribute to a Swedish song tradition of pretty singing and harmless lyrics'', and ``a hobby for the upper classes''. He died in 1987 of liver cancer at the age of 50. But in early 1970, Cornelis went out of his way to make Ronnie Hawkins and myself feel right at home in frigid Sweden. As did our our attractive record company friend whose all-night presence saw me retreating to the sofa.

Up early the next morning for our pre-flight breakfast, there was an growing feeling of termination as we were coming to the end of our world *War Is Over* peace tour. After four weeks and almost 40,000 miles, we were reaching the finale. But somehow as we packed our bags for the flight back into the heart of the British Empire, distant drumbeats of doubt were beginning to be heard. Hints had been flowing into our travelling peace circus for several days, increasing after we'd departed from South-East Asia. It became apparent that while we were out on the road busting our backsides promoting peace, storm clouds were brewing in Toronto and in California.

Even from such a distance, it was becoming increasingly obvious that the road forward was strewn with obstacles. Through the grapevine, I was hearing hints of an alarming scenario. At first I didn't want to know about the implied negativity, but there was no denying the stories of mysterious Peace Festival press conferences where incredibly strange claims were being made of people from outer space attending the festival in flying cars fuelled by psychic energy! There were even rumors of aliens coming to Earth to rescue humans from the hole they'd dug for them-selves on the planet.

Equally unexpected events were unfolding in Toronto, where it now appeared that the projected site for the Peace Festival - Mosport Park, some 40 miles from the Greater Toronto Area - had been sabotaged. I heard that New York State police had travelled to Mosport to show local officials film of the recent Woodstock festival. According to Hugh Currie, a former FM rock deejay who was one of the directors of Karma Productions, which planned to produce the Peace Festival, this film coverage included "the garbage, and the traffic, and all the nudie shots and people fucking ... it really made the townspeople uptight..."

Apparently Ontario Police also had demanded huge bonds be posted to cover every contingency short of a nuclear war. But I was unable to reach any of the Karma directors for a first-hand account of these crucial developments.

In addition to stories filtering in from North America, I also received inside intelligence from the Lennons' personal assistant Anthony Fawcett in London on the view from their camp. The mood about the Peace Festival was not good back at Tittenhurst Park, where the Lennons now lived. Meanwhile the *Instant Karma* single had been released to much acclaim. And the slightly disenchanted peaceniks, John and Yoko, had immersed themselves intensely in the editing of their Montreal Bed-In movie, to take their minds off the faltering peace initiative.

All of this was beginning to bubble up to the surface as discontent spluttered into life around us. As we flew on the final leg towards the United Kingdom, I was having a few second thoughts about our plans to save the world from violence and injustice. I again reflected on the immortal words of British author H. G. Wells, that "The history of the world is scarcely more than a history of crimes against mankind". This was precisely the course we wanted to change. But would it turn out to be an impossible mission?

16. MEETING IN THE LION'S DEN

Returning to London from Stockholm after our eventful voyage around the world was always bound to be anticlimactic. But as a fog of doubt began to descend on our horizons, it now seemed even more so. We'd originally been booked into the Westbury Hotel but after a last-minute consultation, decided to upgrade to the penthouse suite at the Playboy Club on Park Lane.

By now our original travelling party had dwindled to a duo. As Ronnie duly informed London pop writer Ray Connolly, who'd stayed at the Hawkins' homestead eight weeks earlier when the Lennons were in residence just before Christmas: ``When we left home in Canada, there were seven of us. But one by one, all the others dropped out along the way. They just couldn't stand the pace. Now there's just Ritchie and me." (Among the missing members were Ronnie's lawyer, his stock broker and some rich, young and unseasoned Canadian businessmen.)

An early visitor was Anthony Fawcett. Captain Hook, as we affectionately dubbed him, was hankering for party-time, and suggested that Apple Records should be throwing a celebratory bash in our honour at our Playboy Club pad.

Another keen supporter who turned up shortly after our arrival was Phil Carson, a genial gent and earnest music fan who ran the Atlantic Records European office. He was also the former bass player with Dusty Springfield's band. He loved Ronnie's new album and was dead set on an intense promo schedule to support its release. He even funded the filming of a special *Down in the Alley* clip to be played on Top of the Pops, the long-running weekly TV hit parade show which had the viewer power to make or break a single. Phil simply couldn't believe Ronnie's keen sense of Arkansas-styled humour. For a guy who'd basically seen and done it all (including playing fill-in bass for an ailing John Paul Jones on Led Zeppelin's Japanese tour), Ronnie's impact on him was something really special.

Talking of Zeppelin, one of our most eminent visitors at the Playboy Club was guitarist Jimmy Page and manager Peter Grant. Unfortunately they'd dropped by unexpected when we weren't around and we didn't manage to connect up again on this trip. "All I remember from back then,' Phil Carson recalled recently, "was your dedication to peace and how much fun Ronnie was."

We'd been met at Heathrow airport by a small contingent of Hawk fans led by Wild Willie, a rock'n'roll veteran and president of the UK Ronnie Hawkins fan club. Decked out in the traditional black drainpipe pants, described by one eloquent London journo as "tighter than the bark around a tree and hair greased back and pompadored like sticky plumes", Wild Willie was a Cockney character who worshipped The Hawk. Willie proved to be a reliable and ready "go- to" man in London when we needed something to be sorted out. Or to have something procured. Ronnie worked him to the max, especially when the time came for us to fiddle with the finer details of a celebratory party.

Fawcett - still trying to set up a meeting for us with John and Yoko - had stepped up to the plate and organised an Apple-hosted welcome-to-London bash for us. It would be a memorable gathering of Apple staffers and London rockbiz VIPs but the Hawk was less than impressed with the results. Others were obviously amazed by what unfolded. Ray Connolly in the London Evening Standard observed: "It was quite a party. They never had them like that in Ormskirk (a West Lancashire market town 13 miles north of Liverpool, where Ray was raised). God knows who all the people were: record company employees, girlfriends and pick-ups I imagine. There was a lot of drink around too, some really dirty picture books from Sweden (and I mean dirty) for those who had no one to talk to, and a lot of low behind-the-barn Deep South humour. And sitting right there in the middle of it all was Ronnie Hawkins, the host, alternating the shapes of his lips to take sips of brandy, puffs on his cigar and drags on a weedy little home-made cigarette that had a funny smell." That's as good a picture of the scene as you're likely to get.

The 40 or 50 people who'd turned out for the Apple tribute to Ronnie Hawkins' party were apparently delighted about the turn of events and had a great night. They were still talking about the Playboy Club bash years later. But it was a minor-league memory in the scope of what was to come. "Call that a party?,' thundered Ronnie from the doorway of the penthouse of the Playboy Club as the last of our guests stumbled out to the elevator at 2am, "Come back tomorrow night y'all and I'll show you what a real rock'n' roll party is!"

And he meant it, immediately ushering Wild Willie to a corner of the vast lounge area of the penthouse. I instinctively knew they were up to what the conventional world would term "no good", but Ronnie wasn't forthcoming with any details. I knew - after five weeks on the road with the Hawk - that I would be seeing the results of what he was planning in short order. I would not be wrong on this score. It would be pure raunch'n'roll.

The next morning we were up early for Ronnie to meet and discuss album launch tactics with Phil Carson's Atlantic Records promo team, before a stream of interviews with London press movers and groovers. Behind the scenes I kept on hassling Fawcett about an urgently needed meeting with his employers, while Ronnie was running his promo agenda. He conducted a series of music-related interviews, while at the same time admitting: ``It's really very good for me that I met John Lennon because he'd done so much for me. He made all this promotion I've been getting possible.'' At the same time, ``I haven't really ever given the peace thing a lot of thought. I'm not heavy rock like Led Zeppelin. Or like Carl Perkins, who's doing well in country rock. I'm middle-of-the-road rock. I can listen to a lot of different music but I really like the original rock'n'roll.'' And so did a fair number of English folks.

Ronnie was usually forthcoming to media inquiries, even taking on the trick questions. ``I never did get much from marihuana,' Ronnie admitted to one curious journo, before plunging into his traditional rave which I'd heard many times before. This was a spiel that Ronnie had polished down to press-pencil size. ``You know that some cats can have a puff and then wow!, they're as high as a giraffe's cock! I personally never got that much out of smoking marihuana because it usually just put me to sleep. But there was this one special time I recall. I was up at this farm and having a smoke and patting this dog's back when I lolled off. While I was having a stonedout doze, a friend of mine crept up on me. He went and replaced that dog with the smallest horse you've ever seen.

``The horse's body was like that of an ordinary horse but its legs were only 18 inches long. It was a specially bred little thing. When I woke up, I was still patting it, or at least I thought I was. Then I looked over at it and I was quite shocked. I said to a guy nearby, `For goddamn sake, tell me that that damn horse is standing in a two-foot hole!' I shouted out, `Jesus, that is some special hash!' So I guess that experience sort of put me off smoking marihuana for a while ... but I got back into it later.''

And on this special night of the Apple Thank-you Party - chronicled so lovingly by the passionate Southern scribe Stanley Booth - Ron would be smoking anything that came within his reach. Most of the party tragics who had attended the previous night's festivities were in reunion mode the next evening. A fair-sized crowd of new faces also rolled out for the Arkansas version of the party to remember and they would be blown away.

Among the guests were a charming young pair of dark-haired girls who could have been twins. I'd never seen them before but I did see them slip into the master bedroom with Ronnie for a brief period. An hour or so into the flow of the party, they suddenly began to romance one another in a passionate fashion and the atmosphere turned. Hugs and squeezes turned into full body contact as they writhed towards the carpeted floor.

16. MEETING IN THE LION'S DEN

Ronnie sidled over and gave me a knowing nudge. This public Roman orgy-styled development disturbed some guests but delighted others. Horrified wives were seen pretending to be turning away, mortified in moral horror, but were sneaking peeps at what was going down. And that was what happened - these two girls stripped themselves naked and went down on each other, to the general delight of their audience. These young ladies brought new meaning to the word nubile!

Ronnie cheered them on and even performed a sort of running commentary. ``Oh my God, that girl's got more energy than a beehive on Benzedrine. She goes down like a hen on a June bug! Oh my God, look out - that girl could suck a bowling ball up a 50-foot hose,' called Ronnie, providing a play-by-play to the delight of the gathering crowd. The Hawk - through his employed lesbian entertainers - commanded the attention and direction of the party. Ron looked at me and grinned to the assembled audience, ``This is what we dudes in Arkansas call a party, man … I can see that you're digging it''.

Although we naturally had invited them, John and Yoko were too engrossed in their film-editing activities to attend. In any case, they may well have found the entertainment a tad too gross for their liking. The party would go down in London rock'n'roll folklore. On a more formal note, Atlantic Records had hosted a pleasant press reception at a picturesque glassed-in restaurant- bar on the banks of the Serpentine Lake in Hyde Park. But any prospective interviewer who seemed half-serious or met with Ron's approval was invited back to our Playboy Club base by Ronnie for an in-depth discussion.

The Evening News's amiable writer Peter Cole was one of them and after he visited us at the penthouse, he wrote: ``Everything about Ronnie is big - his body for a start, enclosed in a too tight white T-shirt which didn't quite meet his blue jeans, leaving a roll of ample stomach staring at the world, or at least the Playboy Club. The jeans themselves were far too tight, so much so that the zip was only half done up, and looked as though it would go no further. He crossed the room to a suitcase and took out quite the biggest cigar I have ever seen. I exaggerate not when I say it was 14 inches long and an inch-and-a-half in diameter.''

Everything else - apart from Ron and his cigar and the penthouse dimensions - seemed quite small, including the ``sweet thing'' Wild Willie had arranged to come around for a little London entertainment. ``She's as tight as a mouse's ear,' Ronnie confided to his inner circle.

Next morning, a bit the worse for wear, the Hawk dragged what he described as his ``sorry Arkansas ass'' to the Portobello Road markets in company with a group of skinhead extras to film his *Down in the Alley* clip for the following week's Top of the Pops.

I kept nagging Anthony Fawcett to confirm a meeting with the Lennons as the gathering storm clouds from Toronto were interfering with my sleep. ``Come on Anthony, line us up a get-together with them, mate,' I implored. ``Man, they're just so busy in the editing suite and they hardly ever come out of there,' Fawcett replied. ``The only time they leave is when they go back to their hotel to sleep (the Lennons had moved into the Mayfair district from Tittenhurst Park in outlying Ascot while they edited the Montreal Bed-In film and some other film projects). ``And man, really they're just not in a very positive state of mind at present. Give it a day or so, I'm sure they'll come around.'' I kept hassling Fawcett and finally late that afternoon, he called to say that John and Yoko would in fact be able to have a quick dinner with us – Anthony, Ronnie and myself – in Soho near their editing suite that evening.

Over the next hour and a half, I reflected on what the Lennons had undergone in our absence on the International Peace Tour. A month earlier, the John's Bag One exhibition raid had resulted in obscenity charges which would be months in processing. Two weeks earlier, they had joined British Black Power leader Michael X* in a media event at a black commune in the London suburb of Holloway. The Lennons had given him a bag full of their recently shorn hair in exchange for a pair of Muhammad Ali's boxing shorts. Michael X would ultimately auction John and Yoko's hair to raise funds for the controversial commune. (Five years later, he would be hanged in Trinidad for the murder of two people.)

Two days later, the new Plastic Ono Band single *Instant Karma* was released, the same bleak day as reports surfaced in the media that mass murderer Charles Manson had a connection with The Beatles. Apparently Manson was obsessed with certain songs from The Beatles' ``White'' album, in particular Paul's *Helter Skelter*. And in secret - under the alias of Billy Martin - Paul McCartney had begun recording his soon-to-be-announced breakaway solo album. We weren't to know anything about that yet but much heavy shit was hanging in the air.

It was not a carefree reunion dinner with John and Yoko, I am compelled to report. Although grateful for my efforts in storming various barricades on their behalf on the peace tour, the Lennons were equally unhappy about many developments within the Peace Festival organisational ranks. Sitting in a tiny trattoria in the heart of London's West End, we were not enjoying any of the Sgt. Pepper/Magical Mystery Tour kind of atmosphere associated with The Beatles and Swinging London.

16. MEETING IN THE LION'S DEN

As we nervously sipped at glasses of chianti and awaited our Italian food, there were some uncomfortable silences and many unanswered questions.

John and Yoko appeared weary and worn down. I had never seen them in such an agitated and depressed state. They were not the John and Yoko I'd come to know and be inspired by. They had taken a break from the macrobiotic diet which had dictated their culinary lives during the stay at Hawkins' homestead - they'd now moved on to a vegan agenda.

Later John would write in his memoir of the period, Have We All Forgotten What Vibes Are? (published in Rolling Stone, April 16, 1970): ``Ritchie Yorke got to London sometime in late February and told us about his trip; how he had been hearing strange things about the Festival. We said, ` Yes, we heard it, too, what shall we do?' We discussed dropping the whole idea before it was too late. I must admit to wanting `out' many times after Denmark. The pressure and the tale-telling was bringing me down but Yoko kept waking me up again, reminding me of our original intentions. Ritchie then went back to Toronto to see what was happening. The latest news we got was that John Brower (the Peace Festival promoter) was again in New York and so was Rabbi Abraham L. Feinberg - who sent us a telegram (concerned over the Festival's bad publicity) saying his name was at stake (don't worry, Rabbi. God will save you!).''

Under the weight of many heavy pressures, the Lennons had apparently resorted to the painkiller par excellence, heroin. It was only for a short period, and they smoked rather than injected the substance. I never witnessed any use of heroin by either of the Lennons, but John later admitted it had been on the agenda. They had, he sheepishly confessed, done a bit of chasing the dragon. It's obvious that some pretty weird energies were pervading John Lennon's planet at this time. And they certainly were, as he later admitted, ``bringing him down'' and presumably clouding his vision.

This period in the *War Is Over* peace campaign is compassionately described by a Lennon assistant at the time, Dan Richter, in his excellent tome, *The Dream Is Over (London in the 60's, heroin, and John and Yoko)* (Quartet Books).

Fortunately for us, the Lennons' busy film-editing schedule meant they had to return to the job in hand after this brief break for dinner and a review of their peace initiatives. I later realised as we winged westwards to Toronto that the universe had been merciful in our not being drawn into any further futile discussions of what had apparently overtaken and perhaps even permanently scuttled the Toronto Peace Festival.

I merely reiterated to John and Yoko that I would do my best to sort out what was actually going on as soon as we reached Toronto, and would then report back to them. Ronnie just nodded along and said nothing. We agreed to put everything on hold until I completed my private investigations back in Canada.

Soon afterwards, John pulled himself out of his new-decade mental lethargy on the occasion of Yoko's 37th birthday, February 18. With Fawcett's help, John arranged for Yoko to wake up on the anniversary of her birth and be greeted by a bouquet of red roses. And then as the day unfolded, more bunches were delivered to the suite each hour. By evening, it exhaled an aromatic cloud of sweet scents - something akin to a huge rose garden at dusk.

You can readily imagine how wonderful this gesture made Yoko feel as the first anniversary of their March 20, 1969 wedding came into view. John's romantic side gave me a warm fuzzy feeling as well; when Fawcett related the tale to me, I was touched. But out on the reality road, and getting ready to return to base camp and Peace Festival headquarters in Toronto, the vibe didn't feel quite so inviting.

*FOOTNOTE

Michael de Freitas (aka Michael X) emigrated to London in 1957 and eight years later was described by The Observer newspaper as ``the authentic voice of black bitterness''. That same year, he was the first non-white person to be charged and imprisoned under the UK's Race Relations Act. He would be sentenced to 18 months' jail for publicly proclaiming that any black woman seen with a white man should be shot. He later founded the Racial Adjustment Action Society and set up a Black Power commune on Holloway Road. Michael would auction off the bag of Lennon locks (which had been snipped in Denmark in January) to aid in the funding of his Black House commune. The Black House mysteriously burned down in 1970 and Michael and four associates would be charged with extortion. His bail would be financed by John Lennon in January,1971.

A month later, Michael did a runner from the UK for his native Trinidad. He started up an agricultural commune which was inspired by black empowerment. It was located 16 miles east of the Trinidad capital, Port of Spain. He was quoted in the Trinidad Express espousing his motivation.

``The only politics I ever understand is the politics of revolution. The politics of change, the politics of a completely new system,' he said. He launched a new Black House commune which also burned down in February, 1972. That same year, he was tried for the murder of a member of his ``Black Liberation Army'', Joseph Skerritt.

Skerritt had reportedly refused to obey Michael's orders to attack a nearby police station. His body and that of Gale Benson, the daughter of British Conservative Party MP Leonard F. Plugge, were found in a shallow grave by police investigating the Black House fire. Michael X was captured in Guyana where he had fled a few days after the fire. He was charged with Benson's murder as well, but never tried.

The Save Malik Committee was formed (X was also known as Michael Abdul Malik) - members including Angela Davis, human rights guru Dick Gregory, Kate Millett plus high-profile counter-culture lawyer William Kunstler, whose services were provided courtesy of John Lennon. Michael X pleaded for clemency but was hanged in Port of Spain's Royal Gaol in 1975. John and Yoko Lennon had been steadfast supporters to the end.

17. HEADING BACK HOME TO FROZEN LAKES

> "Ain't it lonely, when you're living with a gun,
> When you can't slow down and you can't turn around,
> And you can't trust anyone ...."
>
> (Van Morrison from Who Was That Masked Man, c 1974)

Idle chatter was at a premium as the half-full Boeing 707 jetliner zoomed back across the Atlantic to Toronto from London that Thursday afternoon in late February. We - Ronnie Hawkins and yours truly - were certainly not at our best. We were tired from the nine-day London stay, exhausted from the five-week globe-trotting extravaganza and totally weary of the ridiculous rumor-mongering over the fate of John and Yoko's Canadian-based peace initiative. That good old sound of distant drums didn't sound joyful.

There was much on my mind, not the least the thought of a coming media confrontation: the looming probability that we were likely to be met in a couple of hours at the Toronto Airport arrivals gate by a squadron of media bent on getting the lowdown on the future of the Peace Festival. There had been no shortage of speculation about the possibilities leading up to our return. Was our peace dream all over? Was the festival an organisational shambles? Was our involvement with *War Is Over* over?

As predicted, after landing smoothly at Malton Airport we were greeted at the arrivals gate by several earnest journos along with photographers from the three Toronto dailies. Assuming an upbeat tone for the time being, I assured the scribes we were confident the Lennons would soon return to Canada because ``it's their festival and they've got to do it''. I insisted that John and Yoko very much wanted to be part of a Peace Festival. I further pointed out that I had been speaking to Yoko in London the previous evening and she'd told me she ``would never forgive herself if there was a war and they didn't do the Peace Festival''. Such off-the-cuff grist for the mill got the media off my back and gave us a few days' breathing space.

By now things were spinning along rapidly and it would only be a week before I again fronted the Toronto media, this time to continue boosting

Peace Festival possibilities but only as a side issue. I'd arrived at a crucial crossroads decision. It was time to pull the pin. The main mission was to announce my resignation from the festival's organizing nucleus, Karma Productions, although I left the door open to ongoing involvement with associated John and Yoko's peace initiatives. Key Karma promoter John Brower also attended this press conference and offered his explanation that ``Ritchie has burned himself out on his world peace tour and is just too tired to go on". At the same time as pulling out personally, I tried to bolster the Peace Festival's declining stocks.

``The peace aspect of the festival, which interests me the most, has taken a back seat to details like how many toilets will be needed, where water will come from and things like that. I decided that instead of going along with organisational details something I didn't understand I'd concentrate on my music and peace-related writing career,' I declared.

``There's an incredible response building up all over the world. Kids everywhere are making plans to go to Mosport (where the festival was to be held). It's going to be something like a religious event,' I soothed. I made these statements in an attempt to keep the festival hopes alive, at a time when it was submerging in doubt. There'd been too much severe media damage done to its body corporate.

In addition Rolling Stone publisher Jann Wenner - after reading his own magazine's coverage of the Peace Festival briefing in San Francisco - contacted me to advise that I could no longer contribute to the San Francisco-based counter-culture fortnightly paper if I continued to be associated with Karma Productions, the would-be producers of the Toronto Peace Festival. Rolling Stone had been frightened off by their correspondent's account of a meet-and-brief with the media at the Jefferson Airplane mansion in San Francisco, which had gotten very weird. Wenner's clear message was, "quit the Peace Festival fiasco or you're finished as a writer for this publication!" It was – I now realise an understandable ultimatum.

As it happened, I would in fact quit Rolling Stone within a few weeks, over an entirely different editorial concern which I won't go into detail about. Enough to say that it had something to do with a couple of players named God and Eric Clapton, of all people!

It didn't take me long to figure out many of the things that had gone wrong with the Peace Festival in my absence. But it wasn't all Brower's fault. What I found back at the Toronto home base was a horrible mess. Decay had set in after the desperation stage was passed. Greed had taken over from need as a succession of would-be profiteers seized upon the keepers of the keys at Karma Productions. Everybody seemed to want a slice of something - whatever they could connect with. The American media was strongly attracted to this breaking music story. In mid-February, the influential counter-culture journal The Village Voice sent their well-known rock writer Richard Goldstein to Toronto to write an update piece headlined: ``Canada & the New Age: Peacemaker to the World?''

Since I was off around the world selling the *War Is Over* message to other countries and John Brower was involved in duelling with Allen Klein et al over The Beatles' involvement with the Peace Festival, Karma Productions director Hugh Curry, a former deejay on Toronto rock station CHUM FM, was assigned the task of dealing with Goldstein on an official basis.

``In the short run, we want to produce the most incredible event in history,' Curry had extravagantly claimed. ``In the long run, I would like Karma to be an enlightened and as curious a production company as anyone could possibly imagine. To finance a pop festival, you've gotta be a high-roller. But a lot more than your wallet has to be in it. Your heart has to be there too.''

Goldstein had wisely interviewed Hugh Curry in his living quarters, which featured a number of items of ``Lennonmania''. And Curry readily admitted: ``The first time I saw John, I was surprised because he was stoned and looning about, and since he'd gotten into the peace thing, I thought he'd be more, well, intense. I guess I was looking for Jesus.'' These comments are indicative of the prevailing attitudes of some of the people associated with Karma Productions. There was a messiah-like regard for John and Yoko from many of the staff.

Richard Goldstein must have been impressed with Curry, for he described the promoter as a ``valuable asset'' to Karma Productions. ``With his neatly parted hair and his soft even voice … he's (white American pop crooner) Pat Boone as a hip public relations man.'' Goldstein might have been drawn to Curry personally but his published Peace Festival report was none too positive. Curry nonetheless would leapfrog from peace and love into the world of adult movie making, where he prospered.

The festival had arguably begun sliding off the tracks back in January when the snowbound and newly shorn Lennons had introduced a couple of extremely offbeat characters - a Dr ``Don'' Hamrick and his offsider, Leonard - into the organisational mix. These were people who had followed us over to Aarlborg, Denmark from North America, apparently at John's invitation with input from Melinda (girlfriend of Tony Cox, Yoko's ex-husband). It was part of an effort to help him quit the tobacco-smoking addiction which had long plagued him and Yoko. (And so many other unfortunate victims of Big Tobacco around the world. As a reformed smoker, I have to call it an insidious, evil substance which continues to poison the planet's inhabitants to this day.) John was so on the money when he penned the lyric ``...Although I'm so tired I'll have another cigarette, And curse Sir Walter Raleigh, He was such a stupid git...'' for his White album gem, *I'm So Tired.* Sir Walter Raleigh (1552-1618) was the British explorer who brought New World plants tobacco and potatoes back to Europe. Although both had earlier been imported by Spanish explorers, it was Raleigh who popularised the red man's burden of tobacco throughout European courts.

I personally suffer from severe C.O.P.D., even though I quit smoking tobacco that most insidious of personal poisons in 2001. In order to travel in an airplane, I have to utilize my oxygenator, but it's worth the effort.

I've known heroin devotees who have told me that quitting tobacco was immeasurably more difficult than cutting off smack. John and Yoko Lennon were no different. They had resorted to various techniques to quit their tobacco dependence but to this point had not been successful. That was the cue for the arrival of Dr Hamrick (the doctor prefix being his own invention) into the *War Is Over* scenario. He specialized in aiding addiction withdrawal through hypnotism.

Dr ``Don'' Hamrick and Leonard were members of a psychic cult called Harbinger, named after a place in California called Harbinger Springs, where it was based. The Harbinger group believed they were in contact with supernatural beings from another planet. These beings had plans - so it was said - to make a visit to Earth to save us from our own self-destruction. Another member of the Harbinger cult was Melinda Kendall.

Hamrick and Leonard obviously had bigger ambitions than getting the Lennons off the coffin nails. They quickly convinced John - who might reasonably be described as gullible in his free-thinking approach to most matters - that they should be part of the Peace Foundation, which was to be set up to distribute to worthy causes the projected profits from the Peace Festival and other related endeavours.

Because of John's apparent endorsement of the Harbinger crew, promoter Brower felt obligated to maintain that strange allegiance, no matter how oddball it became. And it certainly did become weird. ``Hamrick and Leonard have been in touch with cosmic spirits,' Brower declared in January, 1970, while I was away on the International Peace Tour. ``The Harbinger astrologers and numerologists have figured out the time and place for these cosmic forces to begin their work on planet Earth. The time is early this summer and it will happen in North America, but not in the United States." Brower had caught the fever. Or at least he was talking the talk.

These revelations notwithstanding, Hamrick and Leonard had also come up with a revolutionary concept for what they described as an ``air-car''. In simple terms, it was a two-passenger vehicle that could travel on the ground or in the air and was fuelled by psychic energy. They apparently had plans for John and Yoko to arrive at the festival on board one of these air-cars to launch the event. Certainly it would have been an attention getter.

That particular idea was fine to digest and contemplate among ourselves. But it was hardly grist for the outside rock mill, and certainly NOT appropriate for public consumption in such a ``house of the holy'' as that owned by West Coast underground music gurus, the Jefferson Airplane. But that's exactly what happened when John Brower took his Karma Productions advance crew to San Francisco in February, 1970, to discuss ways in which the West Coast music fraternity could assist John Lennon's Peace Festival cause.

Their reported task at this briefing was to stir up support for the Peace Festival (which was of course an East Coast-based event), to explain its intentions and to seek input from Californian counter-culture icons such as the Airplane. It was considered vital to have the Airplane's blessing. For that reason, it was arranged for the announcement/gathering to take place in the high-ceilinged and high-class glitzy living room of the Airplane's house/headquarters in San Francisco.

The Karma Peace Festival delegation's spokesman on this crucial occasion was a Toronto musician and greeter named David Britten (aka Sniderman), who acted as master of ceremonies while John Brower watched from the fireplace region of the large room. Britten, another member of the Harbinger cult, opened his spiel with an update on John Lennon. In the last two weeks, he claimed, John had ``really gotten his head together''. The source of this revelation was not revealed. On hearing about it later, I thought it was most presumptuous. But Britten really managed to shoot himself and his cred in both feet when he revealed that ``our interplanetary brothers'' had been contacted about the festival and would, in fact, attend. This outlandish claim certainly raised a few eyebrows and the assembled media felt an immediate need to pursue that line of questioning.

Britten went further and insisted that there were beings inhabiting every other planet in the universe as well as the moon. He said that astronaut

Neil Armstrong had not encountered these beings in his moon landing expedition because ``they live inside the moon''. Stating that he didn't want to go off on a tangent because the meeting he was addressing was meant to focus on other matters, Britten said that he personally had been in touch with ``our interplanetary brothers'' and that they had promised full co-operation.

The Jefferson Airplane's outspoken guitarist Paul Kantner had been remarkably restrained until this point in the preamble, but the ``interplanetary brothers'' shtick had taken matters to a new level of outrageousness. ``You'll have to forgive us,' Paul interjected, ``if we seem incredulous at your promise to bring us some people from outer space. If we're going to believe it, I think you're going to have to show us some proof. If you're going to talk supernatural, be supernatural. You know?''

Britten wasn't up to the challenge. There were many other questions about whether or not the festival would be free, which the delegation did their darndest to avoid being pinned down about. John Brower estimated that the festival would draw ``at least a million people''. One questioner suggested ``The Beatles' probable appearance'' could bring the figure as high as six million. At one point, Brower said that the festival would be gratis. Later he suggested it would be very cheap, say $5 for three days.

There would be no access for Hell's Angels members, who had been entrusted with the security detail at the ill-fated Altamont Festival the previous year at which four people died. A fence would keep them out. Altamont of course had stained the prospects of outdoor music festivals in a very profound way. This line of questioning finally led a bluffed-out Brower to exclaim: ``This thing is just an infant. It's just a baby. We don't have all the answers.'' To which the Airplane's Paul Kantner quipped: ``We're just trying to point out a few of the childhood diseases it's likely to have.''

Many other questions were either ignored or left hanging in the agitated air. Tom Donahue, San Francisco FM radio pioneer, local legend and acquaintance of the Lennons, presented the assembly with much food for further thought when he asked the rhetorical question: ``Why do we need a festival anyway? Why is the biggest festival necessarily going to be the best festival? That's a very American way of looking at things. Who says we need six million in one place at one time?''

Brower and Britten felt such comments represented outright hostility towards the Peace Festival concept. But that was not really true. As Rolling Stone writer Jon Carroll, who attended the briefing, noted perceptively: ``Almost everybody wants the festival to succeed, but the taste of disaster (as in the Altamont event featuring the Rolling Stones) was too fresh. At a time when John Lennon wanted to press the great crusade ever forward, the veterans (and victims) of Altamont wanted to rethink a few assumptions, to see if there's not a better way to get where everybody wants to go. And the Toronto people were so vague about so many important questions, so apparently unaware of the magnitude of what they were proposing, that many found it very hard to put aside their doubts and follow. The meeting didn't end so much as dissolve ..."

John Brower recently provided an interesting and highly relevant perspective on that fateful February afternoon in the San Francisco Bay Area, four decades down the track. "I gathered at the Jefferson Airplane house with an associate of mine named Jerry Hebscher along with two other people I'd brought along at John (Lennon's) insistence. Their names were David Sniderman (aka David Britten) and Leonard Holihan (aka Spaceman). They took over the whole affair. This was what I believed John and Yoko had wanted.

``So I was barely able to get a word out about the Peace festival site difficulties. Nor was I able to massage the bruised egos of the Airplane and Grateful Dead members present at this Peace Festival briefing. There was Grace Slick, Paul Kantner, Jorma Kaukonen, Jack Casady from the Airplane and Pig Pen and another guy from the Dead. Plus of course, there was ... Wenner and underground radio pioneer Tom Donahue.

``So Leonard started in about John and Yoko being aware of this universal shift in consciousness, and the fact that there were alien technologies that were going to be given to Earth that would transform our way of life. Then David Britten talked about the fact that aliens were going to make contact with us through John and Yoko. Then Leonard alerted everyone that John and Yoko would be arriving at the festival in an air-car powered by psychic energy."

Brower sat back to gauge the effect of this avalanche of insider information upon me 40 years later. He'd forgotten that I'd been there too, not necessarily in San Francisco that crucial afternoon but on the Peace Festival wavelength and I'd heard extensive details of all of this crazy stuff before.

"At that point, the whole room erupted with shouting that 'we were all fucked' and if that's what John and Yoko wanted, they could stick it and no one wanted to be part of it. Jack Casady stormed out, followed by Grace Slick. Jann Wenner turned to me, ashen-faced, and said, 'You're fucking ruining me ... this shouldn't be happening'. As you may recall, he was struggling and just keeping the magazine alive issue-to-issue in early 1970. He had gone way out on a limb with Peace Festival cover stories et cetera, but I believe was soon co-opted by (Allen) Klein to bury us. I'm just glad that there were no Hell's Angels there or Hebsher and I might not have gotten out of town. It was that heavy, man.

"Outside the Airplane's house, after the blow-up had happened, I told Leonard and David that they were out of the picture and to stay the hell away from our festival's Toronto office. And to find their own way back to Toronto. I had only bought them one-way tickets and that was the last I ever saw of either of them." Brower laughed heartily over delivering this explanation.

"I liked the way Anthony Fawcett described in his book *One Day at a Time* where he acknowledges that John finally realised the space people had gone too far. But apparently decided, 'Oh what the heck, let's just hang this whole fuck-up on Brower'. I must have resembled a coat-hook at the time."

Rolling Stone magazine's coverage of this extraordinary briefing - published in March 1970 on the same page as a pictorial feature on the Hong Kong border anti-war demonstration featuring Ronnie Hawkins and me - spread like wildfire. More than anything else, it would be the principal cause of a burst of negativity which in effect strangled the Lennon's involvement in the Peace Festival. You can judge for yourself whether that was warranted.

The Rolling Stone story of the San Francisco peace briefing profoundly alarmed the Lennons. In a shrewd ploy, Stone publisher Jann Wenner sent a telegram to John inviting him to get out there and tell his side of the Peace Festival saga. ``When the Toronto Peace Festival thing was looking like it was getting out of hand, I sent John Lennon a letter asking him to explain,' Wenner explained. Lennon responded with a lengthy chronological letter detailing of the history of the Toronto Peace Festival.

In his letter, which Rolling Stone published on April 16, 1970, John firstly acknowledged his initial no-reservations involvement with the concept. ``When Yoko and I were first contacted about the Peace Festival by Ritchie Yorke and John Brower - as usual with anything to do with peace - we said yes and hoped it would work itself out after. We did make it clear that we didn't want - and didn't have the ability - to handle any organisation - but we did want complete control - if our names were to be used to hustle the thing together.''

John then detailed how he had been asked to hustle up high-profile talent (think The Beatles/ Dylan/Presley) to be involved in the Peace Festival. He explained that after announcing the festival he and Yoko had moved on to a retreat in rural Denmark (actually pursuing Kyoko). "We'd had no phone for weeks,' John wrote, "being in a far-out farmhouse. When we finally got a phone, all hell let loose (also, we had been fasting - meditating, energy exchange, telepathy - for days). We got the horrors when our personal assistant A. Fawcett rang saying, 'Disaster, disaster. (Allen) Klein is frightening Brower off! - and the Canadian government doesn't like it and Brower won't touch the festival if Klein is involved!' And a lot more Aquarian paranoia."

John's written response went on at some length about the feud over finances and performance fees between promoter John Brower and Klein. Overlaying all this was John's growing belief that the Peace Festival should be free, which Brower insisted was physically impossible with the sort of upfront costs that local municipalities planned to slug the festival with for holding the event. Meanwhile, according to Brower, Klein was really not interested in peace and was only trying to sell a festival appearance by The Beatles as part of a reunion North American tour he was trying to float for a $2 million fee. It was possible for me to see merit in both sides of the free festival disagreement.

Lennon passionately pointed out that articles in The Village Voice, The New York Times and Rolling Stone were supposed to make his position clear but had failed to do so. So he had been forced to write the formal response. Yet he concluded in the lengthy piece: "In spite of everything - and you haven't heard half - Yoko and I would still like to be part of a Peace Festival in Canada or anywhere else. Our latest idea was to have everyone at the festival singing only Hare Krishna - including all those famous stars I'm supposed to be getting in touch with whom I'm sure will run a mile if I call them now, after all the shit of the last few months - anyway there wouldn't be any money involved in that! No chance! People would have to come for the right reasons whatever they are."

John also reacted to Tom Donahue's earlier questioning of the need for "the biggest festival" in the Rolling Stone coverage of the Peace Festival briefing at the Jefferson Airplane's house.

"Yoko and I still think we need (a peace festival) – not just to show that we can gather peacefully and groove to rock bands (as opposed to the Altamont disaster), but to change the balance of energy power. On earth, and therefore, in the universe.

"Have we forgotten what vibes are? Can you imagine what we could do together in one spot - thinking, singing and praying for peace - one million souls apart from any TV link-ups, etc to the rest of the planet? If we came together for one reason, we could make it together ... We need help! It is out of our control ... We are doing our best for all our sakes - we still believe."

But not, alas, in the Toronto Peace Festival. After Brower sent his revised festival plans to the Lennons in London, John telegrammed back: "Just read your report. You have done exactly what we told you not to. We said it was to be free. We want nothing to do with you or your festival. Please do not use our name or our ideas or symbols."

Unfazed, Karma Productions was busily responding with a seven-page draft press release which began: "John and Yoko Lennon are no longer involved with the Toronto Peace Festival planned for July 3, 4 and 5 at Mosport Park, But the festival will proceed as planned, according to the producers."

And it ultimately did. The Strawberry Fields Festival, as it would be called, took place August 6-8, featuring a significant bunch of artists including Procol Harum, Jose Feliciano, Ten Years After, Delaney & Bonnie & Friends, Mountain, Sly & the Family Stone, Alice Cooper, Grand Funk Railroad, The Youngbloods, Jethro Tull, Melanie and Canadian acts Crowbar, King Biscuit Boy, Lighthouse, Leigh Ashford and Fat Chance.

The event unfolded at Mosport Park, near Bowmanville, despite a raft of objections filed by local authorities who insisted that the venue could only be used for motor racing. The ever-shrewd promoter John Brower - along with festival producers Les Productions Sportive Ville-Marie Inc - managed to evade this difficulty by advertising the three-day event as a championship motorcycle race featuring "some contemporary entertainment". In the north-eastern US, however, the festival was publicized as a rock festival and the heavy-duty star-power-draw name of Led Zeppelin was bandied around. Not that they showed up. Brower did hand over a non-returnable $50,000 advance booking fee for Zeppelin to be part of the show.

The event was only legally permitted to proceed just hours before it was due to kick off when Supreme Court Justice D. A. Keith refused to grant an injunction sought by Ontario Attorney-General Arthur Wishart to stop Strawberry Fields from flowering due to health and public safety concerns. Dramatic stuff on the surface, but less so when one contemplates the subsequently revealed facts that Establishment authorities had always viewed the Lennon peace campaign with suspicion and apparent dread.

Declassified documents released through Freedom of Information laws in 2007 detailed a Royal Canadian Mounted Police report dated December 30, 1969, that the Canadian security service had begun spying on John and Yoko Lennon (and their associates, including myself and John

Brower) after the announcement of the Peace Festival. There was official paranoia abroad, and no wonder Brower had encountered such substantial obstacles on his journey to Strawberry Fields at Mosport. It's almost a crime in itself to ponder the resources and energies expounded by lawmakers and enforcers spying on our peace-believing group, while various criminal gangs and groups were unchecked. If it wasn't so outrageous, it would be funny!

This undoubtedly was a particularly tough time in John's life. As Fawcett would later write about the period: ``(John) withdrew again into the cold, reclusive state that I had come to accept as one of his character traits, having witnessed it so many times before - when he and Yoko had suffered abuse from both friends and the press; the miscarriages; the drug bust; the burden of the peace effort - the list seemed endless. John's personal crisis thus reached a breaking point, and it was not to be resolved until after Primal Therapy.''

The time had arrived for a perceptive therapist to drag John and Yoko out of the swamp of negativity in which they found themselves being immersed. These were tough and trying days in the kingdom of Bag. But would tomorrow be any better?

18. MEANWHILE SOMEWHERE BACK IN ENGLAND

``This man's book (*The Primal Scream : Primal Therapy, The Cure for Neurosis*) came in the post and when I read it I thought it was like Newton's Apple. 'This must be it!' I said. But I'd been so wrong in the past, with the drugs and with the Maharishi ... that I gave it to Yoko. She agreed with me, so we got on the phone ...'' JOHN LENNON

``Primal Therapy is not just making people scream. It was the title of a book. It was never 'Primal Scream Therapy'. Those who read the book knew that the scream is what some people do when they hurt. Others simply sob or cry. It was the hurt we were after, not mechanical exercises such as pounding walls and yelling 'mama'.'' ARTHUR JANOV

It would appear that the sons of Eastern European storekeepers would play an integral role in John Lennon's late-'60s and early-'70s life. First there was Allen Klein, who performed the role of The Beatles' business manager for a short period from 1969 into 1970. And then, as the new decade dawned, there was Arthur Janov, the son of a Russian-born grocer. The psychologist/ psychotherapist, born in Los Angeles in 1924, was the originator of a mode of treatment called primal scream therapy. His book, *The Primal Scream,* is regarded as a significant reference work on an individual's ability to cope with mental pain from the past and moving on from it.

One of the two appendices to the book was a seven-item quintessential guide for those seeking primal therapy. These are to abstain from smoking and drinking, to abstain from drug use, to cease tension-relieving habits, to be totally alone for 24 hours before therapy, to do exactly what the therapist says, not to work or go to school during the initial phase of therapy, and to attend a session with a group of post-primal patients. According to Dr Janov, primal therapy is not effective without strict adherence to these instructions.

In his groundbreaking book, Dr Janov claims that neurosis is caused by unsatisfied needs. He says: "Since the infant cannot himself overcome the sensation of hunger - or find substitute affection -he must separate his sensations from consciousness. This separation of oneself from one's needs and feelings is an instinctive manoeuvre in order to shut off excessive pain. We call it the split."

Dr Janov continued: "Painful things happen to nearly all of us early in life that get imprinted in all our systems which carry the memory forward, making our lives miserable. It is the cause of depression, phobias, pain and anxiety attacks and a whole host of symptoms that add to the misery." *

John and Yoko were instinctively drawn to what Janov was expounding in his book, so much so that in a phone conversation to Arthur Janov's Californian clinic, it was agreed that the learned psychologist would make a special trip to London and work with the famous pair. John and Yoko were, in effect, hooked and who's to say if it was positive or negative. Probably positive because time would show that it enabled him to produce his outstanding first (and penultimate) solo album, *John Lennon/Plastic Ono Band*.

It featured some of John's finest solo songs - *Working Class Hero, Mother, Isolation, Love, Remember* and *God*. This is unquestionably among John's finest work. "It's not really commercial,' John would subsequently reflect, "and some might say its downbeat and miserable, but it's important to me." The primal therapy treatments assisted John in creating these yardsticks of his career.

Two prominent bands from the 1980s were inspired by Janov's primal therapy riff - Primal Scream and Tears for Fears. The latter's Roland Orzabal acknowledged that his early lyrics came through the inspiration of Janov's therapy. "I would never write like that now,' he said in 2010.

"And I don't know why I did it. Other than the fact that I was influenced a little bit by (Manchester band) Joy Division. And their kind of blackness. I got very depressed when I was in my teens. And I think in those days you were allowed to express those feelings. They were almost fashionable."

In 1971, John Lennon offered this appraisal of Dr Janov's therapy:

"His thing is to make you feel the pain that's accumulated inside you ever since your childhood. In my case, I had to do it to kill off all the religious myths. In the therapy, you really feel every painful moment of your life. It's excruciating: you are forced to realise that your pain - the kind that makes you wake up afraid, with your heart pounding - is really yours and not the result of somebody up in the sky. It's the result of your parents and your environment.

"As I realised this, it all started to fall into place. This therapy forced me to have done with all the God shit. Most people channel their pain into God or masturbation or some dream of making it. (It's about) facing up to reality instead of always looking for some kind of heaven."

(From the Red Mole Interview, 1971.)

In another interview about primal therapy during this period, John allowed: "There's no way of describing it - it all sounds so straight just talking about it. What actually you do is cry. Instead of pent-up emotion, or pain, you feel it rather than putting it away for some rainy day. I think everybody's blocked. I haven't met anybody (sic) that isn't a complete blockage of pain from childhood, from birth on. It's like somewhere along the line we were switched off not to feel things, like for instance, crying.

``Men crying and women being very girlish or whatever it is, somewhere you have to switch into a role and this primal therapy gives you back the switch. You locate it and switch back into feeling just as a human being, not as a male or a female or as a famous person or not famous person. They switch you back to being a baby and therefore you feel as a child does, but it's something we forget because there's so much pressure and pain and whatever it is that is life, everyday life, that we gradually switch off over the years. All the generation gap crap is that the older people are more dead. As the years go by, the pain doesn't go away, the pain of living. You have to kill yourself to survive. This therapy allows you to live and survive without killing yourself."

Observed Anthony Fawcett: ``When Dr Janov arrived in London to work with the Lennons, I was surprised by his warmth and youthful appearance. He had the presence and aura of a Hollywood movie star rather than that of a psychologist, but I instinctively felt that John and Yoko would get on very well with him."

The first stage of primal therapy took three weeks. Janov scheduled a session with John and Yoko, separately, every day. It was the first time they had been physically apart for over two years.

After the first apparently grueling week at Tittenhurst Park, Fawcett wrote: ``It was decided that everyone should move up to London. John took a suite at the Inn on the Park Hotel. I went with Yoko, who was in a fragile and nervous state, and checked her into the Londonderry Hotel, a few yards down the street."

In his book, Janov described a patient's typical initial reaction to primal therapy. ``The first few days of therapy seem to parallel the first few years of the patient's life, before the occurrence of the 'Primal Scene' that shut him down. He experiences isolated and discrete events in bits and pieces. As each fragment combines into a meaningful whole, the patient goes into his primal.''

As a close-up observer, Fawcett had some pertinent observations about John's infatuation with primal therapy as a way of easing his pain. ``(His) layers of hurt had been building up since he was five when he was forced to make a choice between his father and mother. He chose his father, then at the last minute ran after his mother, only to be taken to his Aunt Mimi's house to be brought up. When a teenager, John got to know his mother again, but just as she was becoming his closest friend she was killed by a car in the street outside his house.

``The pain of his mother's death was so deep and so traumatic that John never let himself really feel it until therapy. His body shut down to the intolerable pain, requiring something to keep it hidden and suppressed. Neurosis served this function; it diverted John from his pain, and the resulting urgent yet unfulfilled needs were chanelled into his music. The layers of tension stored within John finally were released as he slowly made the connection with their origins. For 29 years he had buried the hurt, the fear, the aloneness. Now he could feel the pain and his own feelings, and he started writing songs again. I, too, had been rejected by my natural - but war-shattered - father. In his post-traumatic phase of shock, he lashed out at those closest to him and my mother and I suffered the violent consequences. It took a long time for me to learn that the cause of my distress was in fact the process of war and the scarring of its participants. It taught me that soldiers and their families are all victims of war.

Significantly, Dr Janov would later comment about his diagnosis of John: ``He had about as much pain as I've ever seen in my life.'' Other celebrities who would embrace Dr Janov's primal therapy were actors James Earl Jones and Dyan Cannon, and middle-of-the-road pianist Roger Williams. Apple's CEO Steve Jobs was a brief enthusiast.

It was around this point of the Lennons' immersion into primal therapy that I flew over from Toronto for my second London visit in 1970. After making contact with Anthony Fawcett at Apple's Bag One offices, I discovered to my dismay that John and Yoko had closed their door and essentially cut off contact with the outside world. They were not receiving visitors - of any persuasion. They were now locked away with Dr Janov in their pursuit of emancipation through primal therapy and could not be disturbed.

Accordingly, I booked myself into the Inn on the Park and proceeded to chase down interviews with such a flock of rock legends as Steve Stills, Eric Clapton and Bee Gee Maurice Gibb and his partner, pop star Lulu. Despite gaining some success with this, I was feeling a strange uneasiness. Something wasn't quite right. Over several days of meandering around the London rock landscape, it became quite clear that a certain weirdness was uncoiling in The Beatles' camp.

I decided to make the pursuit of Paul McCartney for an interview my top priority while in London. Like a true newshound, I'd sniffed something out in the aftermath of the Lennons' departure from the Peace Festival organisation and I wanted to be well and truly across this looming new development. Maybe it would be the next big Beatles' scoop?

Paul McCartney's private phone kept ringing and ringing and was finally answered by a pseudo-Pakistani voice. It was in fact Paul himself, pretending to be a Pakistani to avoid having to deal with any unsolicited calls. I had obtained Paul's x personal number from John Lennon's private phone book, so I knew it was the real deal. Anthony Fawcett assured me it was legitimate, although he admitted with a sly grin that his boss hadn't had any cause to dial it over the past few months. So I kept dialing. But Paul wasn't having any of it. ``No, no, no, zere is no Paul here. You must have zee wrong number,' said the voice. Click!

``C'mon Paul, I know it's you,' I said in the first of several return calls, ``I'm John Lennon's friend from the peace campaign and I just wanted to have a quick chat with you. Just a couple of quick questions, if you would be so gracious.'' There was a slight pause. ``No, no Paul here. Wrong number please.'' I finally gave up and felt like I'd embarrassed myself. But I had to get the message through to him. I just knew something was up.

And so - being reduced to a traditional journalistic back-up plan - I decided to write a personal letter to Paul, virtually begging him for an audience. This was early April, 1970 - there were no emails, faxes or any other medium. It was a phone call, a telegram or a delivered letter. I chose the letter route. Once completed, I asked the concierge if a member of the hotel staff could make a St John's Wood delivery for me.

The young bellboy selected for this task was totally unprepared for what would unfold before his eyes that sunny spring afternoon in London. Neither was I, although I was highly suspicious that there had been serious life-changing developments in The Beatles' camp. I just couldn't put my finger on what they were. And so I sent the bellboy to deliver a letter to Paul McCartney's house in posh St John's Wood, not two miles distant. I ordered up a traditional British room service tea and scones with clotted cream and strawberry jam (when in Rome!) and awaited his return and hopefully, a positive response from Paul. I certainly wasn't ready for the story our eager bellhop told me.

The boy was absolutely horrified by what he'd seen on this journey. ``Oh Mr Yorke, I tried to do what you asked,' he gushed. ``I went by taxi to the address you gave me in St John's Wood and I knocked on the door as you instructed and waited but there was no answer. I could hear noises inside the house so I knew somebody was in there. I knocked again but still there wasn't any answer. So I went back to get in the taxi and that's when I saw the front door of the house open and I couldn't believe what happened next.

``Ringo Starr was backing out of the doorway and he was being shoved quite violently by Paul McCartney! Shoved and pushed, in a most unbecoming manner. It was quite nasty. I just couldn't believe what I was seeing. It was a terrible shock.'' He took a deep breath and you could see he had been deeply moved by these developments. As would the whole world be moved! The boy had been a frontline witness to history unfolding.

Months later the principals involved would in fact reveal what had been behind the fracas. ``We (the other Beatles) didn't want to put out *Let It Be* and Paul's (solo album] at the same time,' John declared. ``It would have killed the sales. There has to be (considered and planned) timing. Paul's was just an ego game. We asked Ringo to go and talk to him because Ringo hadn't taken sides (in our disputes) or anything like that, and he had been straight about it, and we thought that Ringo would be able to talk fairly to Paul. I mean, if Ringo agreed that it was unfair, then it was unfair. Ringo went and asked him and he attacked Ringo and he started threatening him and everything, and that was the kybosh (to the whole thing) for Ringo.''

Further explanation was later provided by Apple's promotions manager Tony Bramwell: ``Ringo offered to go round to see Paul and try to explain to him ... that his [solo] album should be delayed to allow the effective release of *Let It Be*, which resulted in a strong argument and Ringo leaving Paul and deciding to let the album go out on the date McCartney had insisted upon.''

Ringo himself viewed it a tad differently. ``They (John and George) didn't send me around. They, as directors of the company, wrote a letter to him, and I didn't think it was fair that some office lad should take something like that around. I offered to take it round - I couldn't fear him then. But he got angry because we were asking him to hold his album back and the album was very important to him. He shouted and pointed at me. He told me to get out of his house. He was crazy: he went crazy. He was out of control ... prodding his finger towards my face. He told me to put on my coat and get out. I couldn't believe what was happening. I had just brought the letter." Touching times indeed!

McCartney himself would later bare his heart and reveal: ``Ringo visited me, bringing two letters signed by George and John with which he said he agreed. These letters confirmed that my record had been stopped. I really got angry when Ringo told me that (Allen) Klein had told him that my record was not ready and that he had a release date for the *Let It Be* album. I knew that both of these alleged statements were untrue and I said, in effect, that this was the last straw, and 'If you drag me down, I'll drag you down'. What I meant was, 'Anything you do to me, I will do to you'."

Obviously the end-game rot had set in. And if John and Yoko had not been so infatuated with primal therapy (and with the news that Yoko was again pregnant), they might have been more attuned to the approaching storm. On Thursday, April 9, London's The Daily Telegraph reported that on doctor's orders (Dr Arthur Janov) John and Yoko were not talking to each other nor sleeping together. Dr Janov had imposed the restriction as part of his primal therapy treatment, and the couple could communicate only in writing.

Later that day, Paul McCartney put through a call to his old songwriting partner at Dr Janov's private clinic in inner London where he'd set up shop for his therapy with the Lennons. John later said that Paul informed him: ``I'm doing what you and Yoko were doing last year. I'm putting out an album and I'm leaving the group, too. And I said, 'Good!'.''

The next day, when the official break-up announcement was made by Paul, long-time publicist and close friend Derek Taylor openly admitted to feeling very sad, as well he might.`` Because of how it's always been,' explained Derek. ``We live day-to-day here and we live with events, but we sometimes look back to the days when we were younger. When we were all on the road together. While the four of them are alive, there is still The Beatles.

``There is no such thing as an ex-Beatle or a former Beatle or a retired Beatle, because The Beatles are something other than a pop group. Many pop groups have broken up, but The Beatles are not a pop group, they are an abstraction, a repository for many things. I think they fulfil something in the media, for something that's there, that's cheerful and human and rich and, somehow, invulnerable.

"If The Beatles is alive as an idea, The Beatles is alive, then, all four Beatles will respond to that idea, at some time or other and will become Beatles again." Beautifully expressed, I thought.

Even though that wasn't likely to be happening in the near future, Paul had some immediate misgivings for bringing the group's career to an end. "Once it was clear we weren't doing The Beatles any more, I got real withdrawals and I had serious problems,' Paul ultimately confessed.

"I just thought, 'Fuck it! I'm not even getting up, don't even ring, don't set the alarm.' I started drinking, not shaving, I just didn't care, as if I'd had a major tragedy in my life and was grieving ... and I was." Paul was not alone.

John, on the other hand, was extremely angry, and all of us around him instinctively knew it. He - the one who had started the band and had been the first member to threaten to quit - later admitted publicly: "I was cursing because I hadn't done it. I wanted to do it. I should have done it ... 'Ah, damn, shit! What a fool I was ...' We were all hurt that he didn't tell us what he was going to do. I think he claims that he didn't mean that to happen, but that's bullshit!"

Even Allen Klein joined the subsequent (revisionist) chorus, commenting specifically on Paul's well-known dislike of him, both personally and professionally. "It's never pleasant when someone appears not to like you. I think his reasons are sad. They are his own personal problems, but unfortunately, he is obligated to Apple for a considerable number of years, so his disassociation with me has really no effect.'

For their part, the Lennons bunkered down with their recovery mission. At the end of their three-week course in London, Janov convinced John and Yoko that to continue their apparently successful therapy, they would need to move to Los Angeles and continue this work for a further four months. He couldn't stay away from his home base clinic in Santa Monica any longer.

Whereupon John and Yoko – taking his message seriously locked up Tittenhurst Park, shut down their Bag One Productions office, said goodbye to Fawcett (who later chased after Janov's daughter), and John applied for a temporary US visitor's visa to enable him to further his medical treatment with Dr Janov. It was considered vital that after their private sessions, the couple partake in several months of twice-weekly sessions.

War was over for the time being, the peace campaign set aside. The Lennons spent four months living in a rented house in Bel Air watching mindless TV or slipping out to ice-cream (as opposed to I Scream!) parlors. The good doctor had instructed them: ``Don't control yourself in any way - do what your body wants.'' The world's most famous couple would not require a second invitation.

*FOOTNOTE

In January 2011, Dr Janov added to his earlier therapy conclusions in an internet blog: ``As I have reiterated, the only time we can rewire deviated set-points is when the brain retreats to an earlier prenatal time and deals directly with the original causes of deviation. This means getting below repression and into history with every fibre of our being, and that history contains life before birth.

Late research seems to confirm this assumption. Scientists from Massachusetts Institute of Technology have found that the brain becomes much easier to rewire the younger we are. In the journal Current Biology (Oct 14, 2010), lead author, Marina Bedny suggests that as we get older it is much more difficult to rewire the brain. ``Most circuits are pretty well fixed,' noted Dr Janov. ``I wonder if it is not easier to rewire the brain when we go back and relive those very early brain states. It may be why we see such progress in those patients who do successfully relive early imprints. This may defy current research which indicates how difficult it is to rewire circuits later in life.

``Let me be clear about all this: any intervention by a therapist after the critical period can only be palliative. The warm, attentive doctor can only provide a cushion against the impact of the internal pain. That warmth cannot penetrate deep enough to attack the original imprint. Of course, the patient will feel better; she has been palliated, and that feels good, as I have reiterated. The analysis of transference, understanding one's pattern of behavior toward the doctor cannot make fundamental change, nor can any insight therapy; the shuttered sensory window won't permit it. Repression is locked into place. It stops any deep penetration. It keeps us on a superficial level.''

19. THE NEW YORK YEARS

> "Because it is sometimes so unbelievable, the truth escapes being known."
>
> HERACLEITUS, 500 BC

The Lennons, to their credit, stuck at the primal therapy routine for four long months in Los Angeles during that summer of 1970. As the Vietnam War raged and American political affairs were extremely troubling to those who cared, John and Yoko tried their darnedest to make the therapy work for them. When they finally parted company with Dr Janov late that summer, they did so on comparatively good terms.

After declining to star in a promotional film of himself and Yoko undergoing primal therapy (``Who are you kidding, Dr Janov?''), John did offer some illuminating overview comments on his outlook on the treatment. ``I still think that Janov's therapy is great, you know, but I do not want to make it a big Maharishi thing (a reference to The Beatles' work with Maharishi Mahesh Yogi). I just know myself better, that's all. I can handle myself better. That Janov thing, *The Primal Scream* and so on, it does affect you - because you can recognize yourself in there. It was very good for me. I am still 'primal' and it still works. I no longer have any need for drugs, the Maharishi or The Beatles. I am myself and I know why.''

But according to his closest aide in that period, Anthony Fawcett, John Lennon definitely was not ``cured'' by primal therapy. "Cured" is a very big word, of course. But in Fawcett's view, the therapy helped John to cope with his inherent pain and he underwent a ``significant growth experience'' at Dr Janov's clinic. But, says Fawcett, John was ``in more pain when he left California than before, but now he could cope - he could channel it and work with it''.

Given the benefit of a 40-year perspective, Yoko Ono told me in mid 2010 that primal therapy had been ``crucial in John's personal evolution''. ``Dr Janov told us that in order for it to work, we firstly had to sleep in separate rooms. We didn't want to do that but we went along with it. I don't think it went on for more than a week because we couldn't stand it (the separation). But the moment we went into separate bedrooms, there was an article in the London press saying 'John and Yoko are now in separate beds'." (The Daily Telegraph reported on April 9 that "John Lennon and his wife Yoko Ono are not talking to each other and not sleeping together - on doctor's orders".)

"I think that kind of thing made some people happy - the fact that John and Yoko were apart,' Yoko observed slyly in 2010. "The months we spent in LA as patients of Dr Janov was something else. When we were in LA getting it done (from March until July, when they were forced to leave the country), we tried to keep a low profile. We felt a little comfort and freedom (in LA) from the eyes of Fleet Street journalists (in London)"

The results of all of these developments - Paul McCartney pulling the pin on The Beatles, the primal therapy, the personal growth - provided the impetus for a flurry of songwriting, which resulted in the brutally honest repertoire which characterizes his first solo album, *John Lennon/ Plastic Ono Band*. He established some lyrical landmarks in painting a picture of his true persona through the grooves of that album. He spoke truthfully from the heart. He crystallized his outlook into the profound lyrics of his 1970 classic, God: "I was the walrus, But now I'm John, And so dear friends, You'll just have to carry on, The dream is over."

And over that dream would undoubtedly be. Those of us (not including myself, as I was abundantly aware that the race had already been run and there would be no return performance) secretly hankering for the Liverpool lads to abandon their differences and get back together again were whistling up a broken chimney. Anguish was well and truly abroad in John Lennon's life in the early '70s. But his involvement with primal therapy led him away from the flowery and complicated Beatles' post-Sgt Pepper composing style and back towards a more primitive rock'n'roll style. This would be reflected in upcoming musical works.

After the release of his new album, John was permitted by immigration authorities to visit New York as a tourist. Manhattan had been Yoko's home for 15 years before meeting John and undoubtedly she longed to be back in that realm of the avant garde art world. That time had finally arrived. And John felt totally at home in the Big Apple, where the hum of human activity was a 24/7 adventure.

The Lennons returned to Tittenhurst Park in London and stayed there well into 1972. During that period, John and Yoko set up an operating recording studio within their Georgian manor house and recorded the Imagine album. And they organised the shooting of 40,000 feet of album-production film footage to accompany its release. Then the cry of

Kyoko, Yoko's long-lost daughter, came through the clutter of album production - the nine-year old was reported to be in the Virgin Islands.

The Lennons hurried there on a wild goose chase involving a court appearance which ultimately led them to New York and long-term domesticity in the Big Apple. In court, Yoko tabled an application for custody of Kyoko. Her ex-husband Tony Cox, in a legal manoeuvre, challenged the Virgin Islands proceedings in Houston, Texas. Because Cox and Kyoko were living in Texas, the Lennons felt it was time to establish a foothold on mainland US soil. The Big Apple was a natural choice.

Predictably, the radical New Left (true opportunists in the form of two Yippies) jumped on to the John Lennon wavelength the moment they heard his flight had touched down at JFK Airport. As John summed it up: ``I got off the boat, only it was an aeroplane, and landed in New York, and the first people who got in touch with me were Jerry Rubin and Abbie Hoffman. It's as simple as that. It's these two famous guys from America who's calling; `Hey yeah, what's happenin', what's goin' on?' And the next moment you know I'm doing John Sinclair benefits ... I'm pretty movable, as an artist, you know. They almost greeted me off the plane and the next minute I'm involved!''

This would be an involvement with unexpected restraints. It wasn't all positive, by any definition. Rubin and Hoffman were controversial characters. They were not held in high esteem by US authorities and their association with Lennon only invited more surveillance of John and Yoko's life. A new double album, *Some Time in New York City,* was presented in the format and manner of a newspaper with song-title headlines and lyrics reading as articles and news. Its motto was ``Ono news that's fit to print'', paraphrasing The New York Times' well-known statement of purpose, "All the news fit to print". But the album was heavily dissed by critics, including long-time Lennon supporters. The album contained several Yoko songs and John's landmark declaration in a song title, *Woman is the Nigger of the World.*

John called them his ``front-page songs'' and he and Yoko explained the context in a contribution to Sun Dance magazine: ``The songs we wrote and sang are subjects we and most people talk about, and it was done in the tradition of minstrels - singing reporters - who sang about their times and what was happening.'' The album jacket would also feature in the weather masthead box, words from the First Amendment of the American Constitution: ``Congress shall make no law ... abridging the freedom of speech.''

John would later admit: ``That was when I got into the so-called `political songs', which I don't think are the best songs I've ever written, because I was trying too hard. But the concept I was trying to get over was writing about what the people are saying now. And that's what I lost myself in - by not writing what I was thinking and saying. It worked in *Give Peace a Chance*, but it didn't work in other songs."

Some Time would be John's first musical failure, commercially. The critics at large raged against the album. Even long-time Lennon lovers went to town. Rolling Stone's Stephen Holden blasted forth with a claim the album ``was so embarrassingly puerile as to constitute an advertisement against itself ... Only a monumental smugness could allow the Lennons to think that this witless doggerel wouldn't insult the intelligence and feelings of any audience."

More than one observer concluded that John had been listening and responding to and mixing with the wrong sort of people. In retrospect, it seems obvious that John had been led down the wrong sort of garden path by people with questionable agendas. It was all about his open-mindedness in dealing with sundry newcomers. He gave people a chance to be heard but they weren't always good people with noble aspirations. John would reveal in 1974 that although initially he had been fascinated by the antics of media celebrities such as Jerry Rubin and Abbie Hoffman, now ``I prefer to meet people like (Southern playwright) Tennessee Williams.

``I have to admit that some of my early political activities with Yoko were pretty naïve,' John confessed. ``But Yoko was always political in an avant-garde kind of way. She had this idea that you must always make use of the newspaper publicity to get across the idea of peace. The trouble with Rubin and Hoffman was that they never wanted laughter - they wanted violence. I've never been into violence myself ... *All You Need is Love*, like the song says. That's really my ultimate political belief. We all need more love. I found that being political interfered with my music. I'm still a musician first, not a politician."

As his sometime-girlfriend May Pang would note in her excellent candid memoir, *Instamatic Karma* (St. Martin's Press, March 2008): ``John was hurt by the rejection of his (*Some Time in New York City*) music, so he took his new album very seriously." When the London-based general manager of Apple Records, Tony King, turned up on the Lennons' American doorstep, he provided John with a contemporary heads-up on his cred in the music community after the *Some Time* letdown.

King informed John that the world now saw him as an angry radical, which wouldn't boost his record sales. According to King, John needed to make a backward turn towards being ``the jovial, witty guy everyone loved'', in May Pang's words. These observations set the stage for the *Mind Games* album, which represented something of a return to form.

According to Bob Gruen, the New York City photographer who virtually became the Lennons' ``outside in-house'' photographer through the '70s, John was at this time (1973) ``distressed and depressed'' about the election won in November, 1972, by Republican Richard Nixon in a landslide, about the criticisms of *Some Time In New York City*, about his various legal and financial problems - and he was overwhelmed.

"He was drinking a lot. Yoko, in contrast, was sober and anxious to keep working, to keep going. Shortly after the night I dropped him off at May Pang's (John and Yoko had temporarily separated by then), John went to Los Angeles ... I think it was John's friend Elliot Mintz who first dubbed that period John's `Lost Weekend', after the Ray Milland movie (The Lost Weekend) about a man who descends uncontrollably into drink. John's `Lost Weekend' went on for more than a year and was marked by a lot of wild nights.''

Even Ray Charles and Stevie Wonder (who teamed up with him in Burbank Studios, LA, on the only night Paul and John jammed together, post-Beatles) could see that John Lennon was profoundly depressed with his tormented life at this point. All the accumulated early-life baggage and grief (as expressed eloquently in the 2009 film, *Nowhere Boy*) of his life - compounded by the prison-wagon-like encirclement of US government surveillance - had all but brought John to his knees.

It is not the focus of this book nor my desire to delve into this period of John's personal life. My book focuses on John's involvement with the peace campaign. It is not concerned with the trials and tribulations of his often-turbulent existence. What price has to be paid to be a prophet in your own time?

On July 17, 1974, the US Justice Department - under the Nixon regime - ordered Lennon to leave the States within 60 days or be deported. This ludicrous Immigration fiasco would continue for two long and upsetting years at substantial cost to John and Yoko. Understandaly they felt they were in the right place at the wrong time until July 27, 1976, when John 's application to remain in the US as a permanent resident was finally and formally approved. It was an endorsement that had been far too long in coming, and cruel in its intent and impact.

Suffice to say that in a creative sense, John Lennon withdrew from the recording scene and did not release any new music from February, 1975 (the Rock' n' Roll album), until 1980's Double Fantasy (released November 15). Instead he focused intently on being a new-age father to a new-world son, after his reconciliation with Yoko. John would be to Sean the father that his own father Alfred had never been for him. This obviously would be a heavy and all-encompassing emotional experience for a paternally deprived man in his mid-30s, still hurting from the outright rejection by his father when he was two. Lennon was dazed and confused and bitterly hurt - not a good place to be launching out from.

And then there had been Julian, always a painful subject to John because of his inherent guilt that by continually being absent on tour with The Beatles, he had somehow failed his own son, if not rejected him. As his father Alfred had done to him. This might tend to sound too much like soap-opera dynamics but in John Lennon's reality, the enduring pain was an ugly icing on the cake of life.

Julian was born April 8, 1963, to John and Cynthia (nee Powell) Lennon, a few weeks before The Beatles' first barnstorming tour of North America. The demands of the touring life - and the astonishing everyday realities of simply being part of the most celebrated pop group of all time were paid in the form of John's perceived loss of relationship with his son. He would pay an extremely painful penance as Julian grew up ``distanced'' from his famous father. It was a touchy subject that John approached most gingerly in the mid-'70s.

May Pang offers some stunning shots of John and his son in her book, *Instamatic Karma*. May writes in a touching fashion about taking her shots of John with his then 10-year-old son: ``When John laid eyes on him for the first time in four years, he was shocked to see `a little man' and not the small child he remembered.'' For John, the relationship with Julian was fraught with thoughts of what hadn't happened before. May dedicated her book to a number of Lennon associates but drew special attention to John's first son. ``Julian, for all your help and all the smiles. Your dad would certainly be proud of how his `little man' has become a thoughtful humanitarian and talented artist.''

I can only say a hearty Amen to those sentiments. Most recently, Julian was the executive producer of a powerful, poetic and environmentally friendly Australian-based film, *The Gathering*, telling the story of indigenous people's connection with the planet at large and whales in particular. There has also been news of Julian and Sean Lennon linking up in 2009 in both a musical and sibling sense. It makes me feel good to hear that. They needed to spend more time together.

Sean Ono Lennon was born in 1975 on his father's birthday, October 9, and as Rolling Stone magazine's Chet Flippo would write in his incisive account of Lennon's so-called private years, ``both (John and Yoko) viewed (him, Sean) as the perfect child capable of being reared under ideal conditions to become an ideal human being: one free of sexism and racism and all the other-isms that John and Yoko felt were branded upon helpless children''.

This comment very much reflected the Lennons' outlook when I was working on the peace campaign with them. Writing about this takes me back to a sunny winter afternoon in the Ronnie Hawkins homestead a few days prior to Christmas in late 1969, sitting with John and Yoko and pondering a peaceful alternative to the war mentality which surrounded us at every turn. We agreed that it all had to start with the kids. They were the ones who could take on the new reality and not respond to the previous generation's reluctant but regimented response to any call for arms.

We rapped extensively about what might help bring about that awareness. Maybe if we eliminated war games and toys of violence from a child's upbringing, he or she wouldn't grow up with a cowboys-and-Indians attack mentality. Perhaps if we introduced a whole new range of peaceful toys we could subvert the violent streak which seems to thread itself through the human race. But creating new kinds of toys would initially involve huge investments. Maybe we could raise enough money for the International Peace Fund to cover the underwriting of designing and producing the right kind of adolescent amusements. We knew we had to break the pattern of young boys playing at soldiers and imagining violence against other beings. Toy guns had to go - and the thought patterns which inevitably arrived with them.

A penchant for violence tended to accompany the thought processes and protest plans of Jerry Rubin and Abbie Hoffman and many of their cohorts. There can be little doubt - in hindsight that these counter-culture agitators saw in John Lennon's enormous media pulling power a chance to further their personal agendas and interests. And I believe John came to realise that his initially enthusiastic link-up with their agendas became a big negative. It did not contribute anything positive in allowing him to obtain residence status in the United States.

As various FBI Freedom of Information documents have subsequently revealed, the Nixon administration was most alarmed by the Lennon-Rubin-Hoffman relationship. Authorities feared that the combination had plans to disrupt political gatherings and conventions, and set about tailing them and spying on their communications. Further details of this draconian monitoring of John and Yoko's early American life can be found in Jon Wiener's painstakingly assembled book, *Come Together : John Lennon in his Time* (Random House 1984).

Interestingly, Rubin faded from the political scene after being dismissed as an inconsequential phoney by a new generation. He became involved with promoting various health aids and therapies. Hoffman was charged with selling cocaine (he claimed he was set up), underwent facial plastic surgery to disguise his appearance and disappeared from sight, until returning to Wall Street after the end of the Vietnam War. He evolved into an entrepreneur and businessman, and was an early investor in Apple computers. He was struck by a car while jaywalking in Los Angeles on November 14, 1994, and died two weeks later. Strange karma!

Abbie Hoffman, who had bipolar disorder among other disfunctions, claimed to have been influenced in his life by John Lennon, Marshall McLuhan, Che Guevara, Herbert Marcuse and Groucho Marx. During his infamous confrontation with Pete Townshend of The Who on the stage at Woodstock - where he tried to persuade the vast audience to abandon sex, drugs and rock 'n' roll and pledge support to jailed Detroit activist John Sinclair - he was berated by the charismatic guitarist.

``I was in the process of adjusting my amp between songs on the Woodstock stage and this nutter Abbie Hoffman jumps up to the microphone and started yelling out stuff about John Sinclair, the Michigan radical,' Townshend told me during a long interview at his house in South London the following year. He said he had rammed Hoffman with his guitar and told him to ``fuck off from my stage''. Townshend admitted to pushing Hoffman, who later claimed to be on a bad acid trip, off his stage. Six months after this intrusion, Townshend was still seething about the uninvited guest invading the band's sacred stage precinct.

Abbie Hoffman was 52 years old when he committed suicide in 1989 with an overdose of pharmaceutical drugs.

Rock'n' Roll was released in February, 1975. (An anthology entitled Shaved Fish was released on October 24 that year). Sean Lennon was born on October 9 and John retreated out of the music biz spotlight and focused his life on his new son. In a sense, he gave up music for a substantial period but he would return.

John revealed in one of his last interviews that Yoko had suggested to him after the birth of Sean that he didn't have to make new records continually. A regular chain of new discs was not essential in the bigger picture, she explained. That possibility apparently had never occurred to him before, once The Beatles' bandwagon had begun rolling and the protocols of a functional pop group took control of his life.``Walking away is much harder than carrying on,' he observed. ``It was more important to face myself and face reality than to continue a life of rock'n'roll. Could the world get along without another John Lennon album? Could I get along without it? I finally realised the answer to both questions was `yes' ''.

As Yoko concluded in a 2010 interview with me, ``John had been liberated from that kind of thinking. I don't think he felt that he had to dish out (an album) every year just to prove that he could''. So John bowed out of the rock scene and the political scene. His critics have carped on about his not attending the May,1975, *War Is Over* rally on Mother's Day in New York's Central Park, just over the road from where he lived. It was all about the end of the futile and feral Vietnam War.

On April 30, the last Americans had escaped from the roof of the US Embassy in helicopter bailouts. The official death toll was 56,555 Americans dead, 303,654 wounded and an expenditure by American taxpayers of $111 billion. Vietnamese casualties were likely to be in excess of one million. John was missing that day although he'd always pursued the anti-war and anti-Vietnam agenda.

It wasn't that he didn't care. Or didn't feel the non-violent vibe. It was just that he'd long since fought that war on a philosophical level and had personally moved on. He also was not involved in the historic first ``rock'' presidential campaign (1976) fueled by music industry money and endorsements. Thanks to John's leadership in connecting with Canadian Prime Minister Pierre Trudeau in 1969, the rock game was finally getting in tune with contemporary politics.

The Allman Brothers Band and Capricorn Records founders Phil Walden and Frank Fenter (both now deceased) were the initial backers of Democrat Jimmy Carter's campaign in 1976 - and he would be the winner. Although President Carter has taken a lot of stick in recent times over his criticism of the war-fueled agendas of certain nations, he remains a true peace advocate in my book. In addition, his recognition of the rights of the gentler sex in rejecting mainstream religious attitudes to women in 2015, was equally perceptive and compassionate. I had the great pleasure of meeting President-to-be Carter at the Capricorn Records annual barbecue in Macon, Georgia, in 1975. Messrs Walden and Fenter remain etched in my memory as two of the finest and most caring music industry entrepreneurs I encountered in a half-century journey.

John also missed out on being part of the Rock Against Racism festivals in the UK in the late'80s. But he'd condensed that whole story into one three-minute anthem in 1970, the exquisite plea for human sanity, *Imagine*. A supreme universal hymn.

The July, 1976, hearing before Judge Kaufman of the Immigration Service would represent a huge breakthrough in John Lennon's life. He was offered the opportunity to make a statement to the court. ``I'd like to publicly thank Yoko, my wife, for looking after me and pulling me together for four years, and giving birth to our son at the same time. There were many times that I wanted to quit, but she stopped me. I'd also like to thank a cast of thousands, famous and unknown, who have been helping me publicly and privately for the last four years. I hope this is the end of it.''

And an end it was, to one of the most pathetic immigration episodes in US history. When one thinks of some of the low-lifes and assorted scumbags who have travelled in and out of America unimpeded over the 20th century, the campaign to try to toss out John Lennon was not only immoral but absolutely insulting to his great humanitarian character.

The following year, when John's all-time music idol, Elvis Presley, died in a fit of over-consumption in August, John perceptively observed: ``The king is always killed by his courtiers. The king is overfed, overdrugged, overindulged, anything to keep the king tied to his throne. Most people in that position never wake up. What Yoko did for me was to liberate me from that situation ... she showed me what it was to be Elvis Beatle and not be surrounded by sycophants and slaves who were only interested in keeping the situation as it was."

These types are just like the cabal which controls the drug and vice laws in virtually every country - grasping and maintaining a miserable status quo because it suits and profits certain influential groups. These evil forces will continue to campaign to maintain their contemptible control. Greed rears its ugly head yet again. This is one of the major problems confronting the evolution of the human species, in my humble opinion. I believe that John and Yoko shared that outlook.

John did not plan to be a ``househusband'' forever. He merely wanted to maintain a close up hands-on of involvement with Sean's upbringing until the lad was five years old. The concept was for Sean either to go to an appropriate school or study under a tutor at that time. But then he and Sean made a sailing trip to Bermuda where John heard quirky Atlanta pop band the B-52s producing risky but successful music that reminded him of Yoko's earlier avant garde musical work. That's when he finally realised that it was time for the recording of a new Lennon album. He'd been off the scene for long enough. And he stumbled into the album's inspirational title in the most romantic of ways.

Double fantasy is a variety of freesia, the exquisitely perfumed herbaceous spring flower which originated in the Cape province of South Africa. Freesias are named for German physician and botanist Friedrich Freese (1795-1876), who spent considerable time studying the flora of southern Africa. On an outing to the Botanical Gardens in Bermuda, John and Sean spotted these two-color flowers and were instantly attracted to both their beauty and their symbolism. ``It's a type of freesia,' John declared, ``but what it means to us is that if two people picture the same image at the same time, that is the secret.''

``John loved the symbolism of the different colors,' claimed photographer Bob Gruen, who snapped many of the pictures of John and Yoko's New York sojourn, including the final *Double Fantasy* sessions. ``To John, a double fantasy represented two people living together, having the same dream of a relationship, in the same way that the two freesia colors shared the same plant.''

Bob Gruen, who has produced a commendable hard cover art book, *John Lennon: The New York Years* (published 2005 by Stewart, Tabori and Chang), was shooting pictures at the *Double Fantasy* sessions at the Hit Factory. On one of the final nights when they were completing Yoko's brilliant *Walking on Thin Ice*, Lennon became quite philosophical about his future.

According to Bob, at the age of 40 ``John had learned about the happiness that comes from delayed gratification - that if you didn't get high every night, you get an even higher feeling when you see your child learn something. He talked about his ideas of living a responsible life, eating a healthy diet, thinking through your actions. Whereas in years past, he would have chosen to momentarily numb all unpleasant feelings. He told me he'd learned about the gratification that comes from working through those feelings and coming out of a slump through natural - rather than chemical - means.''

Inevitably one has to try to contemplate what his world would have been like now had John Lennon still been alive, in the year (2010) he would have turned 70. It's a tough question. One can only reflect on John's own speculation on turning 60. When I raised the subject of old-age ambition with John as the snow fell down over Ronnie Hawkins' Canadian homestead a few days before Christmas, 1969, he paused for a few seconds and took a long draw on the hash/tobacco joint.

``You know, Ritchie, I sometimes have this vision of sitting back and writing books for children. I always remember how much those children's books like *Treasure Island, The Wind in the Willows, Alice in Wonderland* meant to me. I was so passionate about *Alice in Wonderland* and I drew all the characters. I wrote poems in the style of *Jabberwocky*. I used to live Alice. Those books were really great - they opened up my head to a whole other thing. And to my imagination - they turned a key. You know, it would be really nice to give back to children the same thrill that I felt reading those books when I was young.''

``John was fascinated by *Alice in Wonderland*,' Yoko recalled in 2010. ``We always spoke about it - it was part of our lives. We really respected that sort of surrealism. There were two things that we loved - *Alice in Wonderland* (in literature) and in art, the work of (Rene) Magritte.'' (The Belgian surrealist, 1898-1967, created enduring thoughtful images and his body of work tends to test people's pre-conceptions about everyday subject matter.)``Magritte's paintings were very much like the world of *Alice in Wonderland* in that the surrealism is extremely mysterious but also understandable. There's seriousness in there. I think John would like to have written all sorts of things (later on in his life). I believe that *I Am the Walrus* is very much influenced by *Alice in Wonderland* and it's a love poem to someone.''

As Anthony Fawcett later wrote: ``During his peace crusade, John had focused on a troubled world. His eyes were opened to the human condition, to man's inhumanity to man, and the cruelty of the system. John was part of a general awakening, but his eloquence on behalf of peace revealed the strength of his beliefs, and the part he played was important.''

Along with his partner in rhyme and street performance art, Yoko Ono, John Lennon changed the way the world contemplated peace. And just to think about war and its implications is one long overdue step on the road to stopping it altogether. Could the human species evolve into that enlightened space? One can only wonder. And hope. Because without keeping the hope alive, as John warned, ``we'll sink''.

20. THE INSPIRATIONAL WORLD OF YOKO

"Only people can change the world." Yoko Ono

It is October 9, 2007 (or Year 40 AP) and it would have been John Lennon's 67th birthday. Can you imagine? Yoko Ono can, and does. This is a very special day in her celebrated but controversial history. And of course in her relationship with John Lennon, founder of The Beatles, undoubtedly one of the greatest achievers in the evolution of rock'n'roll music.

Yoko Ono, keeper of the flame for Lennon's exceptional output of words, music, artwork and other creative expression, is unveiling an anti-war flame of another form in - of all places - Iceland. In a moving ceremony on the historic island of Videy in Reykjavik Harbor, where cod fishing fleets have traditionally found maritime refuge over the past 10 centuries, Yoko has inaugurated a beacon of hope for a chronically troubled planet. One which - I suspect - is imperiling its very existence through rampant greed and ignorance.

Beaming high into the clouds above Reykjavik in the northern latitudes at the outer edge of the Arctic Circle, an obelisk of light sends out a message of peace in the grand tradition of John and Yoko's *War Is Over If You Want It* peace campaign. Peace, light and hope - for a new age of understanding and harmony. The very things so obviously missing from everyday life in far too many places in the early part of the 21st century.

Her *Imagine Peace Tower*, dedicated to her late husband, is another plea for sanity in a war-torn world. Another message of hope to a planet that seems unable to free itself from an addiction to violence and aggression. Another plea for sheer sanity in a sea of insanity. Surely the world doesn't have to be like this forever. People trying to kill other people they've never met, because they happen to be on one side of a team. Supporters of the continuing wars in Iraq, Afghanistan and elsewhere might consider it naive, but Yoko implicitly believes that sending messages of goodwill to the world will eventually bring people to their senses and peace to the planet. If only we can wait long enough!

"On October 9, I hope the world will pause for a time and imagine peace. I am unveiling the *Imagine Peace Tower* in memory of John,' Yoko announced to the chilled evening air on the anniversary of his birth. She followed a group of 40 Icelandic schoolchildren who sang John Lennon's peace anthem, *Imagine*, into a bitterly cold advancing-autumn breeze off the coast of Reykjavik, the world's most northern capital city. It was a hot message in a cold place. A genuine beacon of hope in a profoundly troubled planet.

Yoko Ono was joined on this historic occasion by Ringo Starr, John's son Sean and Olivia Harrison, widow of George, and a personal representative of the Dalai Lama (Most Ven. Gyomyo Nakamura of the Ladakh Shanti Stupa World Buddhist Centre) and a select group of friends and peace supporters in a special and very spiritual ceremony. ``I dedicate this *Imagine Peace Tower* to John Lennon. My love for you is forever. I love you all,' said Yoko in a soft emotive voice. The family and friends and like-minded supporters of John and Yoko's peace philosophy - let alone the local dignitaries and caring peaceniks - could hardly fail to have been profoundly moved.

On the swaying ferry back to mainland Reykjavik from the island of Videy, I heard ecstatic raves.

``This is a night I will treasure forever,' declared internationally acclaimed photojournalist Allan Tannenbaum, who had taken some of the last pictures of John before his death on December 8, 1980. Tannenbaum's new photo collection, John & Yoko: A New York Love Story, with a foreword by Yoko, was published in the US by Random House the same day as the *Imagine Peace Tower* was lit up. It's a worthy tome, reflecting America's abiding universal love for Lennon and his music, despite what some politicians and right-wing crusaders might have thought.

I'd been invited with my partner Minnie Cherry to join Yoko and friends for the unveiling of the *Imagine Peace Tower*. By a strange coincidence, it was precisely the day I had announced to my long-term employers, Queensland Newspapers Pty Ltd - publishers of The Sunday Mail, then Australia's second-largest-selling newspaper, and reportedly the most profitable Australian division of Rupert Murdoch's News Limited empire - that I wanted to bring to an end a 20-year association.

Murdoch has gone on to become one of the most extreme right-wing political proprietors in the history of world media, particularly in North America. His support for and financing of the politically conservative Fox News cable TV network says much about his political bias. Fox News has often been described by credible pundits as the propaganda voice of the Republican Party, the haven of the much-maligned George W. Bush. Murdoch is a former Australian citizen controlling more than

70 per cent of the newspapers published in Australia, even though he is no longer a resident or citizen of that country. He is an American, and a stridently Republican one at that! If ever a person could be described as being against the very grain of democracy, opposed to the concept of separate political agendas, it is Rupert Murdoch.

Other countries, the US included, forbid non-resident, non-citizens from owning powerful media empires, which can be utilised as propaganda machines. You have to seriously question their spin and agenda. But when you live in Brisbane, Queensland, the fastest-growing region in Australia, where the daily/nightly, Sunday and local newspapers are controlled by the same corporation, you can't help but wonder about the potential benefits or negatives of this one-dimensional media domination. What other points of view are being presented? What significant developments might be deliberately downplayed or ignored? Where is truth able to present itself? These are big, big questions. Media mind control is a touchy topic, not often addressed by other media players, and more's the pity.

Notwithstanding the ownership issues of Australian media, the timing of my exit was propitious. My resignation announcement from the Murdoch media empire was on precisely the same day that the postman delivered our personal invitation from Yoko's Studio One offices in New York to attend the launching of the *Imagine Peace Tower* in Iceland. It would be the latest in a string of peace-related projects undertaken by Yoko Ono, who had assumed the huge and unrelenting responsibility of keeping the Lennon peace message alive. In doing so, she has somehow brought more vitriol upon herself.

The anti-Yoko ranters could barely hold back as they unleashed a barrage of negative sentiment. Unfortunately, some of that crap stuck and Yoko has - sadly - had to live with it. The anti-woman, anti-Asian backlash against her continued for many years and she was skewered around the planet as some sort of crazy Oriental dragon lady with a control-freak agenda.

``It did hurt me of course, and it hurt John too. He was furious,' Yoko told me in the last month of the last century. ``You know, our lives were very busy; exciting times. But we had each other. We had many great moments together. And that was heavier than the other side (of the coin) in terms of balance in my life. The bad-mouthing kept going on but it was in the distance. (Overall) my life itself was a very blessed one. I didn't think of John as one of the most special people of the century or anything like that. He was just a very attractive guy who was very sexy. So we fell for each other. We were both old-fashioned in those days (1966). Girls didn't call guys and I wasn't a clinging vine just waiting for a phone call. I didn't chase after men - I had other things to do."

Iceland's *Imagine Peace Tower* is the manifestation of an idea that literally beams volumes. In Yoko's 1964 book *Grapefruit,* there was a description of an instructional piece entitled *Light House.* Yoko wrote: ``The light house is a phantom house that is built by sheer light. You set up prisms at a certain time of the day, under a certain evening light which goes through the prisms, the light house appears in the middle of a field like an image, except that, with this image, you can actually go inside if you want to. The light house may not emerge every day, just as the sun doesn't shine every day.''

It was a thought and a vision expressed by John to Yoko very early in their budding relationship. It unfolded during her first visit to his house in Kenwood near London in 1966. ``John talked about having a desire for a lighthouse in his garden,' Yoko told me in a private interview after her press conference at the Reykjavik Art Museum, situated near the harbor. ``Now I am starting to think that here on the island of Videy in Iceland may well be that garden.''

Later she would write: ``John told me that he read about the light house in my publication and if I would build one for him in his garden. `Oh that was conceptual. I'm convinced that one day, it could be built, but I don't know how to do it,' I said with a laugh. `Oh, I thought Americans came up with something,' was what he said. And that was that. I still marvel at the fact that John was touched by that particular concept in my catalogueue, and 40 years ago at that! So this beautiful idea of a building made just from light lay dormant for 40 years.''

She'd been thinking about creating this peace statement as a form of performance art for a long time. Yoko has devoted her life to finding ways of sending a peace message to the world. Back in 2004, she realised the ideal location for her world peace beacon would be in the energy-friendly city of Reykjavik. She had been ``lured'' to visit Iceland some 12 years ago by perceptive civic officials for the installation of an art exhibition. ``There's a lot of caring and concern on a very high sensitivity level in

Iceland ... so it's no wonder I wanted to do the *Imagine Peace Tower* here,' commented an incredibly youthful 73-year-old Yoko in our Reykjavik chat.

Iceland was happy about it, too. ``( We are) honoured,' wrote the Mayor of Reykjavik, Vilhjalmur Vilhjalmsson, ``that Ms Yoko Ono should have chosen this particular place as the home of this beautiful and meaningful artwork - dedicated to such a noble cause and a great creative force. It will no doubt become a true beacon of peace; a testament to great faith and conviction that is so much needed in our world today.''

But why Iceland? ``There is no simple answer,' notes Icelandic writer Sigtryggur Magnason in *Imagine Peace Tower*, a book published with the release of a special commemorative stamp pictured herein, ``just as the story of John Lennon and Yoko Ono is not simple. The answer weaves together the dreams of deceased prophets, thoughts about light and darkness, the clean energy that Iceland possesses, and last but not least, the vision of Yoko Ono and a hope for peace on Earth.''

The historic island of Videy - offshore from Reykjavik and the site of early pioneering settlements in the 11th century - had been the location of a monastery in the medieval era and was the seat of the first Icelandic Governor of Iceland, who took up residence in the Videyjarstofa house. A printing press was subsequently set up on site, and in 2006, the island boasted the country's most state-of-the-art dairy farm. More significantly, it's regarded as an historic, sacred and peaceful region. According to Yoko's Peace Tower announcement, Videy ``abounds with birdlife, grasses and soft hollows, combined with tranquility and the spirit of bygone centuries''. This was undeniable to our eyes.

Its purity was important and needed to be protected. The Campaign Against Military Bases group praised the decision to publicise the importance of fighting for world peace. They were delighted that the city of Reykjavik was keen to promote itself as a centre of peace. In a resolution, the association urged local authorities to announce that, in the future, battleships would be banned from docking in Sundahofn Harbor, near the Peace Tower. ``I think that's just common courtesy towards the artist,' the association's chairman said.

The tower sits on a sturdy platform 17 yards in diameter, at the centre of which a light source emerges from a cylindrical ``Wishing Well'', four yards in diameter and two yards high. It functions like a lighthouse beaming up into the universe. There's obvious symbolism but it works. And it's splendidly designed. Six searchlight streams of beams bounce off mirrors which act as prisms, reflecting and spinning the light upwards. Nine other searchlights combine to provide a powerful vertical flow. It propels a plume of light high into the sky, even in the heavy cloud conditions experienced regularly in this island nation.

The surface of the Wishing Well itself is covered with slabs of pure white glass developed in Japan. The message of Imagine Peace is carved in 24 languages to give visitors the feeling of the message rotating and being received from all over the world. It truly is a universal work of art, reflecting Yoko's stature as one of the world's most celebrated artists - she was awarded a Golden Lion for Lifetime Achievement at the 53rd International Venice Biennale in 2009 along with visual artist John Baldessari.

The official announcement read: "The Golden Lions for Lifetime Achievement are honouring two artists whose ground-breaking activities have opened new poetic, conceptual and social possibilities for artists around the globe working in all media."

Director Daniel Birnbaum also stressed that "Yoko Ono and John Baldessari have shaped our understanding of art and its relationship to the world in which we live. Their work has revolutionised the language of art and will remain a source of inspiration for generations to come". It was a very special moment in a special life. And she responded accordingly, as befits a woman of class and substance.

Message from Yoko Ono: Dear Friends,

When I heard that I was selected for the Golden Lion Lifetime Achievement Award of 2009, I felt like I was in a fog, listening to a foghorn far away!

The fog slowly cleared.

The foghorn changed into the speech the director of the Biennale was giving on this occasion.
So what should I say ... thank you?

John would have been so proud of me.
"I told you, didn't I?" he would say.

I am glad, too.

I feel like I was suddenly given a huge birthday card.
I see myself struggling to hold it in my heart.

Thank you for being there for me all these years.
I am a lucky girl.

yoko

Yoko Ono

1 March 2009 NYC

As a permanent landmark for peace, the *Imagine Peace Tower* each year will remain lit from October 9, John's birth date through December 8, the date of his murder in 1980. It will also be lit on New Year's Eve, during the first week of spring in March, and on rare special occasions as agreed between Yoko and the City of Reykjavik, Reykjavik Art Museum and Reykjavik Energy. With 24-hour daylight in Iceland during the summer months, a light tower would be impractical all year round. The strength, intensity and brilliance of the light tower continually changes as the particles in the air fluctuate with the prevailing weather and atmospheric conditions unique to Iceland.

The electricity to power the tower is produced from geothermal energy, a form of environmentally positive power source in which Iceland is a world leader. "Iceland is a unique eco-friendly country. Eighty per cent of Iceland's energy is provided by water, not oil. Because of this, the air, water and earth are surprisingly pure and clear,' observed Yoko. The energy for the tower is also provided by water. As the world's most active volcanic region, Iceland has a constant supply of water superheated by the hot lava strata which underpin much of the country. The northern hemisphere has recently felt the impact and extent of Icelandic volcanoes.

The morning after the tower's inauguration, Yoko surprised assembled media by addressing a press conference at Reykjavik Energy headquarters. In collaboration with a US-based company called Smart Power, a four-year trial was launched in September, 2007, that could have significant repercussions around the world. Carb-Fix is a plan to store carbon dioxide, the principal villain in global warming, by injecting the gas into Iceland's basalt bedrock where it literally turns to stone. As Yoko pointed out, Carb-Fix provides hope in a scenario which constantly throws up negative messages to the world as we witness the dramatic ever-expanding effects of global warming. As in non-polluting energy creation, Iceland is at the cutting edge of the new technology which the world is going to need in its efforts to deal with the containment of global warming.

Yoko would like to see other Peace Towers installed around the world, as long as they are powered by alternative energy sources. She identifies 140 countries where this could happen and has already sanctioned an effort to set up a Peace Tower near New Delhi. The public has been invited to send in messages of peace to be stored in capsules at the tower site.

As a contemporary vehicle for spreading the peace message, the tower was an instant success. More than 900,000 messages had been received by the time Yoko launched it in October, 2007. If you are so inclined, new messages can be sent by mail to *Imagine Peace Tower*, P.O. Box 1009, 121 Reykjavik, Iceland, or by email to the website www.IMAGINEPEACE.com. Yoko's team was hoping that the one-million-wishes mark would be passed in time for what would have been John's 70th birthday on October 9, 2010.

``Creating the *Imagine Peace Tower* wasn't all that expensive,' Yoko told me backstage at the opening. ``The Iceland government has helped because it will become a tourist attraction. I realised that, with contrasting the two symbolic dates, it gives an understanding of the shortness of life, and the eternity of the spirit. It reminds one how brief life can be and is significant, even for those not interested in John Lennon's life.''

When offered praise for continuing to pursue a peace campaign agenda - when she could join the ranks of the docile and de-fanged rich and famous brigade, Yoko replied: ``I know that there are reasons to compare the present time with the late '60s when the Vietnam War was raging. I'm just doing whatever I can do. Some of the things I don't really know what I'm doing but I just fell into it. It's like a pre-ordained thing. This is a very complex age we live in. The whole idea of goodness seems to be lost. People seem to care more about making money. But goodness is an important thing to be thinking about. We need to create a world of caring and love. There is so much violence and war going on in the world, but I think we can change that. I had been thinking for a while that America is not interested in standing up for peace because the country is at war. But I see now that many American people are standing up for peace. They do not want war.

"Somebody once said that if all the people in China jumped up at the same time, they could tip the world's axis. The same thing applies to peace. If enough of us want it, we can make it happen. But we have to be extremely wise in how we push for world peace. People can look back and see what was good and what was bad. Because of the internet and the global village situation, we are now able to reach out to many people. And this is an inevitable thing which we have to do, because if we don't, we simply won't be here!"

After the unveiling of the tower, a constant stream of intrigued locals gathered harborside on successive nights to check out what one Icelander described as "a lighthouse pointed towards the heavens". There can be no doubt that the tower is a positive step in the ongoing campaign to raise public consciousness about the need to end war and suffering on earth. Yoko declared: "I hope the *Imagine Peace Tower* will give light to the strong wishes of world peace from all corners of the planet and give encouragement, inspiration and a sense of solidarity in a world now filled with fear and confusion. Let us come together to realise a peaceful world. I consider myself very fortunate to see the dream my husband and I dreamt together become reality."

Strangely enough, Iceland might have had a long association with the peace aspirations of John and Yoko. Back in 1969, an eccentric Montreal, Canada radio station proprietor named Geoff Stirling had come up with the idea for a "Peace Radio Network". The concept called for a network of not-otherwise-related radio stations around the world to join up to broadcast messages of peace, from the Lennons and from anyone else who had something to offer on the subject. John and Yoko had even recorded a Radio Peace station ID/jingle for the network.

Hundreds of stations responded to a full-page advertisement I was able to organise in December through my long association with the music trade publication, Billboard. Looking through the list of committed stations while researching this book, I note the very last station on the list was, incredibly, "Naval Station Night Owl, American Forces Radio, Keflavik, Iceland - contact Steve Azlin." Keflavik was the site of the NATO military base from the end of World War II until 2006, when it was closed.

Unfortunately, we were not able to take advantage of the immense possibilities that the Peace Radio Network represented.

But the Billboard ad for the Peace Station Network wasn't greeted that positively by all of the magazine's readers. The Lennons hadn't sighted the ad before its placement and weren't happy about all of the people attaching themselves to the concept. So at around five o'clock one morning, I picked up the bedside phone in Toronto to be greeted by a verbal slapping from Yoko at Tittenhurst Park near London. I'm not suggesting the slapping wasn't deserved but that call prompted me never to place a phone line in my bedroom again. I've maintained that policy until this day.

Iceland is a unique nation, not just because of its proximity to the Arctic Circle or its constantly throbbing and steaming geothermal activity. Icelanders, we discovered, are very tuned-in and perceptive people, and they have a profound connection with their over-heated environment. It wouldn't be long before we discovered an undercurrent of belief in Iceland's mysterious ``little people'', locally known as trolls. This is an open belief in fairies, in a country which is connected directly to its environment.

So much so that plans for new roads and housing developments in Iceland are carefully skirted around their habitation areas, to avoid disturbing the rocks under which they're supposed to live. At one time, local fairytales suggested that the strange lava formations around the countryside were in fact trolls which had turned to stone when caught in outdoor daylight. These special troll habitats of Iceland are clearly marked on regular travel maps, along with known haunted areas. One wouldn't like to describe the Icelanders as superstitious but they are aware of certain energies and forces which may not be so apparent elsewhere.

Yoko has taken this on board as a local feature which may well have substance. She laughs when she talks about the trolls and the travel maps. But her greatest admiration is reserved for the Blue Lagoon, a unique geothermal spa which Yoko believes can help an individual to shed the burden of at least 10 years in a single session.

The Blue Lagoon is an absolutely extraordinary experience. Set up in the natural moon-crater like environment out in the countryside as an adjunct to the local geothermal power station, it is an open-air heated-water hot pool rich in natural silica saltwater. In the course of a visit, one applies fistfuls of this silica mud to face and neck and the longer one leaves it on, the softer skin becomes. Just floating in the dense water as a hot thick mist drifts overhead is incredibly rejuvenating.

After the launch of the Peace Tower, Yoko returned to her Studio One base at the Dakota Apartments in New York and then was booked to fly to Brazil and Japan. She maintains an astonishing schedule and travel itinerary that would deter a less committed humanitarian. She seldom misses an opportunity to spread the word about peace and an end to violence.

Asked if she has found the 15-hour flight from California to Sydney, Australia overly tiring, she claimed to prefer long haul flights because the time span enabled her to work on current projects without interruption.

To tie-in with the 40th anniversary of the Montreal Bed-In in April 2009, Yoko launched her new exhibition as an anti-war activist - *Imagine: The Peace Ballad of John & Yoko*, at the Montreal Museum of Fine Arts. The exhibition ran for almost 12 weeks - from April 2 until June 21 - and admission was, at Yoko's insistence, free. It comprised some 140 works, drawings, unpublished photographs, videos, films, artworks and interactive materials.

Visitors to the exhibition were able to play Imagine on a white piano with a Disklavier sound system, to write down their wishes and attach them to Yoko Ono's Wish Tree, to stamp Imagine Peace on world maps, to read the works of Nobel Peace Prize winners in the Peace Library, to play chess with Play It By Trust and, once daily at an unspecified time, to speak on the phone with Yoko Ono. The museum reported a record attendance of 11,000 during the first two weeks. Ultimately, attendance would reach the colossal figure of 152,239 according to Ms Catherine Guex, press officer for the museum.

We caught up with Yoko and her loyal and exceptional creative assistants, archivist Karla Merrifield and PA Amanda Keeley, backstage at the private launch. It was a warm and - as always - enlightening conversation. Yoko was sitting back on a settee under a huge blow-up of the *War Is Over* poster, sampling a tiny slice of chocolate cake. ``I'm so happy that our dream is still alive and it's spreading and it's expanding. I think that the whole world is realizing that peace isn't all that bad,' she said, with a delicate laugh.

``I think we are very lucky that we are still here 40 years later. When many of us couldn't make it. We are very lucky.'' She indicated that she was thinking particularly of the late Derek Taylor and Timothy Leary. Yoko says she most vividly recalls the positive aspects of the Bed-In. ``Montreal was a place where John and I created a very important statement. We didn't think it was going to be that important at the time but it (made) the beds for our lives.

``I remember that when the journalists in Montreal went home each day around six o'clock after the Bed-In, John and I would turn around and look at the sky. It was a beautiful view. I always remember that. But without Montreal's vibrations and spirit around, *Give Peace a Chance* may not have been born. It was a work between John and I, and our partnership with Montreal."

Yoko felt it was important the 2009 Imagine exhibition be free. ``It's a revolutionary way of doing stuff, but it goes with the idea that peace is for everybody and it isn't something that you have to sell. We share peace between us - together. I think that this is the start of a beautiful age. ``I think of this world as people who want peace, and people who want to solve problems by violence and war. And I think, by now, 99 per cent of the world is very much for world peace, very much for solving things by discussion. There are so many of us, we're going to win.''

Yoko said she felt the election of President Barack Obama had been a strong step in the right direction. ``I think he represents a change and that he represents strong promise - very much so.'' This opinion was expressed before President Obama's expansion of US involvement in Afghanistan.

According to a spokesperson for the Museum of Fine Arts in Montreal: ``The museum is offering a spring of peace. Thanks to the participation of Yoko, this exhibition, while commemorating the 1969 Bed-In, renews their pacifist action in the present, an action made all the more relevant given the current state of the world. In solidarity, an incredible numbers of businesses, suppliers and partners have decided to support this project by offering their services for free, so as to spread this universal message which, it goes without saying, extends beyond the walls of this institution.''

And thus Yoko continues her quest to focus the world's attention on peace, both on a personal and a planetary level. To many people, her life is defined by her relationship with John Lennon. Yet she was always an artist in her own right and write. She was into conceptual art long before she met John and it was her obvious talents in the avant-garde milieu that so impressed and captivated him. Her growth as a conceptual artist can be measured in the exhibitions she has either organised or been closely involved with.

"Art,' she wrote in her liner notes for the 2002 album, *Blueprint for a Sunrise,* "is a way of survival. With this album, I present to you my metronome, my menu, my blueprint for a sunrise." It all makes very clear sense from the first woman to study philosophy at Japan's Gakushuin University (in 1952).

In a relationship stretching back more than 46 years, I have witnessed how Yoko handles herself in a multitude of situations, from the sublime (as in her interaction with Pierre Trudeau, Marshall McLuhan and Dick Gregory) to the most uncouth (as in the Montreal Bed-In confrontation with a snarling Al Capp, or Al "Crap" as we'd quickly nicknamed this extremely nasty human being).

As gracious as she always is, Yoko doesn't back away from disagreements or controversy. What she has to say about peaceful co-existence and poverty and the degradation of our environment is unlikely to curry favour with those in power, political and/or corporate. Her interests and theirs lie in vastly different levels of awareness. Ever the peacemaker, she continues to push us towards embracing the powers of positive thinking as a collective, while exercising common sense and visualising a more holistic approach to everything we do.

She carries herself with amazing grace and humility, no easy task in a celebrity shaped world. But even she was slightly bamboozled in meeting the Queen back in 2002. "I have to say that I was nervous. In getting ready for the meeting, I was going through my collection of jackets, wondering which one was best and which one was proper? Yet on meeting her, I found her to be very warm and very kind. She does have a young spirit about her, and she knew quite a lot about John. She knew that he was a fun person, there was no doubt about that."

She is - in so many ways - the ultimate optimist. But life has not always been easy. One is tempted to write "by a long shot" but that sounds like a dismal pun. John and Yoko were always keen to have children and their medical history of miscarriages clearly caused much pain. "It was very traumatic,' Yoko admitted midway through 2010. "The miscarriages were terrible for me ... and for John, too. One of my miscarriages happened so late (in the term) that we really thought we would have the baby. So we were both crying about that.

"With Sean (born October 9, 1975), we were very careful about everything. John had this idea for the media to make an announcement that ` Yoko is pregnant' - because we were so proud and happy about it. But whenever he announced it, people were hating the fact (of our pregnancy). They were wishing it wouldn't happen. We were the most hated couple in the world because everybody loved John but they didn't like the fact that he was with me. So when I was pregnant with Sean, I said to him, `Please do not announce it'. He finally understood and then decided, ` We're not going to announce it. We are not going to announce it'. But we were going to this doctor and that doctor and people were starting to wonder, I suppose."

Coupled with the constant strain of US government surveillance and the legal bullying over John's immigration status, this obviously can't have been a carefree period in the Lennons' lives. I put that to Yoko in 2010 and she offered a candid response: ``No, it was not a very easy time. But I was amazed at how much a human being can take. I think John was very strong and very determined. And (it helped) that we were together and in love and everything, that was certainly true. But I personally felt so guilty on top of it."

As John poignantly sang, "Nobody told me there'd be days like these ..." But there has been no shortage of them and Yoko must be applauded for enduring through their traumas. But she claims never to have let the downside affect her usually positive outlook. ``If everyone who was nasty to us (John and herself) rotted in hell, as they say, it would be very crowded down there,' she laughs. ``I could keep on either being angry about the traumatic things that have happened to me, but the punishment is that I wouldn't have time to do anything else. I like to do something better with my life." She is obviously still addicted to the politics of change. ``If we don't change our society, it's going to be very hard for us to live in it. But let's be honest - change is so inconvenient for all of us."

Asked about her visions when we were in Iceland, Yoko replied: ``We're all envisioning the future. And what we envision comes true. That's why we have to be careful about what we envision. Many peace supporters say, 'No more war, war, war, war,' and we think about war when they say that. Now we have to start saying peace. And think about the future on the basis of peace, and not war.'

On the brink of celebrating her 78th birthday:

John Lennon and Yoko Ono in bed for peace, 1969. (photo: Public Domain) Imagine Peace 2011

By Yoko Ono, Reader Supported News 06 February 11

Dear Friends,

In two weeks time, on February 18th, 2011, I will be 78.
I know you are asking many questions on Twitter and
elsewhere about what I am really like.
It's something I would love to know, too! One day
it will suddenly dawn on us ... maybe.

The world situation is too urgent for us now to
discuss trivial things, like what I eat for breakfast.

We are at a point in human history when we have to wake up and realise that the only people who can save the world are us.
Every hour that goes by without us doing anything about it
affects us, and affects the world that we love so much.

In his State of the Union Speech, President Obama said
we should do "big things." Well, we are already doing the
biggest thing anybody in the human history could ever hope for.

Together, we are creating a world of Peace,
Love and Freedom, all while the
negative forces try their hardest to stop us.

With their power, they want to control the whole
world. But we will not let them. That's big.

The way we are doing it is by being
conscious of the "Power of Togetherness."

The negative forces do not have that. They are an elitist minority, dipping their heads in arrogance
They always play the same game using violence, changing laws for
their convenience, and seducing us with words to get what they want.

They say if we do things their way, we will all be rich.
Well, that's not happening. It never will. Once there is
great wealth, they will want to keep it for themselves.

They also use fear tactics, saying the world will be in a great mess if we
don't do it their way.
Well, the world is already in a mess. Why? Because we followed them. It's Time for Action. It's Time for Change.

We, the people of the world, are not dumb.
We understand what the "Blue Meanies" are trying to do.
We just don't know how to stop it. And wonder if we can at all.

But we can! We are doing it.

Take a look at this map. Each dot represents millions and millions of people who are all, right now, thinking of Peace: wishing it, voicing it, and hoping that their dream of peace will become a reality.

Map of global locations of visitors to www.IMAGINEPEACE.com 2010-11 from Revolver Maps

The map expresses what my husband John Lennon and I envisioned. I know he is smiling, thinking of how little time it took for all of us to *Come Together*.

IMAGINE PEACE is a powerful, universal mantra that we should all meditate on. With it, we will achieve the impossible. Hopefully, without bloodshed.

Look at all the courageous people who are now being hurt in marches and thrown in prisons for no other reason except for carrying "Peace, Love and Freedom" in their hearts and voicing it.

I don't want you to get hurt. You shouldn't have to.

7 billion of us, people of the world, have the birthright to live with a healthy mind and body at all times.

You should not even get one scratch on you, and you won't, if you don't allow it. So keep IMAGINE PEACE in your head.

Have a clear picture of where we stand, what we are doing, and where we want to be. Know that we are connected in our hearts and minds.

War Is Over, if you want it! I love you!

Yoko Ono Lennon 3 February 2011

"Imagine all the people, living life in peace."

John Lennon

"A dream you dream alone is only a dream. A dream you dream together is reality."

Yoko Ono Lennon

21. MEANWHILE BACK AT THE VATICAN

Warfare is not the only way of inflicting pain and suffering upon the vulnerable. Thuggery and domestic violence are all too common, but when the perpetrators belong to an establishment which claims responsibility for the moral and spiritual welfare of its faithful followers, the sense of outrage, betrayal and hypocrisy is overwhelming.

Shortly after Easter, 2010, the Vatican released a statement to mark the 40th anniversary of the break-up of The Beatles. In the Vatican's newspaper L'Osservatore Romano, it was revealed that the Roman Catholics had forgiven John Lennon for his statement (taken out of context) that The Beatles ``were more popular than Jesus Christ''. The Church's print mouthpiece even described The Beatles as a ``precious jewel''.

``It's true,' the Vatican claimed, ``they took stupefying substances; overwhelmed by success, they lived dissolute and uninhibited years; in an excess of boastfulness they said they were more famous than Jesus; they had fun launching mysterious messages, even satanic, according to improbable declarations ... sure, they weren't the best example for young people at the time, but neither (were they) the worst. (Their) beautiful melodies remain as precious jewels that have changed light music forever and continue to raise emotions.''

Paul McCartney did not rise to the bait of these loaded statements but Ringo Starr had a few apt responses to pass along in a May 2010 interview with CNN promoting his new album, *Y Not*. In rejecting the church's apology, he observed: ``Didn't the Vatican say we were satanic or possibly satanic? And they've still forgiven us? I think the Vatican, they've got more to talk about than The Beatles.''

Amid the present avalanche of claims of pedophilia by priests around the planet - and the Catholic Church's apparent lack of appetite to punish them - its forgiveness of The Beatles can only be regarded as a bit of spin to distract attention from much more serious issues. The legacy of the previous 83-year-old Pontiff was severely damaged by the revelation that in the 1980s he had approved a session of therapy for a suspected pedophile. This man was permitted to resume his pastoral duties while still being treated, and was subsequently given a suspended sentence for having molested a boy. This placed a permanent stain on the Pope's credibility.

One can only imagine that John Lennon and George Harrison - on hearing of the Vatican's belated forgiveness - would offer a wry smile.

One must also wonder about the future. Just how much suffering and injustice - most of it carried out with outrageous righteousness and in the name of some wretched religion - can this planet absorb before we finally realise that enough is enough? It's the biggest question the human species has ever had to face. So far, we haven't been too good at answering it.

22. IS IT THE END OR IS IT THE BEGINNING?

> ``John was the first one to use the song for political purposes, too. To try and improve society. In that way he's more relevant today than ever. John was really against war. We both were. It's crazy how a situation like that repeats itself. Peace is so very important. More than ever, we shouldn't be afraid of saying we want it.''
> YOKO ONO – New York City, August, 2005

> ``The truth will always win.''
> JULIAN ASSANGE - 2010

I grew up in a conservative country town in Australia where all roads led to the right wing of political process and theory. Only now, as we tramp forward in the 21st century, has that town of Brisbane shown signs of developing a contemporary urban outlook. Conservatism reigns and rules in this narrow-minded group of sub-tropical communities.

Another child with a similar Brisbane upbringing is Julian Assange, who has been described as ``one of the great folk heroes of all time'' by an Australian actor named John Waters. Waters makes a acting living with – among other roles his one-man show about John Lennon entitled Looking Through a Glass Onion. The imaginative one-man show has been touring for almost two decades.

If John Lennon was alive now, Waters (who knows Lennon's body of work better than most) feels he would be at the ``cutting edge of political comment. I'm sure that Lennon would be speaking out today because there's a move towards a new kind of right wing politics that is worldwide ... I think he would have been at his best his best to speak out against that. To speak for greater disclosure. I think he would have been thrilled with WikiLeaks. Because it's hysterical that we have a guy who, make no mistake, is going to be one of the great folk heroes of all time and he happens to be Australian, Julian Assange.

``I think the internet has always been potentially a force for freedom of speech and it's proving itself right now. And Lennon would have been just loving that.''

In an article Yoko Ono wrote for the op ed pages of The New York Times on December 8, 2010, a piece that likely also referred to the deeds of

Julian Assange, she said about her late husband:

"The most important gift we received from him was not words, but deeds. He believed in truth, and had dared to speak up. We all knew that he upset certain powerful people with it. But that was John. He couldn't have been any other way. If he were here now, I think he would still be shouting the truth. Without the truth, there would be no way to achieve world peace."

Again we say Amen.

Julian Assange was born in the north Queensland town of Townsville and spent a substantial chunk of his youth living a Tom Sawyer-like existence on nearby Magnetic Island. At a later stage of his adolescence, he was a primary school student at Kelvin Grove State School, an educational institution I had attended myself some years earlier.

The young Assange's conservative Queensland upbringing had a profound impact on his consciousness. As he would write in an op ed piece for The Australian newspaper in December 2010:

"I grew up in a Queensland country town where people spoke their minds bluntly. They distrusted big government as something that could be corrupted if not watched carefully. The dark days of corruption in the Queensland government before the Fitzgerald Inquiry are testimony to what happens when the politicians gag the media from reporting the truth."

The Fitzgerald Inquiry was an historic judicial inquiry into Queensland Police (1987-89). It conducted a thorough investigation of long-term, systemic political corruption and abuse of power in the state of Queensland. As a result of its damning report, the Police Commissioner (Sir) Terry Lewis was charged with corruption and the Premier Sir Joh Bjelke-Peterson was charged with, but later acquitted of, perjury in respect of evidence given at the Inquiry.

The Bjelke-Peterson case had resulted in a hung jury but it was later revealed that one of the jury was a member of the youth division of Bjelke-Peterson's National Party and he had steadfastly refused to convict the party leader, no matter what the evidence. Regrettably, the then-premier Wayne Goss lacked the intestinal fortitude to re-try the 81-year old "hillbilly dictator", as the former premier was described in one documentary book. Several other Cabinet members were jailed. It was a particularly sorry chapter in Queensland's conservative history, but one which had a profound and unforgettable impact on anybody who cared about freedom and true democracy.

These events obviously convinced Mr Assange that protective government secrecy was an abomination, and he would devote his career to what might be described as ``taking the covers off '', unwrapping the realities of our existence. The unvarnished truth. Just as John Lennon had begged for Gimme Some Truth in his 1971 song from the Imagine album (with its anguished protests against random acts of military violence such as the My Lai massacre), Julian Assange would provide a whole lot of truth and honesty to a shell-shocked, media-manipulated world. A world which has been drastically misled and misinformed by what I believe is an established anti-truth agenda controlled by what President Dwight D. Eisenhower described in his 1961 farewell address as the ``military-industrial agenda''.

These are the same gruesome corporations which benefit when any bullet is fired, when any armaments are called upon to inflict a technological victory. These people sell pain and physical destruction. The same expenditures could be used to minimise the suffering and starvation of the poor and the afflicted. It's a lamentable world out there, not improved in any way by the obsession with weaponry and military agendas pursued by so many - if not all - governments.

In his 2010 piece for The Australian, Julian Assange explained: ``(My idea is) to use internet technologies in new ways to report the truth.'' And that's precisely what he has done. In 1987 (TY: Check date, perhaps 1997?) after learning the ropes of internet hacking in Melbourne (having relocated from Brisbane), where he worked as a computer programmer, he began his career at age 16. He began hacking under the name Mendax (which was derived from a phrase of Horace, the foremost Roman lyric poet during the period of Augustus, meaning ``nobly untruthful.'') Sort of shouts for itself.

Moving overseas, he founded the ultimate whistleblower website, Wikileaks. Its purpose was to force a form of open government upon a willing public of all persuasions. The 35-year founder, spokesperson and editor-in-chief initially authored two essays detailing his new site's philosophy: "To radically shift regime behaviour we must think clearly and boldly for if we have learned anything, it is that regimes do not want to be changed. We must think beyond those who have gone before us and discover technological changes that embolden us with ways to act in which our forebears could not."

In his blog he wrote, "the more secretive or unjust an organisation is, the more leaks induce fear and paranoia in its leadership and planning coterie ... Since unjust systems by their nature induce opponents, and in many places barely have the upper hand, mass leaking leaves them exquisitely vulnerable to those who seek to replace them with more open forms of governance".

On November 28, 2010, WikiLeaks published more than a quarter of a million diplomatic cables it had obtained, including 11,000 documents marked as ``secret". The publication was effected through special arrangements which Assange set up with key non-conservative print media including The Guardian, Le Monde, The New York Times, Der Spiegel and El Pais. The content represented the sort of stuff which politicians and governments like to keep a tight lid on. Diplomatic messages which reflected more of the realities of modern life than the official picture we are constantly presented with.

From the Iraq invasion came shocking footage of a US military attack on civilians, including several journalists. There were also more than 90,000 pages of military detailing of the Afghanistan invasion. Army brass loudly proclaimed that their ``innocent informers" had been compromised by the revealing of their names and tactics.

The Establishment was horrified. It was the largest unauthorised release of contemporary classified information in history. Right wingers in the US called for Assange's head. He was described as a terrorist, an anarchist and the most dangerous man in America. In May 2010, prominent neo-conservative, former House Speaker Newt Gingrich, declared: "Information terrorism, which leads to people getting killed, is terrorism, and Julian Assange is engaged in terrorism. He should be treated as an enemy combatant."

And so the pursuit of the leaks began. In trying to get their hands (and handcuffs) on Mr Assange, highly questionable rape charges were drummed up in Sweden, a nation which might have agreed to allowing our Australian-born hero to be extradited to American soil. As I write this, these charges are grinding through British courts. But Julian Assange had the support of a number of influential people including the celebrated human rights lawyer, Geoffrey Robertson. His supporters remained optimistic that real justice would prevail - that David would survive to fight another day against the Goliath of world thought control.

Among those people standing up for Mr Assange's human rights was another legendary whistleblower, Daniel Ellsberg, who was responsible for the leaking of the Pentagon Papers. The documents comprised a top secret Defence Department history of the American political and military involvement in Vietnam between 1945-67.

They documented that four separate US Administrations - but particularly the administration of Lyndon Johnson - had systemically lied to the public and to Congress. Ellsberg provided copies of this damning report to The New York Times and other media.

Shades of the revelations which arose from the WikiLeaks documents. Daniel Ellsberg would ultimately conclude that Assange "is serving our [American] democracy and serving our rule of law precisely by challenging the secrecy regulations, which are not laws in most cases, in this country".

About the much-proclaimed national security considerations for the US, Ellsberg added that "(Assange is) obviously a very competent guy in many ways. I think his instincts are that most of this material deserves to be out. We are arguing over a very small fragment that doesn't. He has not yet put out anything that hurt anybody's national security."

But still American conservatives, led by the arch right-wing media tycoon and controller of the poisoned Fox News, Rupert Murdoch, bitterly complained over the alleged security damage Mr Assange had wrought. To which Daniel Ellsberg observed: "If I released the Pentagon Papers today, the same rhetoric and the same calls would be made about me ... I would be called not only a traitor - which I was [called] then, which was false and slanderous - but I would be called a terrorist ... Assange and Bradley Manning (the alleged source of the diplomatic cables) are no more terrorists than I am."

Conservative forces were outraged. Somebody or something had to be blamed for this intrusion into government privacy. A US soldier, Bradley Manning, the whistleblowing suspect, was subjected to significant mental torture and victimisation through solitary confinement. It made a mockery of the United States' claim to be the democratic land of the brave and the free. Manning was confined without trial or proof. Authorities claimed that Manning had stolen thousands of diplomatic cables and passed them along to WikiLeaks where they were illegally distributed.

In his defence, Mr Assange said: "I'd never heard his name before it was published in the press." He believed that the US put pressure on Manning as part of preparing their case against WikiLeaks. "Cracking Bradley Manning is the first step," Mr Assange claimed. "The aim clearly is to break him and force a confession that he somehow conspired with me to harm the national security of the United States." But such a conspiracy was impossible. "WikiLeaks technology was designed from the very beginning to make sure that we never knew the identities or names of people submitting material. We are as untraceable as we are uncensorable. That's the only way to assure sources they are protected."

As I write this final section of my book, Julian Assange's future remains very much up in the air. In showing us the truth, he becomes the victim of those misinformed and ignorant souls who would shoot the messenger. Let us hope that unlike John Lennon, he will not die a premature death in the pursuit of his beliefs.

Another passionate peace supporter, Roger Waters, the driving force behind British progressive rock band Pink Floyd, called for the names of those who had died in violent conflicts in his Fallen Loved Ones campaign: "Fallen Loved Ones is a request, from me, reaching out to ask you to provide a photograph and personal details of a loved one lost in war. Your loved one's pictures and details would be included, along with those of my father Eric, in my upcoming show The Wall (the name of an iconic Floyd album) as an act of remembrance. The fallen loved one does not have to have been a soldier. Civilian deaths are equally, if not more, harrowing.

"I make this request to you in light of my belief that many of these tragic losses of life are avoidable. I feel empathy with the families of all the victims and anger at the powers that be who are responsible, in equal measure. Please join me in honouring our dead and protesting their loss.

Roger Waters: "I recently came across this quote of mine from 22 years ago: 'What it comes down to for me is this: Will the technologies of communication in our culture serve to enlighten us and help us to understand one another better, or will they deceive us and keep us apart?' I believe this is still a supremely relevant question and the jury is out. There is a lot of commercial clutter on the net and a lot of propaganda but I have a sense that just beneath the surface, understanding is gaining ground. We just have to keep blogging, keep twittering, keep communicating, keep sharing ideas.

"Thirty years ago when I wrote (the song) The Wall, I was a frightened young man. Well not that young, I was 36 years old. It took me a long time to get over my fears.

Anyway, in the intervening years it has occurred to me that maybe the story of my fear and loss with its concomitant inevitable residue of ridicule, shame and punishment, provides an allegory for broader concerns:

nationalism, racism, sexism, religion, Whatever! All these issues and 'isms are driven by the same fears that drove my young life.

"This new production of The Wall is an attempt to draw some comparisons, to illuminate our current predicament, and is dedicated to all the innocents lost in the intervening years. In some quarters, among the chattering classes, there exists a cynical view that human beings as a collective are incapable of developing more 'humane' i.e. kinder, more generous, more co-operative, more empathetic relationships with one another.

"I disagree. In my view it is too early in our story to leap to such a conclusion. We are after all a very young species. I believe we have at least a chance to aspire to something better than the dog-eat-dog ritual slaughter that is our current response to our institutionalised fear of each other.

"I feel it is my responsibility as an artist to express my, albeit guarded, optimism, and encourage others to do the same. To quote the great man (John Lennon): 'You may say that I'm a dreamer, but I'm not the only one'."

- Roger Waters, 2010 Amen and ahwomen!

Meanwhile the wars go on and on and not much changes. One glimmer of hope possibly emerged on May 3, 2010, when the United States revealed for the first time that its arsenal consisted of a total of 5113 nuclear warheads. The announcement was meant to bolster arms control efforts, and we can only agree with that.

"It is in our national security interest to be as transparent as we can be about the nuclear program of the United States," Secretary of State Hillary Clinton said as the Pentagon unveiled previously secret figures. "We think that builds confidence, brings more people to an understanding of what President (Barack) Obama and this administration are trying to do."

The figure represented an 84 percent reduction from the nuclear warhead arsenal at its peak of 31,255 in 1967 during the Cold War, and a 75 percent reduction from late 1989 when the Berlin Wall fell.

But there is always some form of political power which wishes to extinguish its enemies. The only thing which does change is the evolution of evermore efficient killing machinery. My most pressing and persuasive issue is with the murder and maiming of innocent, non-military bystanders and non-participants.

The facts speak volumes. A century ago, 95 percent of the fatalities in war were combatants. The remaining five percent were uninvolved civilians, bystanders and innocent victims caught in the crossfire.

Today, in our supposedly more enlightened times, the statistics have been reversed. In our own time and on our watch, 95 percent of the fatalities are not participants in any military endeavour. They are the innocent bystanders.

As are we.

Back in 1969, we bemoaned the sheer injustice and ignorance of it all. In our youth, we called for an end to the craziness.

Now as we enter our seventies and our eighties, we find ourselves still singing the same old song. One can't help but wonder for chrissake when will this madness end?

After all this time, haven't we learnt any damn thing???? When will we ever learn?

i

Most of us have been conditioned...

Since armies are legal, we feel that war is acceptable; in general, nobody feels that war is criminal or that accepting It is criminal attitude.

In fact, we have been brainwashed.

War is monstrous.

It's very nature is one of tragedy and suffering.

The Dalai Lama

ii

Copyright © Ritchie Yorke 2015

The moral right of the author has been asserted

ISBN 978-0-9944400-2-0 Music History

This book is sold subject to the condition that it shall not, by way of trade or otherwise, be lent, re-sold, hired out or otherwise circulated without the publisher's prior written consent in any form of binding or cover other than that in which it is published and without a similar condition including this condition being imposed upon the subsequent purchaser.

Digital publication

© Ritchie Yorke 2015

www.ingramcontent.com/pod-product-compliance
Lightning Source LLC
Chambersburg PA
CBHW060509090426
42735CB00011B/2154